YANKEE PRIEST

By Edward F. Murphy

YANKEE PRIEST
MADEMOISELLE LAVALLIÈRE
PÈRE ANTOINE
THE SCARLET LILY
ROAD FROM OLIVET
THE TENTH MAN
HANDCLASPS WITH THE HOLY
NEW PSYCHOLOGY AND OLD RELIGION
ST. THOMAS' POLITICAL THEORIES AND DEMOCRACY
JUST JACK
TALE OF TWO BROTHERS

YANKEE PRIEST

An autobiographical journey,

with certain detours,

from Salem to New Orleans

EDWARD F. MURPHY

Doubleday & Company, Inc.

GARDEN CITY, N.Y., 1952

Library of Congress Catalog Card Number: 52-5117

To M. *for memories*

YANKEE PRIEST

I

It BEGAN normally enough, that natal day of mine in Salem, Massachusetts, July 21, 1892, but before noon it went wild.

A blaze leapt up in Mrs. Fogarty's downstairs tenement, as a result of her four-year-old Mike's playing with matches too near a can of kerosene; and the good woman, ably unassisted by the little imp, not only failed to put out the flame with her poorly aimed pan of greasy dishwater but effected considerable increase.

Somebody rang in an alarm which brought out the whole fire department. At the sight of hell on wheels, my sister Annie, who had just made some molasses candy and was setting it to cool in three tin pie plates on one of the second-story sills, fell into a great fear and almost out the window. The plates hit Park Street, so called probably because its very dearth of trees suggested a wealth of them to the wistful nature-loving Irish. The hoofs of snorting fire horses got involved with clattery tin and sticky goo, and one of the animals whinnied so protestingly loud that a distracted fireman squirted his hose right up at Annie instead of into Mrs. Fogarty's. The jet sent her reeling and screaming into the kitchen, and relentlessly followed; and my mother, stumbling from bed to see what she could, scarcely reached the door before she fainted. A section of the much-cracked ceiling, soon soaked, came down with a thud. As Mom often said afterward, "God was good—there wasn't anybody out there but Annie."

Some cabbage on top of the stove was spoiled. A real loss, because that cabbage belonged to us and the house didn't. And when the flames were at last overcome, Clem Ward, the landlord, galumphed up the steaming stairway to demand two months' rent ($15) in advance for repairs which would never be made. As the old skinflint was leaving with the family's last cent, my father burst in, frowning, to announce that he had just been laid off from work and to demand why the dickens a little kindling should cause such a hullabaloo. "It'll be cold enough here this comin' winter, with no fuel for the stove," he warned. "It's down on your knees thankin' God you should be for sendin' us some heat ahead of time, bad cess to it!"

That afternoon Aunt Aggie, a regular breeze, blew in from Lawrence and created more excitement than the fire with her new willow-plumed hat and padded hips. Toward six, Mame Brady, the local midwife, had to be sent for, but solidly committed to a chair and table in Finnian's domestic saloon, she was more interested in grog than babies and refused to budge. At seven sharp, with no assistance save the very best, Providence itself, I made my debut into existence so quietly that everybody thought I was dead—until I denied it with a sudden and resounding blast.

Two weeks later I was christened "Edward" after the holy English king who, 'way back in history, used to heal the sick merely by touching them, and with whom Mom had become acquainted through the medium of a church magazine.

If it is true that man wants but little here below, we Murphys were blessed in having at least plenty of that.

Bulls won fat financial awards at county fairs; but Dad, who seemed to me nearly as big and strong as any of them, and was without a single defect beyond a slight limp in his left leg, never received more than eight or ten dollars a week for the sweat of his brow, though he toiled like a Trojan under a Greek lash at any honest job that offered. Nothing was too menial for him, and this was fortunate, because at that time a good many of the New England Irish were not a great deal better off in some respects than Negroes in the South today; for indication of which I may mention that the help-wanted column of our daily newspaper was not above containing the knell-like clause, "No Irish Catholic need apply."

Fortunately prices were somewhat reasonable, at least on sale days: boys' knee pants, 17 cents, worth 25; boys' double-breasted suits, 89 cents, worth $1.50; good-enough "stickin' pieces" of corned beef, 5 cents a pound, and "flank" 3 cents. When flour jumped to $6.50 a barrel in '98, Salemites might have been a bit panicky, but even then Dad insisted that we youngsters—Will, Annie, Agnes, Jim, Tom Junior, Joe, myself, and baby Frank— slather butter on the wonderful bread Mom used to make. "It's good for the lungs," he would say; and his voice being of a boom-de-ay timbre that could raise the roof in the rare moments when he really used it, I grew up in the belief that he was full of butter, though I'd never seen him eat so much as a dab. Only gradually did I come to realize how well he provided for us by the simple expedient of neglecting himself. There was only one "expensive" habit he held on to, and that was his two plugs of tobacco each week.

Mom was a small woman, with her hair combed back tight from her kind, cameo-like face, and with a large amount of concealed authority in her make-up. Never for a moment did she let Dad feel that he was not master of the home; but never was master more successfully mistressed. Years after, when arrow-eyed women were shooting all over the country for suffrage, I'd think back and smile. Mom wanted the vote no more than the moon. It was enough for her to have the voter, and she certainly did. In due time I happened to learn that she originally gained her handsome mate, plain little pigeon though she was, by the same seeming artlessness that was to serve her wedded life so well.

According to Aunt Aggie, she had come down from Lawrence at the age of seventeen, because the Naumkeag Cotton Mills in Salem paid a few cents more than similar factories up on the Merrimac River; and a swarthy, mustachioed, myopic foreman started ogling her the very first day she went to work. Out of the tail of her eye she noticed Tom Murphy operating a loom a few feet away from her own and hoped that he, too, would do some ogling; but his gaze was glued on the task for which he was being paid. So she used her head, and when the foreman cozened up to her during the noon lull, she merely led him, with a neither-yes-nor-no swerve of shoulder and chin, over toward the unsuspecting Tom and then, with a swift turnabout, throatily exclaimed to the masher, "Why do you persist in annoyin' me?" A spark came to Tom's clean blue eye at that and kindled the chivalry of the days of King Brian Boru when even the fairest maiden, bedecked with jewels, could travel alone from one end of Ireland to the other without a single molestation from any male. A man of few words, he could be eloquent without any. Like a hurled brick, his tight fist hit the foreman in the teeth, dislodging a bicuspid and a molar and busting a lip. Naturally he was fired, and that night he led Mom triumphantly into a booth at the old Phoenix House on Front Street for clam cakes and oyster stew. Not long after, when he had secured a slightly worse job digging ditches, they were married.

Mom continued to comport herself, strictly for Dad, as a delicate creature who needed all kinds of attention and protection, knowing that a too obviously strong woman only brings out the loud weakness in a man and that an apparently weak one is apt to encourage a quiet strength. When Dad was away with his pick and shovel, she would be all energy and efficiency, a Queen Elizabeth ruling her realm; but the minute he crossed the threshold, she'd doff her crown and go limp, and that always changed any possible gruffness of his into a show of meekness. I never heard him say a harsh word to her, even when things went worst. It irked her, perhaps, to keep on playing a part, but I am sure she felt that any other method would have filled the house with din. As it was, we children were reared in a calm which seemed incredible alongside the bedlam of some neighboring households.

When I was still little, we moved from South Salem, largely populated by Irish and French, to Derby Street, where there was a medley of Jews, Poles, and—Irish. Our new home, a weather-beaten nest, had been built almost a century before by an old salt. The smell of the tides lingered in every crumbly wall and rafter of it, mingling with the must of time, and sand fleas infested some of the crannies. The Atlantic rolled only a brief distance away from the rear, a sight that might have been thrilling if it had not been partly blocked by an old tenement building known as "the house of blazes." But my young feet sped me to the shore several times a day, and I became quite familiar with lobster traps, seaweed, jellyfish and starfish, mussels, clams, mackerel, haddock, hake, periwinkles, dories, fishermen, and salty lingo which seemed a part of the sea itself.

Summer nights of my childhood. . . . Lights would go on in the Seamen's Bethel across the street from us, and snatches of such hymns as "Washed in the Blood of the Lamb" and "Throw Out the Life Line" would waft themselves on the mild blue breeze, to the eerie orchestration of beetles and crickets. The big horse-chestnut tree at the corner of Curtis and Derby, so white with blossoms in the spring, was now a silver-sprayed pagoda under the July or August moon. Maybe a spouse-beaten woman would let out an agonized wail from an open window of "the house of blazes." How often I'd shudderingly heard of Mag-this or Moll-that's head being "split open," and pictured a teeth-grinding, red-eyed ogre swinging an ax! But young as I was, I knew that next morning Mag or Moll, stuck up with court plaster, would be smiling again at life as if to suggest that assault and battery was one of the surer proofs of wedded bliss.

If Aunt Aggie chanced to be down from Lawrence (her visits were as frequent as brief, because she could live neither with nor away from her too romantic husband Jack), we'd all sit out in the scraggly yard. Mom would make a pitcher of lemonade—two lemons and a little sugar, all we could afford, but positive nectar to our far from fussy throats. And, as I was eventually to learn, our shaky rush-bottom chairs, purchased from Izzy Kaplin the junk man, were quite as stable as the thrones of royalty across the ocean. As for our ragged hammock, a conscience gift from Kaplin after his overcharging us for the chairs, I now appreciate that no seat in all history was ever half so comfortable. Lolling there between two tilted staves in the ground, Aunt Aggie's arm around me, and my feet adangle, I'd catch up on my stargazing to the delicious tunes of some hurdy-gurdy competing out on Derby Street with the Seamen's Bethel, the crickets, the beetles, and the flow of Auntie's stories.

Her repertoire ranged from the fascinatingly tragic to the crudely comic. I'd prickle all over at her account of the Pemberton, a grim mill in Lawrence which one gray day keeled right over into the Merrimac, apparently pushed by the big hairy hand of Lucifer himself, plunging many of the workers to a watery grave and pinning others in tons of wreckage. And I'd nearly cease breathing when she'd proceed to tell about night coming on before all the entrapped ones could be rescued, and a man entering the ruins with a lantern to search for a relative, and the lamp dropping from his trembling hold and speedily turning the oil-soaked debris into a roaring holocaust in which the last moan melted to silence. My throat would be thick with a hurt of emotion as I thought of the poor, toiling for their daily bread, only to be paid the meanest of all wages—death. But the next moment Aunt Aggie would have us laughing fit to split at Jen Casey, who ran a kitchen barroom and fooled the police by emptying her bottles of booze into a commode under the bed; or at the biddy who tried to cure her husband of drink by paying two laddie bucks to haul him off drunk to a cemetery in the dead of night and scare the devil out of him with an impersonation of a pair of "sheeted ghosts" when he'd come to. The twist of anticlimax in the ending of this particular anecdote struck me as just about perfect. "Begob, where am I?" breathed the old soak, awakening and rubbing his eyes. "In hell *forever*," responded the "spooks" sepulchrally. "Well," said the soak, after a reflective second, and with a sigh of resignation that out of hell there is no redemption and that forever is a long time, "here's a quarter, me

lads. Go get us a half pint, will ye? Y'know the place better than
I do."

Saturday nights. . . . Just around sunset portly Mr. Morgan—
always *Mister*, mind you—would drive his huge-buttocked old
nag Minnie down the street and whoa her to a neighing stop at
each steady customer's gate. Then he'd heave his bulk from his
rickety cart and reach back in to lift up the lid of the wooden
box on which he had been sitting. The effect, as I now recall it,
was like the release of beauteous Eurydice from the underworld
by Orpheus, or the uncorking of a bottle of attar of roses to the
breeze, for there in the box stood three big-bellied earthen pots
exhaling what seemed to a hungry boy the very acme of essences,
the aroma of Boston-baked beans. Those glistening brown gems,
each bathed in its own ichor of perfection! The spiraling, kitch-
eny savor, putting a tingle in the pit of the stomach and sending salivary juices wild! I'd lick my chops, holding out Mom's
yellow mixing bowl to receive as much of the treasure as two
thin dimes could induce the great Morgan to ladle up for our
evening meal. If I'd had a hundred-dollar bill, it would have
seemed too little to give for what I got. Everybody said that he
was much the best bean man in town, and his trio of pots never
passed through our neighborhood without being emptied to the
last luscious scoop. Nobody was his equal, except perhaps Mr.
Fred Johnson, whose candy cart, laden with penny sticks, black-
jacks and Gibraltars, regularly appeared from the Pepper Factory in Peabody. And he was such a convenience, because Saturdays were too busy with housecleaning for home cooking.

The bean banquet would be supplemented at our table with a
loaf of brown bread, thick, cylinder-shaped, hot, full of plums,
from a bakery on Essex Street near Curtis; and no friends of ours
ever dined more satisfactorily on Saturday night, since all of
them had exactly the same fare, only that some—a trifle better off
than others—were able to afford an extra such as ketchup.

After supper Mom would beckon me to the pantry and there
grant the privilege of carrying her own prepared pot of beans to

the Old Grist Mill nearby. It was a neighborhood custom never to burn fuel while we were abed nights, and the mill's ovens were a community convenience for the baking of Sunday breakfast. Soaked for hours in water, seasoned with a sliced onion, sweetened with molasses, and surmounted with a hunk of salt pork, Mom's beans were ready for the goldening that Old Grist could give; and I myself was just as ready to take off, for Mom always slipped me a penny with which to buy for myself at Cahill's Variety Store a red-and-white peppermint twist, a handful of jelly beans, or a fat pickle—salty, warty, drippy. Airily I'd bear the pot by the knotted end of the fresh white towel that she had placed around it. The burden was rather heavy for a little boy, but the little boy's spirit was light. And so, on to the mill, Cahill's, candy, or pickle. Then home to await my turn at a warm, sudsy bath in the zinc clothes tub beside the kitchen stove.

But the serenity of week-end nights in old Salem was only one phase. Saturday was payday, and not a few hard-earned dollars always found their way, as shadows fell, to the several saloons of the neighborhood. My father hated drink resolutely, because as a boy he had seen too many and much of its effects; but his attitude was something of an oddity among the Irish. A joy-loving people could hardly be proof against the temptation to drown out the memory of sorrows and stir up cheer, and their natural heartiness rendered it difficult to know just where to stop. Often, in the wee small hours, I'd be awakened by screams and curses from "the house of blazes" or strains of off-key and sometimes off-color song from celebrators staggering home. But Sunday morning was always as different as a washed face from a dirty one, and both sides of Derby Street would be all proper with people either going to Mass at St. Mary's or coming from it; and I knew that though the Devil might be powerful in the dark, he could never prevent a single sunrise and had to scat at the very first ray.

Winter nights, with a blizzard whirling and howling in from the sea. . . . How cozy our old house then seemed, with its walls and roof still capable of keeping out the monster, even if the arctic breath of him got in freely enough through loose sashes and clapboards. Jim, Tom Junior, Joe, and I had a room all to ourselves, but with only one bed in it, a secondhand white iron thing with weak springs and a mattress that sagged near the middle. Tom would keep his eye on the sag as the warmest and therefore the most desirable portion; and Jim would keep his on it too, but not for himself. The two crazy-quilt coverings, made by Mom and the girls from scraps of cloth and wads of cotton batting, seemed to us like layers of a great love, which indeed they were. Our teeth chattering, we'd yank off our clothes, struggle into our long woolen nightshirts, fall to our knees and swiftly say our prayers, the while we blinked at the glistening of the sentinel street lamp through the thick-frosted window of the room; and then we'd jump up and dive with such energy into the creaky bed as to cause it almost to collapse.

Jim—good, unselfish Jim, so much like Dad—always saw that I, as the youngest of the quartet, got the sag, and he'd even let me ease my icy toes on his legs. Our bodies were huddled together in so limited a space that any change of position on the part of one might have been an annoyance to all, but we had an arrangement to forestall that. Whenever any of us needed to twist or turn, he'd simply murmur the magic word "Shift," and with all the unison of a well-geared mechanism, over we'd go.

Morning. The window would be opaque with frost but sparkling with minuscule diamonds where sunbeams cut in. No other house could ever have had windows like that, we thought; except, of course, each of the "mansions above" which Sister Casimir and the other nuns at St. Mary's School often described to us. And to the charm of sight would be added that of sound: a tinkle-tinkle of sleigh bells. We'd stick out our heads fully from the quilts, but turtle them right in again from the temperature that nipped our noses; yet after a second or two we'd be brave enough to uncover—a little—once more, so as the better to hear the music in the air. Soon, with a heave-ho, we'd be out of bed, aspen but eager, defying the needle-point chill, puffing clouds of vaporized breath, scraping the hoar on the window with our fingernails, and, through jagged little sections of clearance, beholding a world at which we had to whistle. Newborn, dazzling, fantastic. An overnight miracle in white! Depths and drifts of pure downiness everywhere; sheaths of sun-shot ice turning the humble Seamen's Bethel across the street and the red-brick Old Grist Mill behind the chestnut tree at the corner of Curtis and Derby into crystal palaces; prospect of hillside coasting, pung-ride-stealing, snowman-making, snowball-battling.

Gingerly we'd get into our clothes and through our prayers, and streak to the kitchen, which contained the only stove in the house. Mom, assisted by Annie and Agnes, would be already there, preparing our meal. Dad would be missing, because his work required him to be off before sunrise; and we'd glance wistfully toward his empty place at the table, for our awe of him never diminished our affection, and his absence always registered just as strongly as his presence. Will, the eldest of the brood, would be in the yard, dutifully shoveling pathways to outhouse and gate. Frank, the youngest, who had a special cot in a large clothes closet off Mom and Dad's room, would still be sleeping, as the favorite of a family should.

Our family greetings were less expressed than implied. Though we had an unbounded regard for one another, none of us was very demonstrative about it; but that only caused the evidences to crop out the more pleasantly. Annie and Agnes, dainty and fresh in pinafores, would step away from the stove so that we boys might toast ourselves closer to it. Mom remained just where she was, as if realizing that warmth perfected itself for us with her near. She'd give each a pat on the head or shoulder, and she'd smile, as much as to say, "Well, here you are, and here I am, and isn't a new day quite a thing!"

The breakfast wasn't much, but it seemed a banquet. Usually it consisted of what Mom called "turns," pieces of dough from the quantity that she had kneaded the night before and left in a round tin pan in the pantry to rise. These bits, fried in lard to a crispiness on one side and then forked over to be just as well treated on the other, not only tasted but smelled good, especially when served with melted butter and cups of tea or milk. We'd never think of asking for anything better.

And it wasn't just our stomachs that were fed. We had books —dog-eared, finger-marked, fray-edged—around the house, though where they came from, I don't know even to this day. Perhaps Dad picked them up as castoffs from the library of the Father Matthew Hall where he sometimes served as janitor; but that could not have been the full explanation, for there was one called *Home Medical Adviser*. It attracted and repelled me with its full-page pictures of various diseases, and left me liking the others the more, particularly Aesop's fables, Hans Christian Andersen's fairy tales, and Bible history. And the best of all was the last. What amazing things brunette Annie and golden-haired Agnes read for me even after I was old enough to do it for myself! Listening to those scriptural stories, I lived in the first and fairest of gardens which contained a myriad delights and one serpent. I thrilled to the greatest storm that ever lashed the earth, in which rain fell for forty days and nights. I beheld the strongest man that ever flexed a muscle, shaking down a whole temple by seizing and forcing two pillars; the waters of the Red Sea dividing in obedience to the motion of Moses' staff; the walls of Jericho falling asunder at the sound of trumpets; fire pouring down on Sodom and Gomorrah, and Lot's wife, because she looked back, turned into a pillar of salt; the earth opening and swallowing Core, Dathan and Abiron; Elias rising in a flaming chariot to the heavens; angels ascending and descending Jacob's ladder; the little boy Joseph, sold by his own brothers into slavery but becoming the most powerful man in Egypt; the shepherd lad David slaying a giant with a slingshot; rebellious, fugitive Absalom caught by his flowing hair in the branches of a tree and transfixed, as he dangled, with a sword. And stout Balboa, silent on a peak in Darien, could not have been more moved than I was, when, to the music of my sisters' voices, the New Testament unfolded the life of One who died for men.

It was good to know that God and love were the same and that He was always near, for we needed help, it seemed, at every turn. Very special help, at times. Came the day when Christie Shea, one of our playmates and as rollicking a sprite as I have ever known, slipped away from brother Jim and me and some others to hop a ride on the coal crusher down by the Willows Road. That gaunt steel structure with its restless chains and wheels stood like a great hobbledehoy skeleton against the sky, and the jaw of its down-dipping mechanical bucket would scoop out huge mouthfuls from an anthracite pyramid to lift them high into a chopping chamber; then, in small pieces, suitable for domestic use, the fuel would be spewed out upon another pyramid. Little Christie that day longed to go up-up, and here was a substitute for wings. Through the mist of time I can still see him perching on a side of the big bucket, waving his free hand, his face set and eager, a forced smile on lips which were beginning to quiver. Jim and I hollered to him to jump off, but he only shook his curly head, threw a glance skyward, and smiled again, this time genuinely. Jim dashed forward to seize him. Too late. We closed our eyes and held our breath as the bucket, with the minim adventurer to be carried and the coal to be crushed, rose noisily, grindingly.

We never saw Christie again, but only a white casket which "could not be opened," and his mother sitting beside it, too stricken even to move or moan. The morning of the funeral I heard the pastor of St. Mary's saying to her, "Life crushes us all, Mrs. Shea. The child was too little to feel much pain, and God was there to make him whole and take him in His arms." It was then that I noticed her looking up through her tears as Christie himself had looked up, and I was filled with a feeling that Somebody was looking down, because she was smiling just as Christie himself had smiled.

And there was the day when Marie Manski, an unattractive

old-maid neighbor of ours, who used to fluff out her stringy hair in a vain attempt to offset the sharpness of her features, and was the sole support of her ailing parents, came home in an ambulance from the Naumkeag. The loose coiffure had caught in one of the weaving machines as she was stooping to pick up her handkerchief from the floor, and the scalp was torn off with it. That night no lamp shone from any window of the Manski home, and I knew what my mother meant when she murmured something about "dark despair." But the next morning, while standing with some urchins outside that tenement and hoping, boylike, to catch a glimpse of a scalpless head, I saw that, instead of "dark despair," fresh white curtains—embroidered Irish linen —covered the windows; and I remembered that Mom had curtains like those, scented with sachet, wrapped in tissue paper and tucked away in a bureau drawer. They were the only present she received on her wedding day, she'd often told us; and having come from her mother in Lawrence, who had since passed away, they must have been more valuable than ever to her. "The girls will be needing them some sunny day," she would say. Whatever prompted me to go home and peek in the drawer that morning, I do not know; but when I did, the curtains were gone and I knew whence those on the Manski windows had come.

Mom's attempt to lessen the dreariness of an afflicted household brought results, for it started a flow of neighborliness; and Marie, who had taken care of her parents all by herself, was now surrounded by helpers. Nobody had anything nearly so fine as Mom's curtains to offer, but many little gifts—such as a loaf of bread, a slice of meat, a pillow slip, an hour of baking and cleaning, a geranium, a word of comfort—amounted to so much that soon the Manski tenement was almost as happy as any other. And Mom said to Dad at table one evening, "Marie was telling me that if she hadn't lost her scalp she'd never have found her friends."

Our family, with its growing needs, had to have a growing income. True, we could live on little, so long as we had a lot to live for, but even a little needs to be large enough. Will and Annie therefore got themselves some work after school hours; he at Daly's Fruit Store on Essex Street, and she at the Old Grist Mill. Their wages, amounting conjointly to about four dollars a week, paid half our monthly rent, and, feeling more secure, we were inclined to splurge. "If we only owned a piano," sighed Annie, echoed by Agnes, "we could have company." And this caused Dad to remember that the Father Matthew Hall had an old square Chickering which the entertainment committee wished to get rid of—for a reasonable sum. Swallowing hard, he came to a decision. That night he offered the committee five dollars, which, strangely enough, they accepted; and the following morning the door of our musty front room, which contained only some horsehair chairs, a marble-topped table with a thick copper-clasped Bible, and an easel holding up an awful yellow-didied portrait of Grandmother Mahoney with a pipe in her mouth, was flung open to receive the wonderful addition. It looked like a coffin, that Chickering, but we saw it rather as a great oblong treasure chest. I strutted before the kids of the neighborhood as it was being brought in by two hefty knights of labor who astonished me by seeming glad to get rid of it. Now we Murphys had something that most other families lacked.

Annie and Agnes were wild with delight and, desiring everything to be in keeping with this gift from God, tried to remove Grandma Mahoney's likeness. But Mom would not hear of such a thing and looked hurt at the very idea. So they sought to content themselves with edging the easel into a corner where shadows could cover it, and with throwing up the windows and opening the shutters in order that every passer-by might see how swell we had suddenly become. Not satisfied with that, they next decided to put the piano nearer the windows, where it would be kissed by the sun and made all the more visible to the small fry gazing in from the sidewalk. This was a bad mistake, but it became worse when they waved their brothers off from aiding them. The thing was much too heavy to be pushed around on its rusty rollers, and much too old to hold together well. While they shoved as mightily as possible, one of the legs with a worn-out thread in the socket wobbled and gave way. They could not hold up the awful weight, and down came a corner on Annie's foot. The audience at the windows howled with glee.

Mom closed the blinds and carried Annie to bed, where the poor girl had to remain for three weeks, enduring great pain and burning to get back to the Old Grist Mill to help reimburse Dad for the piano and the many visits of a doctor. We all suffered with her, but the joy that she had not been permanently injured compensated for everything, and the June morning when she took her first unassisted steps across Derby Street to the mill was a regular holiday for us. Yet before the sun went down that day she had again become a child of misfortune. The machine that stamped the name of the firm on each saltine biscuit had caught her right hand, even as Marie Manski's hair had been caught by the other kind of machine, and her wrist was broken, to say nothing of her heart. She had to lie abed for many weeks more, and her sweet pale face grew paler, sweeter. The hand healed, but a weakness in the delicate wrist and an ugly cicatrix on it remained to taunt her that, though she'd again be working and life would go on, the music she craved could never be quite hers to learn and give. There are so many kinds of music, though! And the measure of patience and gentleness that came to ener-getic Annie, who might have developed into a little spitfire with that temperament of hers, added to the life of our home some-thing even better than such tunes as "Star of the Sea" and "Whispering Hope."

In as much as we had a piano and Agnes showed aptitude only for keeping it exquisitely polished, and since *somebody* ought to learn to play it, Annie suggested to Mom and Dad that I, as the quietest of her brothers next to Will, be given lessons for which she would gladly set aside the little raise in salary the Old Grist Mill was conceding because of the accident. And that was how one phase of my boyhood ended. Henceforth, Dad and Mom,

determined that Annie's generosity should not go to waste, saw
not only that I took those lessons just as regularly as possible
from Madame Jannery, a dapper little person in South Salem who
earned a living for herself and her small daughters by teaching
"scales" and "pieces," but also that I practiced on the Chickering two hours a day. Gone was a large portion of my freedom to
skip off to the ever fascinating waves that washed the shore; and,
worse beyond words, I was now shunned by most of the neighborhood boys, to whom even the beginning of such sissiness as
piano playing was the same as smallpox.

Clearly I recall the time when, after my slipping away to the
shore from dreary practice, the veil between two worlds was
almost rent for me. Though all my brothers except Frank were
excellent swimmers, I had not yet acquired the art. That day I
waded out too far, and the tide swept me farther still. Lifted
off my feet and over my head, I struggled in a blue-green weird-
ness through which sunlight strained weak and silence thundered. Brine filling my ears, throat, and stomach, and all effort
against it proving futile, I began to relax. Then, closing my eyes,
I found my brief past unscrolling itself with remarkable clarity
and detail within me. It was a strangely soothing record, without
a single serious blemish to cause a keen regret; and my Act of
Contrition, which Sister Casimir had taught me, made it shine.
Only two days before, I had gone to Confession and found nothing in my littleness to tell Father Walsh, the assistant pastor of
St. Mary's, but that I'd "ducked practicin' twice," and "im'tated
a big boy by stretchin' my mouth wide with two fingers an' say-
in' 'Board of health' so that it sounded jus' like 'Go to hell,' " and
"stole once."

"Stole what?" he'd demanded sternly.

"A ride off a team," I'd replied, atremble, expecting to be pen-
anced soundly. But now there was no trembling. Only a great
peace drawing me to itself; such a calm as always preludes repose; the same sort of feeling with which I lay each night in the
white iron bed between my brothers, whose bodies were a wall

of protection from any danger in the dark. Was this death? It seemed rather to be life falling asleep; and, pleasantly tired, I was ready. Through a spinning blur a silvery gleam was coming as if from above.

Suddenly I felt an arm around my neck. It bore me up in its strong vise to air and on through spray. A few moments more and I lay gasping, retching, on the shore; and brother Joe was standing all wet and solicitous over me. "You near drowned," he said. "Good thing I got to you in time!" Good? I wasn't so sure. Out there, under the roof of waters, I had been surrounded and even suffused with a wondrous ease, and here and now I was writhing in nausea.

But on another unforgettable day I saw what I had escaped. A few of us children, coming from St. Mary's, paused pop-eyed at Whipple's Wharf, where men with hooked poles were grappling out of the harbor a gray-brown corpse, shrunken in some parts and bloated in others, the muscles rigidly contorted, the teeth exposed and the nose twisted as if in a final frozen snarl, the cheeks lobster-clawed to shreds. I recoiled but could hardly tear my eyes away, for there in those terrible, pitiable remains was myself as I might have been. Once or twice I glanced out over the gray-blue tide. A sailboat at anchor rocked its dun silhouette on the white caps; some gulls, winging in from nowhere, flashed and disappeared; and the water-logged body on the slimy stones of the wharf dripped, dripped.

Eating was out of the question that noon. The sight of meat sickened me, because I could think only of the half-masticated thing, a blob of refuse that had once been as alive and whole as any other human being. When I told Mom what was bothering me, she stroked my forehead and murmured, "But the man's soul did not drown, Son. It's still living, and you must pray that it's at peace and rest in heaven." And I asked her what a soul was. "Father Walsh or Sister Casimir can tell you better—I haven't the words," she said. "It—it's a pearl of great price. The body's a shell that holds the pearl but soon falls apart."

From then on I began really to think, and my thoughts were more and more of souls. And the nuns at St. Mary's, always harping gently on the same theme, nurtured in me a spirituality which could not but increase. The knowledge that the Lord so prized souls as to have sent His Son to save them, and that men were appointed to carry on this purpose in the Son's name and power, made quite an impression on me; and I pictured myself grown up, searching the sea of life itself for pearls.

Brother Will, who was an altar boy at St. Mary's, watched over me. Tall for his age, deep-eyed, and bearing a resemblance to the paper-lace-edged picture of St. Aloysius that Mom kept in her prayer book from girlhood days, he had a manner which seemed to set him aside from trivial things; yet he could make the little concerns of each of his brothers and sisters his own, and we always liked to have him near. One afternoon when he found me sprawling on a patch of sand at the foot of Blaney Street and gazing off across the harbor toward Marblehead, I learned much.

"That town over there—that's where the first American slave ship was built," he said, sitting beside me. "Father Halley told me all about it, and how the ship was called *Desire*, and how some of the old mansions around here were built out of the profits of stealing and selling Negroes. It was an awful business, Eddie, and New Englanders themselves finally got around to realizing it. But by then the South had any number of slaves. The North wanted to free them, but the South didn't, and a big war had to be fought. Our dad was in it and got wounded. That's why he has a limp in his leg." His voice shook. "Ever since the slaves were freed they've been wandering around in the South like sheep without a shepherd. Father says that, having so little, they need God so much, and that the Church has been calling for priests to go and help them. He himself went, some years ago, but his health failed and he had to come back. He thinks New England owes a lot to the Negroes for having had such a part in selling them into slavery. I think so too, and I want to enter the missionary priesthood. There's a college in Baltimore, he says, where boys are received and trained for that. He's already written there for me and the rector's willing to take me if Mom and Dad say yes. It'll be hard to ask them, because they badly need the money I bring in from Daly's."

Shortly after our talk he approached them with his request. And from then on I never saw Dad with a plug of tobacco; but I did see him hoarding nickels and dimes, and found out that he had gotten himself some extra work at night. And it wasn't long before he said to Mom, "I guess there's just about enough now for that valise at Kaplin's and the lad's fare to Baltimore." And Mom wept, but not sadly; in fact, she looked even happy with the tears coursing down her cheeks. Two days later Will bade us all good-by. And that was not so long after many Salemites, with never a thought of sharing the wealth of the Gospel, were off on the rush to Alaska for gold.

The house seemed to ache with emptiness after he went away, but we were comforted by a feeling that, in following a dream, he had opened a door and let in a breeze from a better world. We had only to think of others so unlike him, to know the blessedness of the way he had gone.

There was plenty of sin in old Salem. Mom and the neighbors would shake their heads and mumble about Moira O'Dare, the fifteen-year-old daughter of a family down the street, being "too pretty for her own good" and having "too much freedom"; and one day Moira disappeared. A few months later I heard hushed references to her fate; another case of drowning, this time in the sea of Boston slums. Moira, whose eyes were vesper blue and whose raven hair was like a nun's veil. Moira, who used to seem to me, as she went to Holy Communion on Sunday mornings, with her head bowed and her hands clasped to her bosom, like a statue astray from a pedestal.

And the others! Helen O'Leary who, not at all pretty, tried to make herself so with ribbons and gewgaws and had to be "sent off" for pilfering from the five-and-ten. Terry McMahon, who hated his stepmother and broke windows and was called "the policeman's pet." Gene Sheehan, Ted MacMurray, Pat Barry, and Leonard Farley, always getting themselves or leading others into trouble. And, thinking of present evil, I'd prowl around that nearby relic of past wrong, the house of the seven gables, where, according to lore and Nathaniel Hawthorne's novel, a man once lived who deliberately sent an innocent citizen to the gallows and was later strangled to death seemingly by the ghost of the victim. Too, Hawthorne's *Scarlet Letter*, the first somber story I ever attempted to read through, moved me beyond my depth and added to my sense of a darkling something in life that must be fought.

Good behavior came easy enough to Annie and Agnes, who were deeply attached to their home. Shunned by the Derby Street kids, I myself was better off than I realized; and Frank, the baby, could not but be safe. But Jim, Tom, and Joe, fun-loving and adventurous, were heading for complications. I knew of their Sweet Caporal cigarettes and their too colorful escapades, but I never told on them, because they trusted me not to, and I was grateful to Jim for giving me the best part of the bed, to Joe for saving me from the harbor, and to Tom for occasionally slipping me a copper. Still, Mom found things out somehow, for she often took the boys aside for talks; and I'd notice that right after they would try very hard to be good. But they never seemed to succeed for long, and a worried look became habitual with her. Surely she wanted to tell her fears to Dad; yet when, tired and hungry, he'd come in at sunset from his hard day's labor, she could never let herself disturb him. And since he scarcely knew his own strength, she must have feared that if he ever laid a hand in anger on any of us he would go too far. Moreover, she was aghast, like so many other mothers in town at the time, at a tragedy in a home on Bleachery Row in Peabody.

There one morning a widow whom we knew well did an unbelievable thing. Suffering a severe headache, and having in vain begged her two children, whom she adored, to cease their shrill game-playing in the kitchen or to go outside, she suddenly lost all control and struck at them with a boot jack grabbed from the floor; then, her mind clearing, she saw in blood and death the effect of her seizure. Mom certainly felt that if such violence could have possessed so good and gentle a soul anything could happen to anybody; so to save Jim, Tom, and Joe from Dad's wrath, she shielded them from his authority. The trial of maintaining this attitude was great, and soon I saw that silver was creeping into her hair.

For the most part, in those days, Salem was cloaked with tradition, the folds of which fell in lines of simple, almost classic, grace. Chestnut and upper Essex streets, with their unostentatious homes and air of cultured ease, and the common encircled by chaste English charm, could not be improved upon and had no course ahead but a process of quiet decay. If the town as other generations knew it was to die, it appeared determined to do so with dignity.

Among my earliest and fondest recollections are the few Yankees who held on to their ancestral property in the Derby Street district which immigrants had taken over; and chief among those few were the two Tarbell sisters, who, white-haired, pin-neat, soft-voiced, courteous to everybody, and so devoted to their fluffy Maltese cats, Ladybell and Sir Launcelot, seemed to me as "nice" as the nuns at St. Mary's. Whenever they beckoned me to their door for a treat of milk and ginger cookies, their wrinkled faces made me think of crumpled silk shedding tiny specks of light, and their dim eyes were moist with a distillation of kindness. It peeved me to hear them referred to as "cheap Yanks" and "black Protestants," because I could see that although they seldom stirred beyond their home they longed to make friends. Was it religion or loneliness? Perhaps a blend of both in an aging town with fragrant but not too lush meadows to the left and, to the right, the constant sermon of the sea. And maybe, too, these sensitive, gentle sisters understood us better than we understood ourselves. At any rate, their timid overtures were little noticed and less appreciated by most of us, for that miserable clause, "No Irish Catholic need apply," stuck in our craws, and our make-up urged us to a blanket resentment of Yankees in general. We chose to interpret their thrift as penury, their strong morale as hypocrisy, their culture as snootiness; and unconsciously we lessened our own worthiness by belittling theirs.

Some of our families, bereaved of breadwinners, were so poor that they had to accept public relief; but they yielded only on condition that it be given under cover of night when, presumably, neighbors would not see. I recall that once, when a good old couple gave me an overcoat which had belonged to their grandson, Mom and Dad made me bring it right back to them. I blushed at a pride that saw fit to slap beneficence in the face, and for a time somewhat doubted my parents' perfection. But now, looking back, I am ashamed of having been ashamed. It was not that Dad and Mom wanted to hurt anybody but only to safeguard their right and duty of doing their own providing. When they needed help, they looked up, not around, for it.

We all knew one Yankee lady, however, whom none of us dared to disprize, so evident were her merits. Though she had the bluest blood of Massachusetts in her veins, her face was pinkly warm with a zeal for human welfare, and she seemed a kind of continual spring, ever bubbling with good deeds. It was she who, like Phoebe in Hawthorne's *The House of the Seven Gables*, dispelled the blight from the estate on Turner Street that I used to prowl around with fearsome interest. Having purchased it, she restored all the gables, planted a garden which attracted honey bees galore and choirs of birds, and threw open gates and doors to everybody. In sum, she made this once gloomy manse again a thing of allure to serve the community not only as a shrine of the good things of Salem's past but as a stimulus to betterment in the future. There she organized little entertainments, which were like so many candles in what she believed to be the drabness of our existence. There she set a standard for our living conditions, copying the efforts of Hull House in Chicago; and as if this were not enough, she mothered the Salem Fraternity, an institution on Central Street, which, supervised by a sterling gentleman named Herbert Farwell, provided much healthier outlets for boyish energy than window-smashing, cat-stoning, and fist fighting. She helped him equip a gymnasium and finance a library and summer camp trips to Rowley for us youngsters. And, at the fraternity, she taught classes in drawing, clay modeling, and painting. This appealed only to a few at first; but the number gradually increased because, so interested herself, she made things so interesting. Her eye everywhere, she discovered Johnnie Brooks, a crippled young man with a yearning for usefulness, and enabled him to find himself in a life of devotion to youth. One of her boys who might have passed on to factory work was to become an architect; another, a civic leader; a third, a journalist; and several, a credit in divers white-collar positions to this lady who thought only of others. And Salem will always remember Caroline Emmerton.

She early detected in my crude but earnest venturings with design and color a promise of talent; and this, together with my piano playing, disposed her to make plans. "When you finish at St. Mary's," she said, "I shall send you to one of the best schools in Boston, if your parents are willing."

Mom and Dad were delighted that such an important person should be interested in me. To have an artist as well as a priest in the family would ring the very bell of privilege. But they winced at the thought of a Murphy being "under too much of a compliment" even to an Emmerton, and wanted to save for my future just as they were saving for Will's. So they put their heads together, and the result was a revolutionary scheme which at first plunged us into debt but soon, as it got rolling along, yielded dividends.

Like all the poor, we had been paying more than the rich for food by buying from day to day in smallest quantities; but now, prodded by necessity, we were awakened to the paradox that we could eat better and lay out less. Apples by the peck instead of the quart, potatoes by the bushel instead of the sack, a whole weekly ham or slab of corned beef instead of mere cuts; these wonders made a royal entry to our larder, and my brothers and sisters and I kept rubbing our eyes. Our only setback came when Mom had to warn us against overindulgence, else we'd end in worse than the poorhouse—*jail*. So we tried to co-operate; and it was not too difficult, for the sight of an ample food supply, after we got used to it, seemed to subdue the appetite with an assurance that our next meals were already provided, whereas a meager amount used to tease it with uncertainty and tempt it too much.

To prepare me for the future, Miss Emmerton sometimes brought me to Boston to visit the Museum of Fine Arts, hear concerts, and see worth-while plays—a great advantage for a little Derby Streeter, but one to which my reactions were not all that she had a right to expect. The museum startled me with its nude statues, and I wondered why she should want me to view such things. I didn't tell Mom and Dad about them, because they might scold me for looking and never let me out of town again. The concerts were far inferior, I thought, to hurdy-gurdies, especially the newfangled kind with mandolin attachment, which made summer nights in Salem so tuneful. But the theater affected me through and through. It was just like turning one's imagination inside out and watching it perform, not in the flat two-dimensional fashion of the magic lantern that Mr. Farwell used to show us at the fraternity, but with the fullness and expressiveness of life itself.

Stock companies often played our town and presented such attractions as Frankie Carpenter, "the star of the East," Jere McAuliffe, "the king of matinee idols," and Corse Payton, "a hundred characters in one." Ten cents could buy me a seat in the balcony of the Mechanic Hall; and there, many a Saturday afternoon, I'd strain forward, hands on knees, eyes apop, mouth agape, ears aquiver. Motion pictures, still in their infancy, had not yet begun their great service of purging the stage by appropriating the blood-and-thunder; and what I experienced was theater plus in such scenes as the heroine of *Uncle Josh Spruceby* almost cut in two by a buzz saw, walls coming together to press a pair of lovers to death in *Queen of the White Slaves*, and the Polish Jew done to a dastardly end by the spine-chilling technique of Thomas Shea in *The Bells*.

To get to any of these spectacles, much more suited to my taste at the time than the far better offerings in Boston which Miss Emmerton afforded me, required enterprise. Through the week, I hunted for empty whisky bottles, which were not too hard to find in our neighborhood and could be sold to Kaplin; and on Saturday morning, unbeknownst to Mom, I'd importantly apply a match to the kindling wood in the kitchen stove of our neighbors, the Goldblatts, who, strictly Orthodox, would rather have died than strike a Sabbath flame before sundown. When the kids found out what I was doing, they called me "Greeny Sheeny," but I didn't mind. Bottles and Goldblatts usually netted me no more than six pennies at best, and if I had not saved two or three more during the week by abstaining from pickles and candy and could depend on brother Tom for yet another, the luxury of a matinee would have been beyond reach.

After the show I'd hang around the stage door to catch a glimpse of the actors and actresses—no, gods and goddesses. On one of those occasions the ethereal girl who had just played the role of blind Louise in *The Two Orphans* stuck her glossy head out of a dressing-room window. She smiled a crooked smile, winked, and invited me from the corner of her rosebud lips to "stick around, kid—there may be somethin' doin'." I didn't "stick," but bolted in confusion down the street.

Thursday nights at the Mechanic Hall were known as "amateur nights," and aspirants to fame who did not "get the hook" were eligible for such wonderful prizes as a five-dollar gold piece, a fish dinner at the Willows—our nearest seaside pleasure resort, or a singing canary, cage and all. One Thursday afternoon a bold idea struck me, producing at first a cold sweat and then a hot impulse. Why shouldn't I, who could play piano, step out before the public and accept an award? How proud Mom and Dad, Annie, Agnes, and Miss Emmerton would be, and how I'd get back at the Derby Street riffraff for contemning me! Squaring my jaw and shoulders, I almost ran to the theater, and in less than ten minutes I was standing backstage, awed at the bareness and dinginess but yielding not a whit to weakness. This was my opportunity to prove myself, and I must offer nothing less than my all.

A stout man was seated at a deal table, chewing a cigar and playing cards with a fellow who looked like a dummy. When he saw me, he snarled, "Whadda ya want, peanut?"

He frightened me, but having gotten so far, I could not retreat—yet. "I want to give my name so's I can be an amachoor tonight," I gulped.

"Amachoor?" He emitted something between a guffaw and a groan. "This town's cram full of kids that think they can act and grownups that act like kids. Get out."

"But I can play 'The Midnight Fire Alarm' on the pianner," I pleaded.

"Me, I can play the fire extinguisher over there," he boomed, pointing to the nozzle of a hose coiled on the wall, "and gad if I won't play it on *you!*"

He lumbered up, his stubby fingers stretching.

An addled puppy, I turned and made for the door.

For an eternity of fifteen minutes or so the world was one big black cloud. But as soon as I got home Mom made me see sunlight again by putting something in my hand, the very first thing of its kind I had ever received. "It just came, and I opened it," she said. "It's an invitation for you to play your pieces at a party uptown."

I read and reread that note. *Your presence is requested at the home of Mrs. D. Trask at 3 P.M., March 1, 1904, 4 Liberty Street, to help celebrate her daughter Della's birthday. Please bring your music.* And when I got my breath, I still could not speak my surprise and pleasure. Curiosity seethed in me. Who was Mrs. Trask? And Della? And why should I, who had just been shooed out of the Mechanic Hall despite my ability to make music, be invited to a party because of it?

"Somebody, maybe Miss Emmerton, must've told this Mrs. Trask you're a fine musician," said Mom. "Slip off that blouse so I can wash and iron it. It's your only one, and March the first is tomorrow. Look at your shoes! All scuffed, and I haven't a dollar to buy you a new pair. Go in the front room and practice for all you're worth."

That night I tossed and squirmed so much in bed that Tom and Jim were almost as wide awake as myself. And I had to say "Shift" so many times that at last Tom growled, "Aw shet up'n go t' sleep."

But the next day the party proved to be worth all the excitement and anticipation. Mrs. Trask, trim, little, with wavy black hair and violet eyes which were somewhat tired-looking but very pretty, took me right under her wing. She quite dispelled my awkwardness at being among well-dressed boys and girls in a house that surpassed my own home as much as a mansion a hovel. It was only a boardinghouse, as I was later to learn, but so spacious and attractively furnished, and with such rich gas chandeliers! She kept me near her, imposed quiet when I sat at the piano to play, worked up some applause, talked to me later about my family, school, likes and dislikes, and filled my stomach and pockets with candy. Della, the daughter, perhaps no older than I but with the air of one who has seen much and learned fast, shared the mother's attractiveness and daintiness. She wore an accordion-pleated white dress with a yellow sash and did a *pas seul* for us in which the skirt whirled like the petals of a stem-spun daisy. "Della with her dancing and you with your playing could be a vaudeville act," said Mrs. Trask to me, unconsciously salving the sore of my Mechanic Hall defeat. "I'd just love to see you both at Keith's in Boston."

The boys and girls indulged several rounds of "post office," "spin-the-cover," and "drop-the-willow." But I preferred to look on, because taking part in kissing games would only have made me as red as a beet; and I wanted to talk with Mrs. Trask, whose voice was the softest I had ever heard. The party concluded with my playing a waltz, "The Wedding of the Winds," to which everybody danced. It was a long piece. Mrs. Trask, sitting beside me on the piano bench and turning the pages, let her left arm curve lightly around me. A lilac fragrance emanated from her, and somehow I thought of a kitten sprinkled with cologne. She bent her head and whispered, "You must come back often, Eddie. We're going to be great friends." I had to ask, "But how did you know about me?" Again she gave her bright smile. "I was at Madame Jannery's one day when you were taking a lesson," she said. "I saw you, but you didn't see me. I was waiting in the next room. When you left, she spoke of you and your parents. I hope you like me, because I—I——" She put a hand to her throat and held it there, breathing deeply. After a second or two, she exhaled. "Don't grow up—ever. Men can be so terrible."

That evening, when I gave Mom a report, including the remark about men, she said nothing for a while. Her finger on her cheek, she just stood, thinking. Then she told me that I'd better not go there any more.

"But why?" I asked. "She's so good to me!"

"It could be that she's not so good to herself." Mom's chin tilted a little. "Some of the neighbors say she's divorced and takes in—roomers. If I'd known in time it was such a place you'd been invited to, I'd not have let you go. You're much too young to understand—things."

I tried to stay away. But since Mom's words were "You'd better," not "You must," it did seem that she intended—well, somewhat—to leave the matter to me; so the next day there I was, with my face scrubbed pink and my hair combed smooth, ringing the doorbell of the house on Liberty Street.

Della let me in and tiptoed down the hallway, beckoning me

after her and cautioning me to be as quiet as herself. The interior was dark and gloomy today in comparison with yesterday's brightness and festivity. A brindled cat pressed close to the foot of the side staircase, arching its spine but not emitting so much as a single miaow. Presently I found myself in a big kitchen, and when I asked Della why we had to be so still, her explanation only confused me the more. "There's a man—Joe Hastings—upstairs," she said. "He hates everyone Mother likes, on account of he wants to have all her liking for hisself." And I thought what a queer person this Joe Hastings, whose presence could muffle and chill a whole house, must be. I wanted to know more about him, but she abruptly changed the subject by saying that if I cared to have something to eat, there was plenty in the ice chest. A chicken leg? Sure!

And while I was munching, munching, the sound of footsteps and a door either opening or closing could be heard. After a few moments Mrs. Trask appeared, and she stood there before us, hardly noticing Della or me, tears brimming in her eyes. "Why do you put up with him, Mother?" asked Della, and I was quite surprised at a little girl talking like that. But Mrs. Trask merely moaned; then, dabbing her lids with a frilly handkerchief, she smiled. It was only a ghost of a smile. Her lips were white. "There's such a thing as fear, my dear," she said, and turning that violet gaze of hers fully on me, she murmured, "I'm glad you're here again so soon, Eddie. A little music will do me good. Let's go into the parlor."

Again she sat beside me, and I played from memory for her. The lilac fragrance was still there, but now it seemed that a withering had set in, and I sensed a pathos rather than a perfume. After all these years I can see her as she was that day, her slender fingers lying entwined in her lap, her cheeks drawn, her big dark-lashed eyes gleaming into space. Once more she made me promise to return. And I did—the very next morning.

When Della answered my ring and let me in, I shrank back, disbelieving what I saw. The place looked as if some maniac, bent

on destroying everything, had blazed through it. Who? Why?
Della's eyes flashed as she said, "Joe Hastings—he did it! He
thinks Mother has someone else. She made up her mind only last
night to leave him once and for all, and this mornin' she acshally
went. I was supposed to get a few things together and follow her
to Grandma Culver's in Beverly where she'll hide out awhile;
but hidin' won't do any good, because Joe'll find her. I told her
that, and she just wouldn't listen. She's such a baby!" A sigh.
"Before I could get out, Joe got in with his latchkey and went
ravin' crazy at not findin' her. We haven't had any boarders with
us for weeks on account of Joe was jealous and acted mean
whenever Mother was nice to them as she had to be, so I was all
alone here, and I hid in the coal bin in the cellar till he finished
readin' the note she left on her bedroom bureau. And I kept hid,
you bet, when I heard him bustin' around smashin' and tearin'
things. It took a long time. He left only a few minutes ago, and
it's good you didn't come sooner. I'll show you upstairs. It's
worse there—mattresses and pillows yanked open, feathers everywhere, mirrors all broke. Awful."

"I don't want to see," I said. My teeth were chattering, and my
chin swerved over my shoulder. Mightn't the man dash back
through the door any minute to complete the chaos and include
both of us in it? "Let's get out right away. You should've gone
straight to Beverly. I'm goin' home and—and stay in all day, I
guess."

The next noon when I was walking down Derby Street from
school, I heard some newsboys yelling, "All 'bout the big murder
in Beverly!" *Beverly?* That was where Mrs. Trask and Della
were. *Murder?* I had two pennies in my pocket and bought one
of the papers; the front page affected me like a blow between the
eyes. Squatting limp on one of the stone steps of the old custom
house where Nathaniel Hawthorne used to be chief executive
and of which he wrote, "Neither the front nor the back entrance
opens on the road to paradise," I read about Joe Hastings prowl-
ing around the Culver house in Beverly through the night, wait-

ing for Mr. Culver to leave for his day's work, and then breaking
in; and about Mrs. Trask running in terror from him, only to be
cornered and shot through the head.

Not a wink of sleep was mine that night.

When the body was brought to Salem the following day, Mom
let me visit the undertaker's, because, after all, Mrs. Trask had
been kind to me. The Essex Street funeral parlor, the rear of
which was right next door to the house on Liberty Street, seemed
to indicate the nearness of death to life. And standing beside the
dove-colored coffin, I could not take more than one look at the
waxen, tortured face. My wet lids squeezing together, I turned
away, thinking how much Mrs. Trask had liked to hear me play
and that there'd be no music any more for her. People were already saying bad things, but I knew she was good. I'd seen that
goodness. I'd pray for her, and that would be a kind of music
which the live part of a dead person—the soul—could maybe
hear.

On the way home I went into the little chapel behind St.
Mary's Church; and there, kneeling at the altar rail, under the
ruby sanctuary lamp, I became older than my years, thinking of
little Christie Shea, whose span had been only a day, and of a
man's corpse drawn up on hooks from the dark of the harbor,
and hearing within me an echoing of the words, "There is such
a thing as *fear*." After the ruin I had beheld with my own eyes in
Mrs. Trask's house, I understood her fear and felt that it both
explained and pardoned any fault of hers; but how such a kind
lady could have had any fault, I did not see.

Days dragged by and etched sharper my image of death stalking life, for more news of the murder was issuing from the press.
Hastings had been arrested and put in the jail on St. Peter's Street
to await trial and, possibly, capital punishment. For reasons
too strange for me to grasp, the body of his victim was exhumed
for an autopsy in the same funeral parlor from which it had been
taken. How terrible men could be indeed! Why didn't they let
even the dead rest? And one drizzly morning I stood in a small

group of the curious on Liberty Street, watching a long box being removed from a hearse.

The effect was that of a skeletal finger tracing my spine and,
when I woke in the night, penetrating my flesh. Jim and Tom's
warm bodies could not keep it away. I grew scared of the dark,
and even during the day a tree-shaded street could make me
shudder. Often I seemed to hear footsteps behind me and looked
over my shoulder, sure that somebody was following. The
chapel was just about the safest place, and during the recesses at
school I regularly went there. Thoughts of brother Will, calm
and secure in a holy college down in Baltimore, from which he
wrote us such good letters, made me wish to be with him, doing
what he was doing. I especially felt that way when Sister Teresa
Carmel, who had a flair for lurid stories with a moral, taught
Sunday school.

From such lips as Sister's I was certain that only absolute truth
could come; and one of her tales, quite in keeping with my glumness, knotted my nerves. She told it to us on a murky autumnal
afternoon when winds were wailing like a horde of lost souls and
shaking the casements of St. Mary's in passing. With her sense of
timing, she *would* have to tell it on a day like that. It was the
story of a boy who struck his mother in rage and, through shame,
did not confess the sin. Sometime later he became ill and died and
was buried in an isolated spot in a big lonely cemetery. The sor-
rowful parent came daily to kneel there, and one bleak evening
when snow was falling, she discerned in the cold half light an
awesome thing: an arm, with the clenched fist that had once
dealt her a blow, protruding stiff and stark from the mound in
which the body lay. With her bare finger tips she tore away the
hard frosted soil and tried to bend the member back into burial,
but it kept springing forth like a tough yet pliant bough of a tree.
In horror and dismay she went to her priest, and he ordered her
to go back to the grave with a switch. "You did not chastise the
child when he struck you," he said, "and now you must do what
you failed to do then. Whip the sinfulness away." Obediently

she forced herself, and under the strokes of the belated beating the stubborn arm slowly sank into the depths.

Shortly after Sister Teresa Carmel's adding to my gloom with this pious fable, New England itself went morbid over a female torso which had just been found in a suitcase off the coast of Winthrop. The papers were full of grisly details, and the suspense of waiting for the head and limbs to turn up was terrible. When the restless tide swept to the shore a second suitcase containing the arms and legs, I felt that my own body was falling apart, just as Mom had said that all bodies eventually did.

There was a rather odd ring, the papers said, on one of the dead fingers; and a smart Hub reporter made it his business to get to see and examine it. He remembered a similar ring worn by one of the dancers in a publicity picture of *The Shepherd King* —a scriptural drama which I myself had managed to witness when, after a Boston run, it played the Salem Theatre. And this slight clue led him to a certain Geary household in Cambridge, where he learned that the daughter, Susan, had joined the "Shepherd King" company and had not been heard from for some time. So an identity was startlingly indicated, and even before the day the salt waters yielded forth a satchel with the head, the mystery was completely solved. Under the stage name of Ethel Durrell, Susan Geary had been with the company in Salem months before and had left for Boston in order to undergo treatment for a delicate condition. She died in the doctor's establishment, and to escape the consequences, he dismembered and disposed of the corpse.

Habitually I kept souvenirs of the shows I'd seen, and when I took from my pasteboard box the program of *The Shepherd King*, I discovered the name Ethel Durrell tucked away at the bottom. With a pencil stub and a shiver I heavily underscored it.

Moodiness was setting me farther apart from youngsters of my own age. Books, each one an escape from too keen-edged reality, had a special appeal for me, and trips to the fraternity or public library were now a steady necessity. One afternoon, while hurrying to return my copy of *Quo Vadis* and avoid a two-cent penalty for keeping it overtime, I could not resist the temptation to reread the famous episode of the giant Ursus strangling the bull in the Roman arena and rescuing his beloved Lygia; and crossing Essex Street, my eyes glued to the graphic pages, I was knocked down by a horse. Asprawl under the belly, I might have been hoofed into kingdom come, but an alert policeman got to me in time and dragged me away. Even so, I had to be taken to the hospital on Charter Street for treatment, a bone in my arm having been cracked.

Mom and Dad saw that books and brooding were making me too peaked and pale, and decided that what I must have was a vacation, not at the fraternity camp in Rowley where strenuousness was the rule and practice, but down on some good farm. The problem of just where to send me was easily solved. Steve and Martha O'Toole, distant relatives of ours who had always kept in touch, were briefly visiting Salem that June and they offered to take me back with them to their home in the vicinity of Lime Rock, Rhode Island.

Of that vacation away from Massachusetts I recall mostly that I missed the sea but soon appreciated the billowy grass and grain all around me, that I gobbled up Martha's deep-dish apple pie, and that I met John Nelson Goucher. "Come on in," a clear voice called to me one morning when I wandered toward a pond not far from the O'Tooles' house, and glancing out on the glassy surface of the water, I spied a sun-bronzed, well-shaped head. It looked severed, like—like Susan Geary's, but the face was attractive, with a grin reaching almost from ear to ear. "How deep?" I hollered. For answer the head disappeared and a hand rose. Then the hand itself went down and only a swirl of ripples with a bubbling in the center could be seen. "Show-off," I thought, and started to turn away; but a liquid sound renewed my interest, and twisting around, I saw the swimmer himself, sitting on the bank and swooshing his skin with his palms. "It's twicet over my top," he said, "and that makes it fun. We need a springboard, though. How 'bout you'n me makin' one?"

There followed some sprightly hours in which, with materials from Steve O'Toole's workshop, we worked on our springboard and became very well acquainted. Everything about Goucher pleased me, particularly his Yellow Kid ears, his abounding energy, and his explosive smile. His convex of personality fitted right into my concave of loneliness.

"I'm goin' to run away," he confided.

"From home?" I asked, not too brightly.

"Nope. *For* it. Y'see, there's seventeen of us in the family, and that's a heap of mouths to feed. I reckon one less will be a help."

I whistled. Seventeen! "Where do they all come from?"

"Oh, Pa's a powerful man."

"Is he big like Samson in the Bible?"

"Nope. He's little, like most Canucks. But Ma's big and Irish. She's got pink cheeks and blue eyes. A cancer too. A milk one."

"Gosh."

"Uh-huh." He seemed quite proud. "She's been op'rated on, but you'd never know it. She's always laffin', 'cept when any of us gets hurt or some of the neighbors have troubles. She helps everyone as needs it, and they all think she's grand. Me 'specially. That's why I'm goin' to run away and make money and build her a house with a lot of windows in it. She wants everything sunny."

"I'd sure like to know her," I said. "A cancer and all those children and always laffin'! She must be the best mother round here."

"Uh-huh." Stooping, he plucked a blade of grass and ran it zingingly through his very white teeth. "Wish I didn't hafta leave her."

I had learned to swim since the time, three years before, I nearly lost my life by not knowing how. My injured arm, already out of a sling, was not too much of a handicap, and the good one worked extra well. We dove and stroked and splashed until sundown, and then, not even thinking of going home for supper, we stuffed ourselves with huckleberries from the bushes that

rimmed the pool. And every time my mind reverts to that
meal I think of one of the several Thoreau paragraphs that a
fondness for outdoors has imprinted on my memory: "It is a
vulgar error to suppose that you have tasted huckleberries who
never plucked them. A huckleberry never reaches Boston; they
have not been known there since they grew on her three hills.
The ambrosial and essential part of the fruit is lost with the
bloom which is rubbed off in the market cart. As long as Eternal
Justice reigns, not one innocent berry can be transported thither
from the country's hills."

John Nelson Goucher and I, sated, lolled by the water when
the risen moon was using it for a mirror. Flat on our backs, with
our hands under our heads, we looked steadily skyward; he at
the stars coming out, and I a bit beyond them. And we talked of
how it would feel to be up there gazing down, and whether there
really was a man in the moon, and what we'd like to be. "I was
kept after school for shootin' spitballs in class one day," he said,
"and my teacher made me mem'rize some lines of a poem. I can
mem'rize great, only I forget right after. But I won't ever forget
a special one of them lines." And he quoted earnestly, " 'All are
architects' "—he pronounced it arshitects—" 'of fate, working in
these walls of time.' " And that inspired me to quote a text which
had lingered with me from Sunday school in Salem: " 'Unless
the Lord build the house, they labour in vain that build it.' "

I saw a great deal of Goucher during the rest of my vacation,
and met his mother. She really did have the jolliest face and the
heartiest manner, and seemed to draw everything and everybody
to her. I told her that she didn't look at all like my mom, but that
she made me think of her just the same; and she smiled and said,
"You make me think of her too, darlin'. Yerra I'll be seein' her
someday"—she winked warmly at John Nelson—"when I get
that automobile I've been promised." And he assured her, "I'll
get it for you, Ma." She laughed and said, "I know ya will, son.
But how?" And he answered, squinting into the dazzling future,
"Oh, I can sing, can't I? People tell me I got a good voice. Wasn't

I clapped out twicet when I sang Pop's old song, 'Lac St. Pierre,' in the church hall?"

My summer went fast, but the good effects of it were to last a long time, and I've never forgotten those Rhode Island scenes: the temple-like groves of junipers, white spruce and beechnut; the limpid streams alive with trout; the tangles of pickerel weed, and sloughs and bogholes deep in shade; the sun gliding so goldenly through boughs and leaves by day, and the myriad silver candles illuminating the altar of the skies by night. Oh, we did such prosaic things as nest robbing and shin scraping, Goucher and I, acting pretty much as boys on the loose in the midst of nature usually do, yet I derived from my vacation a feeling of communion with somebody—somebody with a capital S. And when I got back to Salem, my memories of the Beverly murder, the autopsy, the arctic touch on my spine in the shadows and the dark, Sister Teresa Carmel's stories, and the case of Susan Geary—all were so covered over in my consciousness that I was little troubled any more, even if they should stir again and never let me be quite the same. Besides, Della Trask and her grandparents had departed New England for their native Kentucky without leaving a trace. So it was that Puck of a Goucher, with his plan to run away, who kept in the forefront of my thoughts, crooking a finger to me with his ambition. I wished to imitate him but could not see myself as an "architect of fate." And why run off, if God was everywhere?

God everywhere. This teaching, prominent on the very first page of the catechism which I had learned from cover to cover, gave me much pause. " 'In Him we live, and move, and have our being,' " Sister Marie Concilio, who taught the ninth grade into which I was admitted that fall, quoted to us pupils in her initial talk. "He is to each and every one what the sea is to a fish. And more! Fish merely move in the sea and displace tiny portions of it, but God not only surrounds us—He *saturates* us. That is, if we don't expel Him by sin; and if we do, we die—like fish out of water." Then, relinquishing the figure of sea and fish, she declared, "He is to the soul what air is to the lungs. Without air the body cannot live. Without Him the soul——" She threw up her hands and trembled.

That last phrase, unfinished, affected me like a return of the icy hand. It made me think of a universe all dark and cold, "void" as in the beginning of Bible history, Decemberish, swept with a midnight wind. Heavy imagery for a boy in his thirteenth year, but natural enough to one who, by that time, had skimmed over several of the soul-tossed Hawthorne novels and been too much alone. Moreover, that home of ours, no matter how far Jim, Tom, and Joe were eluding its influence, was replete with solemn suggestion. No room in it, except the front one which had the Bible, lacked a sacred picture, a crucifix, or a statuette of some saint; and in my sisters' bedroom stood a miniature replica of the high altar of St. Mary's Church, which Dan Sully, one of Dad's cronies, had cleverly whittled to the last detail. Many an evening Mom and Dad would have us kneel before it to recite the rosary, after which Annie and Agnes would harmonize in a hymn and we'd all join in the chorus. Then heaven really seemed to absorb us, and God was everywhere. But indications of His absence and of evil were at other times strong. Having already seen and felt some of the somberness of life, I was rather unable to reconcile it with a belief in His continual presence, and one day during recess at school I haltingly expressed myself along this line to Sister Marie Concilio.

She picked up the beads that dangled from the cord around her waist and let them glide through her tapering fingers. With a faraway look in her eyes, she slowly replied, "God is truly everywhere; above by His glory, here by His providence, and even below by His justice. He never sleeps, and His love and care and justice always were and always must be. Even when men do wrong and cause a cloud of confusion in which He seems lost to them, He remains at hand, ready to forgive, soothe, heal, and turn evil into good. They think He isn't there because they can't see Him. But who ever saw his own mind and heart? If God were not actually present to men and in them, they couldn't think or feel anything at all or even exist. All power is from Him."

"But, Sister, don't we expel Him by sin?" I asked. "I've heard you say we do."

She kept looking into space. "Yes. But in the sense that we close our minds to His way and His will by opening them to our own. He tries to repair our mistake. He is the Good Shepherd who desires that no sheep be lost. He loves sinners because they need Him, and He seeks to raise them up from moral death. Ever He works through His chosen ones who, like Him, know the value of souls."

All this, though beyond my grasp, satisfied me for the time being. But other perplexities soon sprang up like weeds in that young brain of mine, and I had to look for further explanation. Two posers were the worst: first, Carrie Donovan, and, secondly, the Polish church on Herbert Street.

Sister Marie Concilio taught her class that through each and every good soul God's own beauty shone like sunlight through crystal. But Carrie, whom Mom always called "that good soul," seemed to me a strange advertisement for "God's beauty." A well-known character in town, she habitually appeared on the streets in dingy clothes and an old sailor hat. She shaved like a man, and, like a man, sometimes looked unshaved. Nobody ever saw her do a day's work, but she was often seen in St. Mary's Church. Too, she would often stand on corners to hold busy but tolerant people by the ear with her little sermons about the dire state of the world and the near approach of doom; and sometimes she could be found even at home—a tenement in a crowded tinderbox of a building. It was said that when there one day, she discovered a sooty chimney burning, and without the least thought of warning any of the tenants, she ran over to the church to pray.

As for the Polish congregation, they staged a battle which I chanced to witness on my way to St. Mary's one Sunday morning and which shocked me into wondering what good religion really was, if people who had so much of it could be as bad as those who hadn't any. Just as my Irish parents had taught me to look on God's house as sacred and on every priest as another Christ, so these Poles had doubtless instructed their children; yet here were fathers and sons, mothers and daughters also, shaking their fists, hurling stones at a holy door, and loudly demanding their pastor's removal.

The next Saturday afternoon, when I went to St. Mary's chapel for Confession to Father Walsh, who had prepared me for First Holy Communion and Confirmation, I mentioned how I felt about the fight and about Carrie Donovan. He put his hand to his lips, perhaps to cover a smile, then cleared his throat and said, "After I've absolved you and you've performed your penance, go into the sacristy and wait for me. I'll be there as soon as I hear the other penitents. We must have a little talk."

The little talk gave me a better perspective on the Poles and Carrie. From thinking of the woman's peculiarities, Father quickly had me considering the causes beneath them: the past years of hardship, struggle, and bewilderment, leaving defects in a personality, just as the Old Grist Mill had left a scar on my sister Annie's wrist. And the Polish fracas was explained as the all-too-human result, not of a hatred for the new pastor, who had yet to prove himself, but of a love for the old one who had served his people long and well. "To be sure, it would have been wiser for Carrie first to warn the tenants about the fire in the house and then slip over to the church to pray," he said; "and it would have been wiser for our Polish brethren to restrain themselves. But human beings are not perfect, my boy. They are, at best, merely striving for perfection; and God's beauty shines through whatever effort they make, because it is He who is behind it. Admire in all souls the good you see, and don't look for the opposite. People are less ridiculous than pitiable when their emotion, getting the better of their reason, causes them to act queerly. Always turn to God when you can't understand His creatures. He alone knows them fully. As their Creator, He has the key to what's going on inside them."

And he went on to tell me about a trip he had once made through Italy. "The peasants in a small town beyond Naples were making a novena to Our Blessed Mother so that she'd persuade her Son to send down rain on their withering fields," he said. "Each evening they would walk in solemn procession through the countryside, singing hymns of praise and reverently bearing her statue. But on the ninth night the skies were still locked, and the air was even hotter and heavier. They waited trustingly until the last hymn was sung and the last prayer of the novena recited. Nothing happened. Then, frankly disappointed, they frankly showed it. They took up stones and fistfuls of dry soil and hurled them at the statue. Childish? Absolutely. But all men are childish when they let themselves go, and childlike when they bow their heads to mystery, as Mary herself did when she murmured to the angel, 'Be it done unto me according to thy word.' "

Mellow Father Walsh. After so many years I have only to close my eyes to see his full-moon face and pleasant smile; only to shut out the sounds of the world again to hear his voice. And it was there in the sacristy, during our conference, that I was seized by a desire to serve him as his altar boy. I asked if I might, feeling all warm and satisfied within now, and not at all wanting to run away as John Nelson Goucher intended to do, but to stay near the sanctuary which seemed but an extension of my own good home. He not only gave me permission but promised personally to teach me the Latin responses and how to serve Mass.

There were three priests at St. Mary's: Father Timothy Murphy, big, dignified, aloof; Father David Murphy, thin, boyish, alert, and given to such humorous remarks as, "The Murphys are everywhere—even in jail"; and my own Father Walsh. But I could often see in my mind's eye a fourth—frail, ascetic, more spirit than flesh. That was because we had in our house a cherished photograph of Father Halley. We kept it near the miniature al-

tar, and I'd often study it, remembering what Will told me about
the missionary zeal of this former pastor of ours who had since
gone on to a church in Malden. Whenever I stood at the foot
of Blaney Street or down on the tip of Derby Wharf and gazed
over Salem Harbor to Marblehead, I'd think of the first slave
ship, and walking on Chestnut Street or around the common, I'd
remember that some of the mansions in our town had a connection with ugly profits from a bygone traffic in Negroes. There
was an echoing within me of the plea of the Church for shep-
herds to care for the dusky fold in the South, and I could almost
feel Father Halley beside me, whispering the same things that
had sent Will out on an ideal road. It kept occurring to me that
home was where the Lord dwelt, and that since He was everywhere, I needn't hesitate, when the time should come, to go
ahead.

I worked hard that year, both in the classroom and out. No
matinees in the old Mechanic Hall or the new Salem Theatre
drew me; I was saving for a purpose. Selling whisky bottles and
striking Hebrew flames appeared out of keeping with that purpose, and so I acquired an income now in a wholly different way.
We Irish were feeling our oats in Salem, and had even shown ourselves strong enough to boost into the mayoralty of the town our
own candidate—John Francis Hurley, as trim-whiskered, be-
ringed, tall-hatted, and jaunty a person as ever stepped out of a
Hibernian dream. We aptly described him as "right on deck."
And having bulged our political muscles once, we did it again,
keeping him in office and proving to our own satisfaction that no
Yankees could hold us down in this land of the free. Also, a kind
of cultural movement to suit the new state of affairs began to
show itself, and several families in the Derby Street section
bought pianos. Accordingly there was something of a run on the
local market for music teachers, and a fair musician by now,
who could play such intricate compositions as "The Twittering
of the Birds" and could be had cheap, I found myself being paid,
a dime a lesson, to impart my accomplishment to other kids.

I might have been quite taken with my importance, only that snuffy Jackie McCabe, the most resentful and resistant of pupils, guaranteed my humility with a treatment against which I had no defense. He hated me for obtruding on his precious freedom; hated me with an intensity I could well understand but which wasn't any the less uncomfortable on that account. He would stick out his tongue at me and thumb his freckled, drippy nose whenever, in the course of an instruction, his stout mother, who usually sat near us in her parlor to see that I gave the woolly lamb only my best, waddled to the kitchen to attend to something burning on the stove. And one Saturday morning, when about to report for duty at another household, the O'Keefes', I stood outside their door for a few moments, listening to a wailing little Micky getting from his ma a thrashing for "not practicin'," and overhearing her accuse herself of being "a double-darned fool" for "enrichin' them uppity Murphys thit don't have nothin', with nickels out of poor hard-worrkin' Dinny's pants pocket."

Happily there was something to balance the effect of the McCabes and the O'Keefes. We had just moved to another house, a bigger one on the corner of Derby and Daniel streets. A drugstore occupied the ground floor, and this seemed to me quite distinguished, because the store sold liquor on the sly and ice-cream sodas in the open and was very popular with old and young. Mom and Dad had thought long and hard before making the change, in as much as they feared to have Jim, Tom, and Joe exposed to alcoholic temptation; but their scruples were lessened by their realization that the whole neighborhood teemed with that sort of thing. Besides, our old place, so damp and mildewed, had given us too many coughs and colds; and this other offered such advantages as ten sunny rooms, a built-in tin bathtub, and a landlord who wouldn't hound us for the rent but let us come with it at our own convenience. All for only two dollars more per month than we had been paying.

And now each of us boys had a room to himself, a condition

which would have been delightful were it not that we missed the greater intimacy of less space and felt a certain drifting apart. Sleep never seemed the same to me after the old white iron bed with the saggy mattress landed in Kaplin's junk shop, giving way to neat cots. But soon we took to our new existence like growing ducks to a larger pond.

Annie, Agnes, Jim, Tom, and Joe, now with jobs in Brown's Shoe Factory, were helping the family finances, and a disposition to put on airs again rose in us. We papered and painted our new home, adorned the parlor windows with draperies, saw that young Francis was combed and scrubbed until he howled, and started to pity people who still had to live in "dumps" like "the house of blazes." But all the wind was taken out of our sails the day when Agnes, weeping, came home from work to tell us what Nellie McCarthy, a Brown's stitcher, had said: "You Murphys think you're mighty special, don'tcha? Special, my foot. We Mc-Carthys wouldn't *consider* living over a *saloon*."

The very next day Mom, who had been doing some serious thinking, restored our spirits by buying a fairly good ice-cream freezer from Kaplin and informed us that henceforth we'd adopt a policy of having the neighbors in for refreshments and to see for themselves how decent a home could be, even when it was over a saloon. Many a social gathering followed, the kind that Annie had planned before the piano fell on her foot. Two nights a week, come eight o'clock, we'd receive our company and sit with them in our parlor, which was so spacious that it swallowed up our few sticks of furniture; and around nine we'd serve our well-meant but not too rich dessert and be entertained by Jim, who of late had learned to play the Chickering by ear better than I by note. Too, he could sing. The sweetness of old Erin was in his throat, and the guests would listen entranced, their ice cream melting, their eyes misting. When the weather was hot and we had to raise the windows high for a little cool air from the harbor, a crowd would gather down on the corner, and their spontaneous applause at the end of each of Jim's renditions always made us Murphys feel "mighty special" indeed.

Then there was for me the joy of an old barn which belonged to Johnnie Geary's family. Johnnie, a delicate youngster who served Mass at St. Mary's, had a wealth of friendship to offer and few takers. He did not care for athletics but liked to read and think; and he often induced me to stroll with him up North Street to St. Mary's Cemetery to visit the tree-shaded grave of his sister Kitty, a child as fair as the dawn, the neighbors said, before a diphtheria epidemic came to close schools and deplete many a home. "It's so peaceful here—like heaven," he'd murmur, kneeling.

But no place seemed to me so suited to our daydreams as that ugly, abandoned, fascinating structure directly behind Johnnie's home near Grant Street. Filled with nothing, it afforded us all kinds of space in which to expand, with its weather-beaten walls shutting out the world, and its half-missing roof letting in the sky. There we'd talk about the books in the pages of which we had lived; and we'd make up stories, drawing on our brief past and illimitable future. Johnnie said that he'd prefer the priesthood to any other kind of life, and when I told him all about Will and Father Halley and the Negroes waiting to be saved in the South, his eyes glistened.

In a warm moment we decided to be unselfish and share the bliss of the barn with some of the other boys of the neighborhood. Ten accepted the invitation to join our "club," but soon we had to try to get rid of them, for they wanted a regular roughhouse—"lotsa biff-bang." When we said they'd have to go, they threatened to burn down the place or bust it up, but Johnnie's father, heavy-chested and iron-jawed, stepped in and booted them out. And they kept away until one Saturday when Johnnie and I brought some old chairs from the attic of his home and put on a show to raise enough pennies for an excursion on the trolley that had just started running direct from Salem to Boston. Although it wasn't much of a show, the few women and children who attended were well pleased with Johnnie's tame recitation of "The Charge of the Light Brigade" and my third-rate vocalization of "You're as Welcome as the Flowers in May" and the other little numbers we had haphazardly arranged. At least they appeared to be until one tiny girl blurted, "Ma, it's rainin'—I feel it on my head," and another chimed in, "Me too." At that all looked aloft and were horrified, for the ousted members of the club had quietly climbed onto the roof of our rustic theater and, through the ample opening, were deliberately spitting down on the performance and the audience.

The show ended in a stampede for the door, and every penny had to be returned. Johnnie and I never did get that trolley ride to Boston. Instead, we arrived at a conclusion that there was so much nastiness around us that henceforth we must keep absolutely, if possible, to ourselves. In consequence we transformed the old barn more definitely than ever into a castle, or rather a cathedral, in Spain; and Johnnie, considering the misdemeanor on the roof a sacrilege, even went so far as to sprinkle the place with holy water.

That year of mine in the ninth grade at St. Mary's passed mostly on a high plane. Association with Johnnie Geary and John Carroll—another altar boy, much livelier than Geary but very well behaved—was helpful, and I got such good marks in my studies that Sister Marie Concilio chose me, along with John Bradley, George Chambers, Eddie Coffey, and Jimmy Armstrong, to represent St. Mary's in a breath-taking event, the archdiocesan competition in Boston, which annually offered a Jesuit scholarship as a prize. Nothing seemed more desirable. Sister had told us that the great Order of Jesus was like a sword, with the hilt in Rome and the point all over the world; that it had given the Church such saints as Ignatius, Francis Xavier, Stanislas Kostka, Francis Borgia, Aloysius, and Peter Claver— the apostle of the Negro; and that its type of training was almost a guarantee of noblest success in life. Hence we five hopefuls were keyed up for weeks, and especially on the Saturday morning when, at our pastor's expense, we boarded the train for Boston where the examination was to be held. But I had a sinking feeling on the way, as I measured my fellow contestants. Bradley, lithe, well-tubbed, cool-eyed, looked as if he could answer any question effortlessly. Chambers had the kind of intelligent, clean-cut face that is used in advertisements for junior military academies. Coffey already showed signs of the trigger personality that, in years to come, would repeatedly make him mayor of our city. And Armstrong—the very name!—exuded confidence. Obviously I did not have a chance.

A scholastic met us in North Station and took us to Boston College. There we entered a huge classroom filled with boys of our own age from all over the archdiocese, and without ado the ordeal began.

I wrote tersely but torturously, and finished among the last, wishing that I could start all over again and especially fearing the examiner's possible reaction to my handling of the following points.

Question: What part of New England is known as "the Cradle of Liberty" and why? My answer: *Boston. But the title really belongs to Salem, because it was on Salem's North Bridge that the Colonists first raised armed rebellion against British authority. The Boston Tea Party and Paul Revere have been overstressed in history.*

Question: What caused the Civil War? My answer: *Slavery, Harriet Beecher Stowe, and Marblehead. It was Marblehead, away back in the summer of 1636, that built the first real American slave ship, which was well named* Desire *because it represented a lust for gold; and Mrs. Stowe, two centuries later, with a book called "Uncle Tom's Cabin"—the best novel I have ever read, next to "Quo Vadis"—got everybody excited.*

Question: Why did Columbus sail the sea? My answer: *Because he wanted to go as far as he could and did not believe that he would arrive at the end of space and fall off. And he had an idea that, by finding a shorter route to the Indies, he could bring all distant peoples into the circle of the true Faith and so save innumerable souls.*

Late that afternoon I returned to Salem, washed out. Bradley, Chambers, Coffey, and Armstrong, on the contrary, stepped off the train in our home-town depot as sprightly as from a refreshing swim. "Cinch," they all said.

A week passed. And one morning a letter from Boston College reached me. It was signed by Father Rockwell, the president, and it informed me—what?—that I had attained the highest average (96.4%) and was therefore awarded the scholarship. Holding my breath until I could read the news a second, a third, and even a fourth time, I was able to think only that by means of some heavenly intervention my answers must have been made to read wholly different from the way I had written them. I'd prayed. How I'd prayed! And from now on, I felt, I'd never stop. Why, prayer was Moses' staff and Aaron's rod welded into one!

When I brought Sister Marie Concilio the letter, she smiled fondly on me. "I knew you would do well, Edward," she said, "but this is so much better than I expected. Always remember, nevertheless, that God, not you, answered all those questions. He answered them *through* you."

Did He? After much reflection I could hardly hold that Divine Intelligence had pronounced Salem more fame worthy than Boston, or peaceful little Marblehead a main cause of the Civil War, or Columbus as free from personal ambition in his exploits as a baby's chin from whiskers. Rather, I knew that there had been plenty of me myself in those answers and suspected, years later, that the Lord had given His good Jesuit Fathers in Boston a sly sense of humor.

Life was now rose-tinged for me. Father Timothy Murphy, pleased as Punch that one of his own boys—and a Murphy at that!—should win such an honor, wrote a lengthy article about it in the Salem *News* and gave me a week's vacation at his summer home in Swampscott. He let me take a friend with me, and I chose Johnnie Geary. Those few days were an uninterrupted joy, filled with swimming, dorying, fishing, and good eating. And when I got home I was greeted with a burst of surprises. My pastor had handed over to Dad and Mom for me a twenty-dollar gold piece in a plush-lined box. Annie and Agnes proudly displayed pictures of me clipped out of the Salem *News* and Boston papers, and Dad said, "Will and you make everything seem worth while, Son." Neighbors sent in homemade cakes, and there was a letter of congratulation from Miss Emmerton in which she wrote, "Now you are ready to step up toward a career. You will not need that scholarship. I am making arrangements——"

No, I'd not need that scholarship. But little did she realize that circumstances had been making arrangements independently of her. How was she to know what had been going on inside me? She would have me build a beautiful life, but I had dimly learned that if the Lord did the building the beauty would take care of itself. When I went to the fraternity to tell her that I was thinking of following my brother Will and becoming a missionary among Negroes, she took my cheeks between her palms, searched my eyes, and said, "But I can't understand. You have talent, and you owe it to yourself and your family to develop and use it." And I, who had answered so many questions in the archdiocesan examination, could find no words for a fitting reply.

Steve and Martha O'Toole were revisiting Salem that week and had told me that John Nelson Goucher, my chum down in Rhode Island, had recently run away from home. I knew what they didn't know, namely, that he was trying himself out as an "architect of fate." But I still believed, from my memory of Aunt Aggie's story about the ill-built Pemberton Mill in Lawrence falling over into the Merrimac, and from my glimpses of human wreckage along the path of my few swift years, that only the Supreme Architect's work could stand. He seemed to be directing me to pass through the door my brother had opened. I was anxious to get going before it closed.

Miss Emmerton was not the kind to surrender a pet project readily. She came to my home and argued with Mom and Dad, trying to show them what a help and credit I'd be to them if, after studying at a select private school in Boston, I chose art for my future. But in the light of their faith they saw the inferiority of the rewards of time. "God will be makin' something of the boy, instead of the boy makin' something of himself," Dad told her. "If he has the callin' to go South, I won't hold him back. I'll help him." And Mom said, "That's how I feel too, Tom."

The next day I wrote to Will, who had just graduated from Epiphany College in Baltimore and was about to take his philosophy at St. Joseph's Seminary down there. He promptly answered, "Very good, Eddie," and had Father Saint-Laurent, the rector of Epiphany, send me an application blank, which I immediately filled out and which Mom and Dad signed. A letter of acceptance, telling me to report in early September, soon arrived.

I left Salem more showily than Will. He had had only an old valise, but I owned a brand-new trunk, bought and paid for with Father Timothy Murphy's gold piece. There was a limit to luxury, however, and economy still had to be served; so Dad, to save a few cents toward "the books and things" I'd be needing, unashamedly carried the trunk on his shoulders to the depot.

Johnnie Geary and John Carroll were there to see me off. "I'll be with you in Baltimore next year when I finish grammar," said Geary. "So will I," said Carroll. "Write," said both.

And I now blink as I think back. Strange that I should have been chosen and not these two excellent youngsters, so eager to offer themselves! Well, John Carroll is at present just as excellent a father and grandfather as he might have been a priest, but Johnnie Geary—after many lonely, yearning years—lies beside his little sister in the shady spot in St. Mary's Cemetery that, as a boy, he found "so peaceful—like heaven."

II

In north station, Boston, I was met by Larry Landrigan, an Everett-ite a few years older than myself, who also had applied for admission to Epiphany College that summer and been accepted. Directed by Father Saint-Laurent, he'd paid a brief visit to Salem the week before to make my acquaintance and promise Mom and Dad to look after me. Larry was a pensive but pleasant fellow, big-brotherly enough to suit any boy, and already I liked Epiphany because he would be there.

We took the "el" to South Station, then the boat-train for the Fall River line to New York. My thoughts kept racing ahead and my feelings flowing backward, or *vice versa*, and Larry helped me to get hold of myself just by letting me be. His silence had all the warmth of a handclasp.

That night we stood on the deck of the S.S. *Priscilla*, leaning over the railing and watching the dancing reflections of the stars in the black tide. Needing to talk now, I told Larry most of the somber things that had influenced me to leave the old life—not so old—and seek the new; also the past joys that, alive in my memory, were distracting me from the future. He put his hand on my shoulder. "It's the same with me," he said. "I've had good times and bad. But the bad only made the good seem better, just as stars are shinier the darker it gets. My pastor says that God wants to give His blessings all the time but that people are selfish and forget even to say thanks. That's the trouble, selfishness—thanklessness. He can't keep giving if it only makes people ungrateful——"

He was talking rather at random, it seemed; but I felt much impressed when he went on to suggest, "Let's not ever forget to say thanks, and then—well, then I guess we'll be sure of having, wherever we are, not only the gifts of the Giver but also the Giver of gifts."

He smiled that lopsided little smile of his, pleased and perhaps surprised at his ability to turn a phrase so neatly. *Gifts of the Giver. Giver of gifts.*

We could not afford a stateroom, since the Lord's generosity, even for the would-be grateful, evidently stopped at certain points. But mattresses were available for deck or salon sleeping, and when we got sated with hearing a pianist and two fiddlers repeating themselves over and over again, we decided that we had better retire. It was then that the Devil, surely annoyed at the sight of a boy and a youth going off to study for the priesthood, attempted to work on us. He did it by means of a sleek middle-aged man who, peeking through a slit in the curtains of one of the windows of the salon reserved for female repose, crooked a finger and hissed to us, "Come and see what I'm seeing."

Larry promptly grabbed me by the collar and drew me away. Maybe I'd not have looked anyhow, but just the same I was suddenly conscious of the allure of a little swerving from "the straight and narrow" and sensed that an undeviating course would not always be so easy as the Curé d'Ars' succinct advice for access to God, "Go quite direct—like a cannonball," which Sister Marie Concilio often quoted, had made it seem.

Early next morning, as the boat fog-horned its way toward a docking in Manhattan, skyscrapers loomed hazily before us. My first feeling was one of disappointment that they did not literally scrape the sky, but this was soon followed by a sentiment that the Lord, in dwarfing and blurring these great monuments of earthly enterprise, was letting me see His own architecture as vastly superior. Why, the heavens stretched boundlessly above the tallest man-made building! And New York, interpreted as so great and important by Horatio Alger, most of whose stories I'd read, was nearly blotted out in the very least of the Lord's creations—a mere mist. Since then, of course, my every glimpse of our greatest city has added to my astonishment; but so has my every glance at the higher masonry, and Rockefeller Center ranks in my appraisal as a child's heap of play blocks in comparison with the Pleiades, and the atomic bomb as a firecracker alongside Genesis.

We went to Mass and Communion that morning at St. Peter's Church on Barclay Street. And afterward Larry brought me to one of Childs's restaurants for a breakfast of flapjacks—with plenty of butter and syrup, a meal of which I'd have enjoyed each mouthful only that I couldn't help thinking of Mom's "turns."

Next we rode uptown on the "el," and in swift transit viewed many tenements that were worse than "the house of blazes" in Salem; or perhaps they just seemed worse to me because of the fire escapes zigzagging an italics of poverty on the façades. But Thirty-fourth Street, even on a hazy autumnal morning, showed so magnificent, with the sun now struggling out of clouds and dripping gold down on mammoth buildings, that my mouth opened wide and my eyes bulged, and I kept staring, staring, feeling smaller and smaller, yet not quite lost. Could anyone, anything, be really lost, with God everywhere? Still, despite my talks with Father Walsh and Sister Concilio, echoes of past doubts returned to me. How about that fat man who had peeked last night at females undressing, and what of the poor colored people in the South wandering like sheep without a shepherd? Weren't *they* lost? But mightn't the Lord, by setting before the peeker such a good example as Larry, have helped him to find himself? As for Negroes, wasn't He sending Larry and me to help find them?

I disclosed my inner questioning to Larry when we boarded the train for Baltimore. "I'm confused, too, at many things," he said. "That's why we have to study a long time before we can become priests. We must learn, I suppose, to get our five senses under the control of our reason, and our reason under the control of——" He broke off, as if unable exactly to recall something that he had read or that his pastor had told him, but his unfinished sentence was to remain with me, the logic of life itself eventually supplying the last word—*grace*.

During that trip on the Pennsylvania Railroad from New York to Maryland, I had a feeling that, for one so very young, I was wading out pretty far into the unknown; a fear that I might be drowned. But the same light from above that I had sensed in the gray-green waters of Salem Harbor the day I nearly came to an end was still shining; and I was buoyed up when Larry spoke to me in simple language, as we rode down through Philadelphia and Wilmington, about Herbert Cardinal Vaughan, the English prelate, who believed that Providence had permitted a branch of the African racial tree to be wrested away and transplanted in the New World so that it might become a vital part—perhaps a test—of an Americanism committed to a belief in human dignity and equality. He said, too, that, when Cardinal Vaughan founded a missionary order and asked the Pope to what section of the world the new missionaries should be sent, His Holiness indicated the United States and Negro need, and that this was the origin of the work of the Society of St. Joseph to which we were going, the only organization of its kind on these shores to be devoted exclusively to the spiritual interests of the colored. "It's named after the foster father of Christ, because it fosters Christ as he did," he explained. As if brother Will hadn't already told me all this! But I let Larry talk on, because I could hear Will in what he was saying, and that was what buoyed me up.

On our arrival in Baltimore we rode a trolley to Walbrook, the suburb where Epiphany College was located. The building proved to be tall, gabled, wooden, and atop an incline. A porch, like a jolly open mouth, spread across the front of it, and its ample wings appeared as inviting as a pair of open arms.

Father Saint-Laurent, well-upholstered, square-jowled, keen-eyed, received us unsentimentally and led us straight to the chapel to give our first greeting to God. Then he directed us up a dark mahogany stairway, the only ornate feature of the whole interior, to our appointed rooms.

Alone, I stood in the middle of my "cell," knees shaking, heart pounding. The blankness of the walls was an erasure of almost everything I had known, and I could gaze only at a small crucifix lying on a pine-wood table. But that crucifix, almost the same as the one in my room at home, shed a ray in the gloom; and I found myself thinking of something I had read in a book in the Salem Public Library about an artist who always insisted that those who came to see his paintings should wait a while in a bare dim anteroom before entering his studio, so that their sight might be free and fresh for appreciation. And now I could somewhat grasp that the method of religion was similar, because when I stepped over to the single window, I saw nature richer and more colorful than ever before. A sun-swept lawn of velvety green sloped to a sylvan glade, and in the far distance, under an azure sky, the Chesapeake glimmered and glistened like strewn gems. I threw off despondency, and my relief increased as I looked down at a large stone statue on a pedestal right in front of the college. It was a masculine figure of gentleness embracing purity in the form of a child, and I was able to make out an inscription carved on the pedestal: "Go to Joseph." More. I fancied something of Dad in Joseph's face, and that caused me to picture Mom, for I could never think of the one without the other. But this meant a second wave of glumness, since thoughts of their goodness caused me to miss them poignantly, and I turned from the window with a sigh.

By five o'clock that afternoon Larry and I had met most of the students, some of them older than he, a few as young as myself, all eager and anxious to get adjusted. And brother Will had managed to obtain permission to come from St. Joseph's Seminary on Pennsylvania Avenue in the heart of the city to spend a little time with me, a circumstance which pleasantly scrambled geography by making Salem seem a suburb of Baltimore. Will was taller and even more otherworldly than when I last saw him.

but now there was a smile in his spirituality, and a quiet humor too. He spoke so cheerfully that I asked him, "Don't you miss home at all?" His eyes twinkled. "Why miss what I have?" he said. "Studying for the priesthood is like going up a hill. You turn your head and there below you have what you've left, only you see it as part of a bigger plan and from a better angle. Understand?"

No, I didn't understand. Not yet. It struck me as rather disloyal to Mom and Dad and our brothers and sisters that he could be contented with just a retrospect—a memory—of our home; and it would be some time before I'd advance to the point of discerning and cherishing the truth of Thomas à Kempis's teaching in his *Following of Christ*, "Leave all and you will find all."

Life in Epiphany College was run strictly according to bell—the voice of God, so we were told. But in the beginning I could not associate God with that persistent summons from sleep, recreation, and practically everything pleasant. High, petulant, twangy, it sounded like a temperamental creature with a bad head cold; and I abhorred it until, on reflection, I came to feel, at first vaguely, then unmistakably, the lesson it was trying to instill: the value of minutes and the necessity of not squandering them. Though it obtruded on the enjoyable, it also brought the irksome to an end, keeping the one from cloying and the other from depressing. It was prudent and beneficent, and at length it seemed even musical.

We students had to be up and out of bed with the rising of the sun. Enough time and no more was allotted to washing and dressing. Then we were tolled on down into the chapel for prayer, and the chapel being too poor for stained glass, the simple windowpanes, kept crystal-clear by many a scrubbing, freely admitted all the glory of dawn—facsimile of Creation!—to our obtuseness. During these too early spiritual exercises, some young apostle, like Peter, James, and John, who themselves fell aslumbering even in Gethsemane, would be sure to emit a snore; and

Father Saint-Laurent, all dignity and recollectedness, would frown from his official *prie-dieu* and motion that the offender be poked awake. To prevent a general dozing, he tried out a system of dividing the morning meditation into three parts, during the first of which we'd kneel, in the second stand, and in the third sit; but it was only partly successful, for some of us became adept enough at reflex action to go through all three movements quite asleep—except in the deep-winter months when the janitor took his time sending up heat to the few radiators the chapel could boast, and an acute chill kept us wide awake. Epiphany, I found out, had been built for a summer hotel, and it might well have remained just that. My old home on Derby Street in Salem had never seemed nearer the North Pole.

Mass, which we students took turns at serving, followed meditation. And from the Sanctus on to the Communion a stillness enfolded us, a solemn but tender stillness in which the divine and the human almost palpably blended into a renewal of the mystery of God becoming man that man might become God. In those sublime moments, at least, everyone of us was devoutness itself.

After our thanksgiving we'd file off into the study hall for a half hour's coping with textbooks. The effort to force something into our heads while our stomachs were empty and shrieking in their own mute way to be filled was mostly futile, and the local baker, visible through the windows as he drove his wagon up the side path of the grounds to deliver his yesterday bread (very cheap) to the kitchen, reminded me so keenly of old Mr. Morgan in Salem, with his nag and his three pots of piping-hot beans, that my hunger usually became ravenous. Forgetting the Holy Sacrifice from which I had just come, I'd think of the innumerable good meals that must have gone into the making of Tommy Burns, the butter-fat boy at the desk in front of me. Occasionally some of us would raise hands to the senior student acting as prefect and receive a nod of permission to leave the study hall, ostensibly for a visit to the lavatory in the basement but really for the purpose of stealing to the back porch and doing business with the college's first daily visitor. By pooling our coppers we could buy from him two or three stale sweet-potato pies, which we'd devour on the spot. To me those pies were almost as wonderful as Mr. Morgan's beans, because of the flavor that only a growing boy's appetite can find in any kind of edible; and they never spoiled my breakfast, but always sharpened the craving for more substantial food, just as in my later life nearly every minor satisfaction was to stimulate a yearning for the better things that the Lord's bounty would provide.

Sisters, whose convent occupied the rear section of the building, prepared our food, washed, ironed, and mended our clothes, and with their utter humility, kindliness, and self-effacement were as so many reflections of Mary herself in Nazareth. It seemed to me, when I had sense enough to think about it, that their merit almost exceeded Mary's, in as much as she had had the ecstasy of serving the faultless young Christ, and theirs was the drudgery of serving us. Mary had been so close to the Child and so able to see every sign of His growing in grace and favor before God and man; but these nuns had their lives apart, their enclosure, their rule; and we saw them mostly, if not merely, as gentle shadows moving along the farther bank of a flowing stream. Sometimes I wondered whether we were to them just a series of stomachs to be appeased thrice a day—with a four-o'clock snack of bread, jam, and milk thrown in for good measure, or so many pairs of socks and suits of underwear to be retrieved.

Not until the day when the rector sent me with two other boys into the little garden behind the convent to help them build a rockery around their statue of the Blessed Virgin did I have the least inkling of what each one of us really meant to them; for then Mother Albertina, a thin person with a pale face which the whiteness of her coif made paler, and with frail hands gnarled from toil, turned on me the bluest eyes I had ever seen and asked softly, "How are the folk in Salem—your parents, Anna, Agnes, James, Thomas, Joseph, and Francis?" I nearly keeled over.

"Fine, Mother," I blurted, "but how do you know the names —like that?" Smiling, she indicated a bed of asters in a circle of green, and murmured, "Your brother William planted and cultivated them for us. Does that answer the question?" It did, perfectly. Right away I could see that the warmth of Mother's gratitude must have opened Will's heart to her. But I did not say so, waiting eagerly for her next words. And they came so sweetly that it almost seemed as though Our Lady herself was speaking. "The families our boys come from are as dear to us as the boys themselves, and we like to remember in our prayers as many names as we can." *Dear to us? Our boys?* Then it dawned on me that we seekers of the priesthood were to these good women as close and personal as Christ to Mary, and a simile different from that of a dividing stream suggested itself to me. I could see a wall built by reverence between them and us, but also the vines of many a maternal concern creeping over it.

Their needle art was extraordinary. Knowing that most of us had only the sketchiest financial means, they performed marvels of repair on our wardrobes. And the tattered, threadbare things, relics of vigorous games of handball, baseball, and football, that we'd put in our laundry bags! Father Saint-Laurent protested. "You send two buttons and expect a shirt to come back on them," he'd say. "Try to remember that Sisters are not slaves. Slavery was abolished in 1863!"

I suspected that Mother Albertina and her community would gladly have starved themselves to spread a luxurious table for us, but the rectorship had charge of all supply, and since we were in missionary training, Father Saint-Laurent saw no reason why we should be pampered. His own tastes were of the simplest, and his girth was merely the result of desk work, study, and lack of physical exercise. Never had any of us met, nor would we ever meet, a more scholarly man. He could have been an ornament to any university, yet sought nothing better than to give his best to those who would labor among the poor and be forgotten with them. So under him we dined *à la Delmonico* mentally, but otherwise not. Breakfast: prunes, a cereal or French toast, and skimmed milk. ("Gosh, there's a lot of milk in this water," Billy Marshall, a lath of a boy with a big Adam's apple and a snaggle-toothed smile, who sat next to me at table, used to mumble between gulps.) Dinner: a soup so light and innocent that we named it "baptismal water"; meat and fish so good but unlavish that, while it was being passed, pleas like, "Have a heart," "Go easy, bud," and "Hey there, I'm here too," were whispered through the prescribed silence; a dessert—usually bread pudding with just enough raisins in it to emphasize the fewness. Supper: hash, bread, potatoes, and weak tea. But cherries and apples from the college trees made a seasonal supplement beyond compare; and the four-o'clock snacks, to say nothing of the occasional sweet-potato pies, rounded out the requirements of the department of the interior almost to a nicety.

The boys were of two types: the merely pious, and the pious but not merely. The former, expecting heavenly bliss on a silver platter, were disappointed and did not last; but the latter were able to take the bumps and to profit from the experience. I remember when Vincent Warren, a real upstander from Germantown, Pennsylvania, received in silence a severe reprimand from Father Saint-Laurent on account of the "untidiness" of his room —unmade bed, books scattered, floor littered. And Vince the neatest of us all! The explanation of this injustice was that some of the fellows, having heard from the janitor, whose ear was everywhere, that the rector intended to make an inspection that day, had slipped into Vince's room and created a havoc which, they naïvely trusted, would not tarnish his reputation too much but have the effect of comparatively polishing up their own. Looking back now, I can see that the same strength of character that then enabled Vince to keep quiet under rebuke manifested itself in speech years later when, as pastor of a colored church in Norfolk, Virginia, he was kidnaped from his rectory by the Ku Klux Klan and confronted in a weird spot outside town with the grossest and most bigoted questioning. Never, perhaps, were

Klansmen more simply, directly, and dignifiedly answered; and dropping the whip that was to have drawn blood, the Kleagle ordered that the priest be taken back with safety and respect.

Then there was Alex LaPlante from Nashua, New Hampshire, who kept his hair combed and his nails pared so neat that we considered him a kind of "softie." But that was our mistake. The time would come when, an ordained Josephite, he'd show himself a hero throughout a catastrophe brought by a great tidal wave to Galveston, Texas.

And Charlie Winckler! Sometimes this roly-poly boy from Brooklyn, with his banjo eyes, seemed a personified buck-and-wing to me. Nobody else found life so bright and sunny, and at the same time practiced spirituality more seriously. On Saturday evenings, during the recreation period between supper and study, he'd round up some of us younger students and, under the early stars, have us march along the edge of the campus to recite the rosary in reparation for the week-end sins—of all things—to be committed in the city of Baltimore. Left to ourselves, we'd hardly have given a thought to week-end sins in Baltimore or anywhere else; but with him acting the part of a moral Paul Revere, our imagination was alerted and perils without became pictures within. And not content with promoting the rosary, he felt called upon to increase chastity by having us wear under our clothing De Montford chains, of which he had secured a supply from some religious bureau. These chains were not to be removed even in bed, and the consequence, in my case, was the very opposite of his intention. The links so chafed and tickled that they kept me awake at night, tossing, turning, thinking; and I felt that they would do better on the back of a chair than on me. When I asked my confessor for permission to doff them, he scolded me for the donning and roundly ordered that hereafter I take spiritual direction only from the duly qualified and authorized. But Charlie meant so well; and his spirit, pruned and perfected in the long course of training, was to qualify him for a truly blessed and fruitful ministry.

On the other hand, Joe ——, an old man of fifteen, was far from concerned about other folk's sins or the practice of penance. A narrow ledge ran around the exterior of the third floor of the college, and one thin-mooned night, after prayers and the lights-out signal of the bell, he crept along the catwalk to my room. "You'll get caught," I muttered as he tapped on a pane and I raised the window. "This place is too dead for that," he said, coolly seating himself on the sill. I looked out, right and left, to see whether any lights were still on in other rooms, and was startled to behold a crucifix thrust from an open window. "Tony Miele in there must've seen my shadow when I passed by and thought it was a spook," explained Joe. He laughed. "To heck with the holy ass! Let's chew the fat. Nobody'll hear." And that was how I got my first blunt introduction to the so-called facts of life.

I had seen and heard only good in my own home, and though I'd savored the opposite beyond it, seaminess had never really preoccupied me. My dissociation in Salem from most of the boys of my own age had been a safeguard from venery, and a deep sense of the eye of God and an angel guardian, together with frequent Confession and Communion, had more than helped. True, Joe had had the same sort of training, but he had run around freely, before entering Epiphany, with companions as different from Johnnie Geary and John Carroll as poison ivy from a clover patch. "Why did you ever want to study for the priesthood?" I asked when he finished his detailed account of "fun" back home. "Oh, I wasn't bad in what you'd call a loud way," he said with a shrug. "I'd get ashamed of myself and try to be good. My pastor thought I was, the way I served Mass and helped around the church grounds. I just fooled myself and everybody else, I suppose. Well, I've seen so much of the real thing here that I know I'll never fit." He grinned a sickly grin in the pallid moonlight. "My mother sent me fifteen bucks today, and I'm leaving tomorrow."

The next afternoon he bade us good-by, and I was never to see or hear from him again, but what he left in me was hard to dispel. The more I pushed it, the more viscous and sticky it became, until Father Hanley, my confessor at Epiphany, took over. "The mind is as flexible as the fingers," he said. "You can turn it any way you will. Don't think on a plane surface. That's like crawling on your hands and knees and getting all muddied, no matter how much you'd like to keep clean. Look up—up."

I did look up, steadily enough to get a crick in my neck. It seemed to me perilous to look around at all, and during that period I missed many of the common-sense examples of most of my fellow students. My head was in a cloud of scrupulosity. But one evening at Benediction, which I chanced to be serving, I was to become aware of exceeding Father Hanley's good advice by taking it too literally. When it was time for the monstrance to be elevated, I went with my mind and eyes heavenward to the side table for the veil that had to be draped around the shoulders of the kneeling and awaiting Father Saint-Laurent, who was celebrant; and unwittingly I took the tablecloth too. Returning, I put both veil and tablecloth, as one, on him.

The hush in the chapel was invaded by a sound incredibly like a titter. Shocked that students for the priesthood should find anything funny in a holy ritual, I quickly knelt and bent so low that my nose touched the nearest altar step. Then I straightened up and lifted my eyes. Father was now at the center of the altar, wrapping the stem of the monstrance with the loose ends of the veil, and I saw to my horror what I had done. A section of the tablecloth, tightly held under the drawn folds of the veil, was showing wide and absurd from beneath. Leaping to my feet, I thrust forth a hand and made a great grab at it, but it refused to be dislodged, and my spasmodic act jerked the rector so hard that he and the monstrance almost fell.

Purple with surprise and indignation, he regained his balance and went on with the ceremony as best he could, tablecloth and all, while my cheeks burned and I wished it were possible for me to melt into nothingness. When he had blessed us and come down to kneel at the foot of the altar and recite the divine praises, I took the veil and the tablecloth from his shoulders with aspen fingers. But that was not the end. Oh no. The very removal of my mistake seemed to cause a fresh awareness of it, and the titter returned. A little later, the organist, convulsed, struck the opening notes of the recessional hymn, "Mother Dearest, Mother Fairest," so uncertainly that the choir thought it was "Nearer My God to Thee" and sang accordingly; but then, realizing the error, they broke down ignominiously. And Joe Lally, the thurifer, shaking with a merriment which was all the worse for his too earnest effort to control it, spilled live coals from the thurible over the sanctuary floor, causing the carpet to smoke; whereupon he did a sort of Highland fling to stamp out the possibility of flames.

Never in the whole history of the Church could there have been a worse celebration of Benediction. And all because I had so badly sought to be so good.

Of our teachers at Epiphany the most distinguished-looking was Father Charles Uncles, the first native Negro in the United States to become a priest. Back home I had seen only imitation Negroes, performing in *Uncle Tom's Cabin;* and a genuine, splendid specimen like Father Uncles fascinated me. I'd sometimes heard the word "nigger," but never felt the essential insolence of it until the morning when, while I was buying one of those sweet-potatoe pies, the baker warned, "Cheese it! Your Frenchy rector's forbade me to spoil you boys' breakfast by sellin' stuff to you, and that nigger priest—what's his name?—is comin'. Look out." I glanced from the back porch and noticed Father Uncles strolling from the campus where he had evidently been taking a constitutional and filling his lungs with good fresh air. He caught my eye, smiled, nodded; his whole manner seeming to say, "Don't mind me, son. Boys are always hungry. I understand." The pie didn't go down my gullet easily that morning, and I found myself so disliking the baker for having said "nigger" that I resolved not to patronize him again.

Father Uncles was as frank as Father Saint-Laurent was formal. He loved to laugh, and his laughter shook the cobwebs from our brains and we had to laugh with him. But he puzzled us with a certain peculiarity, a habit of going around to throw up all the windows in the college—except those of his own room, which he kept closed drum-tight. We welcomed this ventilation in warm weather, but it tried our patience in the wintertime. Why so genial a man should care to set himself and us ashiver, we could not fathom. "If he ever gets to heaven, and he certainly will," said Billy Marshall to me, "he'll find it a purgatory of a place unless it's full of windows to fiddle with. He won't mind St. Peter having the keys so long as he himself can work the sashes."

Along with five priests, there were some lay teachers in Epiphany. One of them—Professor Gookin—appeared even more saintly than the clergy themselves, and we students wanted to test whether he was real. Tall, spare, remote, with high cheekbones and tight skin, he would have looked more appropriate in a niche than at a desk; and we thought it almost ridiculous that he should wear coat and pants instead of robe and mantle. But his sanctity did not save him from the practical jokes that even aspirants to the priesthood, happy in their vocation and as healthy as the next, often play. His wardrobe included a pair of white duck trousers which some thoughtless friend or thoughtful enemy must have given him, for surely he would never have made such a purchase himself; and Tommy Burns, the pink-fat boy, gurgled and purred the day when he saw him, in those immaculate ducks, standing at the base of the main stairway and awaiting the bell for class. He winked at me, did Tommy, as he darted into the refectory. Emerging in a moment, his pocket bulging, he motioned me to follow him to the classroom; and there, open-mouthed, I watched him spreading mustard, out of the jar that he had borrowed from the faculty table, on the professorial chair which would presently be occupied.

When the bell rang and the boys assembled, Tommy delivered himself of much whispering through his fingers, so that an air of amusement and expectation pervaded the room as the innocent teacher entered and began his usual little preliminary speech about the necessity of making the most and the best of our God-given opportunities. We thought the man would never get seated, but he finally did. A squirmer by nature, he surpassed himself that day, because he must have found the chair slippery; and we knew that those pants of his were not faring well. At the end of the period, he rose with dignity and passed out of the room, wholly unconscious of the smeared area beneath the back of his very brief alpaca coat. Down the corridor he proceeded, and the afternoon being bright and sunny, he took his straw hat from a peg in the wall and strode out of the college toward town.

When he returned around suppertime, Tommy Burns and I, purposely loitering on the front piazza, overheard him saying to Father Saint-Laurent, "I've had the oddest experience this afternoon. Almost everyone I saw seemed to be grinning. At what I can't imagine!" And the rector, whose quick eye had already taken in the situation, smiled wryly. "It isn't customary for anyone to appear in public with the seat of the trousers like—that," he said. "You'd better go to your room right away and change." Bewildered, Mr. Gookin touched the back of his pants and then held his hands up to his flaming face. "Who could have done this?" he cried. And Tommy Burns and I, nearly exploding, disappeared.

Another day Mr. Gookin became much displeased in class with Tommy Tully, an apple-cheeked boy from Akron, Ohio. The trouble was that Tommy, a habitual mouth breather, appeared to respond only with a yawn to a request that he cease yawning. Three times the request was repeated, and so was the seeming yawn. Then Mr. Gookin, no longer himself, left his chair to administer some kind of chastisement. But Tommy, naturally disfavoring the move, made a dive for the door; and so did the professor. Out of the room and down the corridor the two dashed, and Mr. Gookin's voice, lifted in prayer as his long legs kept going and even increasing their speed, trailed back to us: "O holy Mary and Joseph, don't let me catch him! Don't let me catch him!" Thoroughly co-operating with the plea, Tommy remained uncaught; and thereafter, more than satisfied, we students never deemed Mr. Gookin's piety superior to that of our well-poised priests.

Saul's armor was so large for us Davids that we had to grow into it. The process took time, and meanwhile foolishness, as a relief from intensive regularity, continued to have its entries. There was the night when a pair of us, Billy Marshall and myself, sneaked into Gookin's room and loosened the screws in the frame of his bed. It was Billy's bright idea, but I'd fallen readily into cahoots, for I still rather resented the professor for his holier-than-thou-ness, and thought that a little downfall would be good for him. But the little downfall, when he threw himself on the bed about nine forty-five, turned out to be a big one—a veritable crash, audible all over the second floor. Billy had taken care to sprinkle some carpet tacks outside Gookin's door, and Gookin now sprang forth, probably to warn the college that Beelzebub had taken possession of it or that the end of the world had come. So the crash was succeeded by a burst of ouches and yelps. Abed and all ears, I doubled up with such un-Christian glee as I'd never known to be in me.

But jokes have a way of outdoing themselves and backfiring, and it was not only our professor who happened to be the victim of this one. I heard another door swinging ajar and, jumping up, cautiously opened my own a crack to peek. Great Caesar! Father Saint-Laurent, aroused from his study, was rushing slipperless down the corridor. I breathed a prayer to all the saints to withhold him from the prickly area, but they turned from me, and I saw him about to seize and thrust Gookin back. Suddenly there was a second outburst, for the tacks were penetrating the soles of authority itself.

Billy Marshall and I came near being expelled the next day,

and the whole student body found their privileges much curtailed for two months on account of us. "There is nothing more expensive," I wrote in my notebook, "than a bit of unwise fun." But the lesson faded and the wrong spirit rose again.

We had a colored student in Epiphany—Clifford Tureaud, quiet, likable, and not a little superstitious. And one night Billy Marshall, whose daring had established him as a hero of sorts in my estimation, whispered to me after chapel prayers, "Let's waylay good old Cliff in St. Teresa's corridor—it's mighty dark there —and wrastle him. He'll think we're a couple of demons." And I said all right. But once more a plan went haywire, for darkness worked both ways. If Tureaud could not recognize us in St. Teresa's dinginess, much less could we recognize Tureaud, a fact which we had curiously overlooked. I pounced on a form which turned out to be not our man but Tommy Burns, who was twice my size; and the mauling Tommy gave me left marks for a month and a memory forever. As for Billy, he fared worse, the person he fell upon proving to be—of all people—the rector himself. Hence for weeks Billy and I had to sojourn in a new little doghouse, and we thought that surely this time we'd get out only to be put on a train for home.

With such experiences I began to see that, even at Epiphany, I could get along far better by cultivating some of the solitude that had been mine in Salem, and I took to reading more. From Charles and Mary Lamb's *Tales Founded on the Plays of Shakespeare*, I proceeded to the works of Shakespeare himself, and was elated that Epiphany had a custom of annually presenting for the Sisters, faculty, and students a cut version of one of the great plays. By begging Father Carroll, the director, I was entrusted with the very slight role of First Commoner in *Julius Caesar*. Short and thin in those days, and trigged up with tunic and sandals, I must have no more suggested a Roman artisan than a kitten a lion, but I felt as important as Pompey, and when fiercely addressed by Flavius in the opening scene, "Speak, what trade art thou?" I piped at the very top of my voice my only line,

"Why, sir, a carpenter," and could not at all understand why the audience laughed. And in the big scene in Act III where, fired by Mark Antony's speech, the mob (consisting solely of me and Tommy Burns, because costumes cost money) rose up to "pluck down forms, windows, anything," I almost knocked myself out by charging headlong across the stage—only to find the door on the opposite side locked and to thwack my head resoundingly.

The best that could be said about that performance of *Julius Caesar* was that it did absolutely nothing for Shakespeare; but Shakespeare, on the other hand, did very much for me. Those mighty sentences and phrases of his, far more effective when heard than when merely read, rolled and flashed through my brain; and I now knew that the Bard of Avon was to Horatio Alger as Hawthorne's *The House of the Seven Gables* to *Mother Goose*. With this stimulus, solitude became still more precious to me, and each recreation period and free day I'd ascend the stairs of the college to the topmost floor, which had many empty rooms, and curl up with a book from our library in the deep-silled alcove of one of the gambrel windows. Away off over the sea of trees and roofs I could glimpse the ever silver Chesapeake and indulge daydream on daydream. Lifted high above immediacy, alone but never quite lonely, I'd discover new worlds, one a week: Dickens, Thackeray, Austen, and in time Shelley, Keats, Francis Marion Crawford, and Canon Sheehan. I read and reread Francis Thompson's saga of Christ's love for souls, "The Hound of Heaven." But most of all I perused the New Testament with its firsthand, inspired account of the story of stories which Fulton Oursler, a future friend, was to weave into a narrative that all America would love. It linked this distant college with my relinquished home, because every word of it away down here in Maryland lay in the big copper-clasped Bible that still, as my family's prized possession, occupied the same old marble-topped table in Salem. A feeling of the timelessness of religion and truth, and of the nearness of earth and heaven, would fill me; and my sisters' voices, which had first brought me the vision beautiful, would return like a strain of music. Too, I could trace Dad's worth in the terse but pithy texts about Joseph, foster father of Divinity; Mom's gentle features in Mary's meekness; and the blueprints of the best scenes of my childhood in the simplicities of Nazareth.

At last I was at least beginning to understand what brother Will had said to me the day of my entering Epiphany. *Studying for the priesthood—it's like going up a hill. You look down and have what you've left—have it as part of a bigger plan—from a better angle.*

III

FIVE years passed and the day of brother Will's ordination came. The ceremony took place in Baltimore, with James Cardinal Gibbons officiating, and with all the glory of a ritual, enriched by twenty centuries, brimming the souls and senses alike of a large congregation. Thirty were made ministers of the Gospel that late May day, but in the course of the event I saw only one, the eldest son of Tom Murphy and Johanna Mahoney, who had denied themselves that the Lord might have a servant who would do the same for others. And I thought of the boy who used to rise so early on frigid New England mornings to shovel a pathway through deep snow for the family's convenience; whose unselfishness had rendered him a second father to his sisters and brothers until he was called to prepare for a larger life; whose heart asked of the future only an opportunity to help those who, having the least, needed the Lord the most. And even more I thought of Dad foregoing his two weekly plugs of tobacco and pinching pennies and nickels; or rather building, bit by bit, toward the beauty of this day. He and Mom had reared a tabernacle of their own, and a living one too, just as truly as the Irish in New York, with their dimes and quarters and boundless faith, had achieved—as I'd been told by Charlie Winckler—the splendor of St. Patrick's Cathedral.

"We've chosen the better part," murmured Will when he gave me his first priestly blessing.

I returned with him to Salem where, at St. Mary's, he would celebrate his first Solemn High Mass. And Mom and Dad received him on their knees in the tenement over the drugstore. It was many moments before they could see him through their tears, and it almost seemed that they'd never take their lips from his consecrated hands. Looking on, I shared his feelings. How much both of us wanted to kneel to these, our first, best, and dearest teachers!

Annie and Agnes had fixed every room so neatly, lavishing special care on the one that Father Will would occupy, and only a trifle less on my own. They had grown very pretty, and it pleased us to be informed that each now had a beau: Annie, a fine young man from Peabody; Agnes, an attractive Charlestowner. We studied Jeffry O'Connell and Walter Brennan, the fortunate fellows, when, the very evening of our arrival, they came to call; and we nodded to each other approvingly. Then we smiled on our sisters and they smiled on us; and satisfied that all their tomorrows would be in good hands, we were free to worry about Jim, Tom, and Joe with whom, we suspected and were too soon to learn, all was not well.

We took Mom aside and put direct inquiries, wanting her to have the relief of unburdening herself, and insisting on frankness. "There's not much to tell," she said, facing us; but the strained look in her eyes said differently. "Sure they wouldn't harm a fly, and everyone has the good word for them. It's only that they can't say no to anyone, and that includes themselves. When they're paid on Saturdays, bums wait for them at corners, and the thirst is there, and sometimes your father and me don't see them till the last cent is gone. But they're that repentant every time—and 'tis only sorry, never bitter, I can be. Over and over they've took the pledge from Father Dave Murphy and broke it." She gazed yearningly at Will. "Maybe now, with you—their own—to give it to them, they'll be all right."

But Will's lids were locked tight, and a drop trickled down his cheek, and I knew the self-questioning that was wounding the joy of his early priesthood. Should he, the eldest, have gone off when needed most, and left his parents without the kind of help that only the eldest could give? If he had remained in Salem, mightn't he have succeeded in winning his brothers to sobriety and strength? Why had he dreamed of saving souls so far away while his own flesh and blood were being lost?

"Your father's health isn't so good any more," said Mom. "You must've noticed how gray and bent he's got. Sometimes his mind wanders a little, and I talked him into givin' up his work—savin' his pride, because I had word that his boss was goin' to lay him off anyhow. Poor Tom! Sure I always thought I was keepin' trouble from him, but I guess he knew everything down deep all the time and had to fight like sixty to keep quiet. I overtrained him at holdin' back his feelings, I did. That's what finally tore him apart inside." And she repeated, wringing her hands, "Poor Tom—the best man that ever drew a breath!" We could not speak, and she maundered on. "He disappeared a few months ago. We found him in the hospital. He'd gone there to try to get fit and spry for your ordination, Father Will; and he told the doctors and nurses that they'd *have* to make him well, because he was an old soldier and had rights."

Will and I did our best to comfort her, our own hearts heavier than they had ever been before. And that night in Will's bedroom we discussed the state of affairs till dawn came in on us. It was Sunday, and the Lord seemed to enter with the light. And we saw that, since He had called us to careers in His farther fields, He himself would somehow attend to the business that, in obedience to His will, we had had to leave unfinished here at home. "We can help our brothers," said Will, "by applying the merits of our lives in religion to their souls. I'm certain that, no matter how bad things look now, they'll end right, because we're consigning them to the best hands, the only ones that never make a mistake. Besides, we have so much to be thankful for. Our sisters are just about perfect. Frank's growing up without any serious fault . . ."

Devoutly he made ready for his first Solemn High Mass, which was scheduled for eleven o'clock. As the hour neared, I proposed that he let me accompany him to St. Mary's and carry his satchel for him, but he said no, there were matters that he had to talk

over with Someone on the way. So, with young Francis, I helped
to spruce up Jim, Tom, and Joe, who had sheepishly, asham-
edly, kept in the background since our return. Annie and Agnes
looked lovely in muslin, home-sewn gowns and flower-wreathed
leghorn hats; and Mom, matronly and modest in a plain gray
dress and toque. But Dad—where was he? We searched the house
and the neighborhood. In vain. And there now remained just
enough time for us to get to St. Mary's. It would have been
unforgivable to be late on such a day! We simply had to start
out, trusting that he would turn up as we hurried along.

When we arrived at the church, there he was, kneeling in the
very first pew. While we had been bothering about appearances,
he had had only one thought, his son's first Mass. My throat con-
stricted and my eyes smarted as I saw him, his silvered head
down, his well-worn beads clasped firm, his whole attitude a
prayer. He had forgotten to put on a coat, and his time-darkened
galluses, crisscrossing his bent back like a symbol of life itself so
patiently borne, made the whiteness of his shirt shimmer in the
morning sun.

Two weeks later Will left Salem for what was to prove a long
and arduous ministry. And right after, Dad, who had kept living
only for that first Mass, visibly failed. "Persevere, Son," he bade
me repeatedly. He spent his last days on his knees; and one night,
to the pattering of rain on the windows, he closed his eyes forever.

As long as I could I lingered in town to help console the family
and catch up on my former associations. Some of the people I met
did not remember me, and others hardly knew I had been away;
and life impressed me somewhat as a painted river, static in its
very flow. I focused on the old landmarks: the Seamen's Bethel,
the Old Grist Mill, the house of blazes, the Marblehead steeples
across the harbor, St. Mary's Church and School, the house of
seven gables, the fraternity, the public library, the custom house,

and particularly Derby Wharf extending its long gaunt finger toward the sea, as if indicating the source of a commercial prestige which had once caused natives in the Indies to consider America a small town in the great country of Salem. And strolling the now denuded stretch of rocks and weeds, which before the Embargo Act in the War of 1812 had teemed with an activity rivaling Boston's, I meditated the present meaninglessness of the city's once proud motto, "To the richest port of the far East." But it pleased me to think that, even better than in her heyday, Salem was now embarking, however unconsciously, on a spiritual enterprise. The same missionary urge given by Father Halley to Will had been passed on to me, and I was determined to share it. My lively imagination could already envisage a band of Pauls, Xaviers, and Clavers—all Salemites—setting out for the southland as vessels of the Faith.

Johnnie Geary and John Carroll, whom I'd so wanted for my first recruits, were at present like trees with roots too deep for transplanting. They still inclined to the priesthood, but felt that it required more quality than they possessed, and sadly surrendering the hope of their ever being with me, I was doubly grateful for the grace of having hearkened to the call in the time of boyhood when dreams beckon more effectively than self-analysis retards.

Whom else besides Geary and Carroll might I seek to stimulate? There must be others. But five years of separation from Salem had caused my acquaintanceship to decline. Surely, though, when I should return as a priest, not a mere student, the Lord would grant me access to young hearts and use me to win apostles for Him. I made that trust a prayer and mingled with it a resolution that, if the time should indeed come for me to enlist a local interest in the Negro, I would counsel speed; for I now felt, from the thwarted cases of my two friends, that to keep heaven waiting was one of the surest ways of missing the call.

That September I was received into St. Joseph's Seminary in Baltimore. The toll had been heavy in the class with which I started out half a decade before. Satan, or the Lord himself, had sifted us, and from a total of eighteen, only two remained: myself and Joe Lally—a fine Bostonian. Now, in foretaste of the priesthood, we survivors could wear the Roman collar, the cassock and the biretta, a privilege which caused us already to feel almost ordained.

The seminary, a plain brick building on the main colored thoroughfare, stood so solemn that one might well have expected sin to locate itself at least a mile away; yet right across from us a brothel flourished, its old gray banners of roller curtains defiantly high. From our windows we could have looked directly into it, especially when the lights went on at night, but we merely pulled our own curtains down and wondered why the police seemed remiss. One seminarian, however, spoke so often and scandalizedly about the "den" that we began to suspect him of peering. He resented this and gave us to understand that he had stacked up all his textbooks on the study table at the window in his room so as to guard his vision entirely from shame. Why, then, was his mind so beset? The answer came and struck like a whimsical bolt from the blue one evening when, going to his room to borrow some ink and opening the door without knocking, I caught him perched on his table and gazing out over his barricade of books. A few weeks later he left the seminary and returned to the world, probably to spend the rest of his days wistfully looking back at the good life from which he had uncontrollably looked out on the bad.

Colored people, of whom hitherto I had seen few, were now a frequent sight. Every Wednesday afternoon we seminarians visited the Negro wards of hospitals, and each Sunday we taught catechism in the mission churches of our order. My fingers on a black child's cheek felt softest silk; and the whites of the eyes, whiter by contrast with the melting dark irises, had the gloss of lilies. I liked all the kinky-haired little ones I met, and did not see how anyone could deem them odd. They had as many faculties, nerves, arteries, and potentialities as other children. That their skin was sable seemed to me but an added and interesting detail.

I knew, from the literary browsing of my boyhood, that Indian babies in Massachusetts in colonial days were born somewhat light in color, and that the east wind and New England sunshine soon produced a tawniness. Would not the more exposed conditions and far hotter sun of Africa have caused in a susceptible race a tintage capable of becoming through the course of centuries a transmittable variation? The old Grecian explanation of the origin of color, which I had also read in my green years, now returned to me: the myth of the sun god Apollo letting his importunate offspring Phaëthon drive the flaming chariot of dawn, with the consequence that a very inexpert performance brought a scorching heat so near to the land of Ethiopia that blood rushed to the surface of human beings there and made all epidermis dark. There could be truth in fantasy; and this story, told along the Aegean shores when thought was young and fresh, at least argued that the most civilized of pagan peoples found no essential difference between Negroes and whites. Why should any Christians look on pigmentation as an unpardonable crime? I had already discovered Montesquieu for myself with wonder and relish, but his remark that "the noses of Ethiopians are pressed so close to their faces that it is almost impossible to pity them" was almost enough to make me drop him. And the Darwin-inspired notion that evolution represented an ascending scale with the white man on top and the Negro at the bottom! What harm it had done a humble people, and how badly needed was a deeper conviction of the brotherhood of men to offset it!

This was my seminarian mind as I walked among the underprivileged group whom I, like Father Will, now lived to serve. But there were jolts for me in the hospitals. Having pictured the Negro as stretching forth his hands piteously for the gifts of understanding and sympathy, I was crestfallen when this or that patient failed to welcome my brisk, bright approach and even turned the flat of his back on me; and I came to realize that before planting the Gospel seed it might be necessary patiently to retrieve a soil which, like that of old Carthage after the Roman conquest, had been plowed under and strewn with salt.

One day, a few weeks after I began philosophy, Father Pastorelli—our rector and ablest Josephite—took me into his office and tendered some advice. "Talk to the colored as if they were white, and they'll like you as if you were colored," he said. "Never say 'You people,' and seldom use the word 'Negro' when you're with them. Don't be gushingly sympathetic, or you'll only remind them of their lot; and how can they welcome any reminder of what they cannot forget? Don't think for a single moment that you are doing them any favor by going to them. It is a blessed privilege to bring hope and healing to anybody, and a feeling of sacrifice is not justified. What sacrifice is there to a life of accumulating treasure where moths do not consume and thieves do not break in? Always remember that Peter Claver gloried in being the slave of slaves, because it made him a full servant of God."

When I told him about the rebuffs I had received in the hospitals, he replied, "Perhaps your very enthusiasm made the patients all the more conscious of their being ill. The colored get so little attention that they incline to be uncomfortable and suspicious when it comes; but once they're convinced of our sincerity and altruism, they respond well. Claver used to say that we must speak to them with our hands before speaking with our lips. Give them something—a medal, a holy picture, a rosary—and they'll be less apt to identify you with those who have taken so much away. Let a quiet Christian attitude be your speech until you see that they are ready for your words."

There was far less leisure for us students in the seminary than there had been in the college. Time took on a swift tempo; but it was so referred to heavenly aims and purposes that no little of the peace and dignity of eternity itself permeated the place.

Still, becoming more and more sensitive to my imperfections as I studied ideals, before long I stumbled deeply into what St. John of the Cross might have called "the dark night of the soul," a period of diffidence, groping, and gloom which lasted for weeks. My spirit was at its lowest the day when, wandering through the seminary library, I came across a quotation from Voltaire in a historical essay, an acid comment on human intelligence: "They needed a mathematician, so they hired a dancer." And I asked myself, if God needed a missionary, would He—could He—have selected me? Ah no. I myself must have done the selecting, and who was I, so inferior to Will, to offer myself to divine service? True, the rector and my confessor seemed satisfied that I'd do, but they were so charitable, and I could see myself only as nothingness equipped with presumption, or as a bunch of faults tied together with a mere wish for worthiness. I doubted that I could have made even a good hod carrier, for surely I lacked the quality of my own father who dug ditches; and here I was, seeking the very highest of estates.

But driven back to my New Testament as my only escape from cynical Voltaire, I found, in the manner of an entirely fresh discovery, my answer. "You have not chosen me, but I have chosen you." And reflecting that the Twelve Apostles themselves had been pretty negative until the Paraclete came upon them, I further recalled the text about the Lord using the foolish to confound the wise. As a result, an extra calm sleep was mine that night, and ever since I've had a sneaking regard for the wizened thinker who obliquely helped me to see daylight again. Moreover, I've cherished the thought that Providence allows so many sophisticated voices to be heard in this world of ours because, however unwittingly, they do—sometimes—force the spirit to such medicament as can be found only in simple faith.

St. Joseph's Seminary, like a small brother, was more than fostered by the great St. Mary's Seminary across the campus which both separated and joined the institutions; and the students of the two schools mingled in classes and recreations, for the excellent Sulpician Fathers in charge of St. Mary's were only too happy to grant us Josephites all their facilities free, a favor that none of us would ever forget. And so my memories of the one are entwined with those of the other.

There was the instance in which Father Duffy, an ardent Sulpician advocate of temperance, who had inspired many of us to take the anti-alcoholic pledge for life, called on me to stand up during Scripture class and synopsize very briefly the Book of Ruth. A little self-conscious, I began, "Ruth, the Moabitess, was gleaning in the fields of Bethlehem and found Booz." At that, the seminarians burst out laughing, since my pronunciation of "Booz" made the name sound like a beverage and put in their minds a funny picture of whisky bottles cached in holy places. Worse, I went on to insist, "But that's what the Old Testament says!" The amusement increased, and Father Duffy, stroking his chin, eyed me not too pleasantly. "I know, Mr. Murphy," he drawled, "but the word is usually pronounced 'Bo-oz.'" After thanking him for the correction, I got through the rest of the narrative hurriedly and was glad to sit down, but when the session was over, a few of the St. Mary men surrounded me in the corridor, pumping my hand and thumping my back. "Good, Murph," said one. "Père Duffy thinks that booze is Dante's Inferno, and here you slip a supply into Bethlehem!" It would have been futile for me to explain that I had had no intention whatsoever of poking fun at our teacher's heavy championship of teetotalism, so I accepted the accolade with a forced grin.

The Josephites and the St. Mary students often exchanged accounts of their respective forts; and I've always remembered a certain episode, told and retold till its variations were just too many, that happened during a meal in the Sulpician refectory one noon. The gist of it was that an Irish "sem," while reading from the rostrum Bourdaloue's panegyric on Mary Magdalen, distinguished and almost extinguished himself. His brogue being fairly thick, he kept pronouncing the great penitent's name so peculiarly that it sounded less like "Magdalen" than "Mag Dillon." Finally the patiently presiding Father from Saint Sulpice in Paris, whose duty it was to make corrections, put down his knife and fork and cried, "My good man, *qu'est-ce que c'est que ça?* Is it that this saint was an *Irish* woman, that you should be calling her 'Mag Dil-long'?" And the reader, leveling his gaze rather injuredly at him, retorted, "I'd not be thinking she was Irish, Your Riverince, because the way she had of washing feet with her tears and dhrying them with her hair would seem more like *French. N'est-ce pas?*"

Right after hearing this for the first time, and chuckling over it perhaps more than I should, I made some amends by going into our library and soberly weighing every word of Bourdaloue's sermon. It moved me deeply, that tribute; particularly the observation that though the Magdalen's vice was that she had many lovers, her virtue was that she loved much. And years later I was to recall it in a way that would affect my life strangely.

Our studies grew absorbing; philosophy deepening the mind, Holy Scripture exalting it, and science lending objectivity and precision. And Father Pastorelli's earnest conferences in the assembly hall, together with the Sunday sermons which we took turns preaching in the chapel, attuned our souls to the Infinite. Sometimes, however, the young preachers, insufficiently prepared, would become rattled, and then we'd break into smiles. But the smiles were never big, for the realization that we ourselves would too soon be on exhibition was more forbidding than the rector's frown. Well I recall one of our orators nervously trying out a Delsartian gesture or two and getting his arm so solidly into the air that he could not draw it down; and the mishap of our most brilliant student's mind, in the midst of a memorized flight of rhetoric, going completely blank; but chiefly our utter astonishment when a normally levelheaded fellow whose subject was Catholic education and who, carried away from his moorings by his flow and floundering in mid-stream, desperately shook his fist at us poor celibates and shrieked, as a

filler-in, the old reliable slogan, "Send your children to the parochial schools!" But in general the sermonizing was good and the
delivery not bad, and some of the young men who, in the wider
ranges of the Epiphany landscape had practiced throwing their
voices against the breeze and improvising speeches as they rapidly
paced along, gave indication of future perfection.

Because I could play I now fell heir to the position of organist. At first it was an annoyance, because of the plain chant
to which we had to adhere. Such flat, defunct tunelessness!
But gradually the realization came to me that, exactly the opposite of operatic, this music had a remarkable merit of its
own, calling no attention to itself, hence giving everything to its
theme. The wise old Church disapproved the use of florid compositions which glorified human genius rather than God, and
once I caught the significance, plain chant appealed to me, in its
modesty and serviceability, as an improvement on the ecclesiastical best even of Mozart and Gounod. It made me contrast the
simple charm of Nazareth and Bethany with the artificial splendor of the halls of Caesar. Moreover, since some few of the
seminarians could hardly carry a note, I further appreciated the
thoughtfulness of Rome in providing and prescribing the barest
and most facile system of vocalization.

On the small pump organ in the chapel I played every High
Mass and Vesper service, and as my fingers stroked the keys, my
mind often went back to my sister Annie in Salem, whose little,
hard-earned savings had been spent for the lessons that were now
making it possible for me to serenade the King.

The good fortune that made me a winner in the Boston archdiocesan competition years before had not abandoned me; and
at the end of my two-year philosophical course at St. Mary's, I
received not only an M.A. *cum maxima laude*, but also a prize of
books which could be personally selected. At the suggestion of
Father Baisnée and Father Redon, my teachers, I chose the works
of St. Thomas Aquinas, and consequently turned more diligently

to the greatest mind of its kind that Christian civilization ever produced. With my vocation to the Negro apostolate ever before me, I searched the master's profound yet lucid Latin pages, treating of myriad problems, for some special principles to guide my missionary steps; and what was my surprise to find that, five centuries before Thomas Jefferson, he had written what might well have been a preamble to the Declaration of Independence! Human dignity, equality, anti-tyranny, inalienable rights—all were there in black and white. I marked whole passages in the *Summa, De Regimine Principum*, and *Contra Gentiles*, and made copious notes which, it occurred to me, I might someday elaborate into a book.

Why not, I thought, a little practice in writing even now? It was quite urgent for me to try to earn a few dollars on the side, because the economic condition at home was uncertain and I could not go on accepting help which involved too much sacrifice on the part of my selfless sisters. Between the lines of Mom's letters, always breathing of an effort to cheer me up and withhold any cause for worry, I could read that times were hard and inferred that Jim, Tom, and Joe were still contributing practically nothing. Annie was about to be married, and how I wanted to send her a present! As for Agnes, her prospect of wedded bliss had just ended with the sudden decease of Walter Brennan; and knowing her as I did, I was sure that no one else would ever take his place in her life. Soon, despite her own need for rest and comfort, she would have to be the chief support of the family, for Frank, going to school, could not yet put much of a shoulder to the wheel. So in my few spare moments I produced and polished an article and sent it, with a stamped self-addressed envelope enclosed, to *America*, the national Jesuit weekly, chiding myself for daring to hope that it would even be glanced at.

A fortnight later a letter of acceptance and a check for ten dollars from Father Tierney, the editor, reached me. Rudyard Kipling, as I had just read somewhere, was getting a dollar a word for his output. (It was alleged that somebody had written him a note, enclosing a dollar and requesting one of those precious, peerless words. Taking the cash, Kipling simply wrote back, "Thanks.") But to me ten dollars for an article was equivalent to a hundred, and Father Tierney's note of encouragement, to a thousand. He even proposed that I let him see other manuscripts, as if anything could keep me from doing so!

By the light of a candle, and long after everyone was asleep each night, I worked out contribution after contribution. Such a variety of themes! "World Peace," "Pan-Americanism," "Social Justice," "Tuberculosis," "Divorce," "Birth Control," "Female Suffrage." What I did not know about these subjects was much, but I strove hard in the library and reading room to learn something, and evidently there was enough originality to my style or personality to my earnestness to catch the editorial eye, because Father Tierney bought a number of my brave attempts. Soon he raised me to sixteen dollars and suggested that, since I was appearing so frequently and some contributors were complaining about not being able to get into *America* at all, I use a pen name or two. I did—a pair of very select pseudonyms, "Edmund Sinclair" and "Edmund Saint-Hilaire." And I was beginning to feel chesty, because religious journals were reprinting me, and even some secular papers were quoting such important conclusions of mine as "World peace should begin in men's souls, not in Switzerland," "The future of the Western hemisphere lies below the Panama Canal," "A free man must be a fed man," "God made marriage a sacrament, and man would make it an experiment."

But "Female Suffrage" was almost my undoing. Mindful of my mother's devotion to the home and her apathy toward most things beyond it, I went into really high gear against "these modern women who lack sense enough to see that in gaining the vote they may lose the voter"; and explosively I warned that a two-headed family was as anomalous as a two-headed baby. *Miserere.* A hive of hornets was stirred, and letters from extremely articulate females, of whom I had never imagined there were so many, stung my ego deeply. When Father Butsch, who was Father Pastorelli's assistant and our prefect of discipline, took me aside quietly but firmly to say that public controversy was incompatible with seminary decorum, I almost wished that I had never dipped a pen in ink. But Annie, thanks to Father Tierney and those articles, got her present—a silver-plated tea set. Mom received enough wherewithal to meet several months' rent; Agnes, a new dress; Jim, Tom, and Joe, prayerbooks; Frank, shoes and a suit. And though limited by Father Butsch, I was not silenced. Short stories appealed to me as a better-paying, non-polemical field, and I was not disillusioned. *Extension Magazine* purchased my very first offering for twenty-five dollars, and soon I was getting as high as sixty.

I smile now at that fiction spree of mine which at the time made me feel not too unlike Hawthorne. In one tale I had a character ascend three flights of stairs in a factory, and some paragraphs later, forgetting that he was so high up, led him to a window to receive a letter from a postman in the street. (After this mistake had slipped into print, the editor, genially and forgivingly enough, wrote me: "How far can one's fancy and psychological suspenders stretch?") Like most religious yarn spinners, I was bent on morals more than facts, and on idealization than realization. My eyes were starward and I still got Benediction veils mixed up with tablecloths.

Like philosophy, theology increased the reasoning powers of us seminarians, and like the tyros-in-thought we still were, we reasoned on everything under the sun and even above it, hopefully jumbling our bright key into even the tightest of locks. Not until I was nearing the subdiaconate did I fully recognize the audacity of this. "Let God have at least a few secrets," Father Butsch told me. "Reason is to faith as a candle to the sun. It lights up the immediate dark in life, but only faith can illumine life itself. Would you prefer the far less to the far greater?" Yet being Irish and obstinate, I challenged him: "Then it does seem strange that the Church puts us through such a long mental course. Didn't St. Peter Claver himself ask why so much theology was necessary in order to receive Holy Orders and baptize a few poor Negroes?"

He shook his head and smiled. "That was his zeal to get started on his quest for souls," he said. "Later in life he would have been the last to belittle the need of minutest preparation for spreading the Gospel. Mind and talent are most needed where problems most abound, and that may be why Claver's own great Jesuit Order has always had a policy of sending some of its very best men to the hardest missions. Study is not a substitute for faith—the things of faith need no proving for believers; but it is absolutely necessary for the purpose of our answering nonbelievers and furnishing motives of credibility to them and turning them toward truths beyond reason. In this sense Claver, Xavier, and every other apostle kept studying throughout life."

I appreciated this exposition, yet could not withhold a final thrust. "But reasoning—analysis, deduction, induction—has a tendency to draw us from faith, doesn't it, even though we use it to lead others to faith?" I asked, veered by overconviction to a new angle. And he replied gravely, "The priest has his Mass, his office, his rosary, and the grace of a mighty sacrament."

My three years in theology passed swifter than those in philosophy, and I found myself at last holding a B.S.T. sheepskin—"the triumph of the sittest," joshed Joe Lally—and standing at the goal.

The night before ordination I lay wide awake, marveling that even with heavenly help I had gotten so far. From Derby Street to the New Jerusalem! And I wondered what might have happened if the fat man backstage at the old Mechanic Hall in Salem had given me a chance over ten years ago, instead of shooing me away from the amateur-night performance. Would I have been like Susan Geary, the little Cambridge-ite who opened the door of the theater only to discover the opposite of what I now know from the pure pages of Thomas à Kempis to be the Way without which there is no going, the Truth without which there is no knowing, and the Life without which there is no living? On what small hinges a door—a destiny—swings! Would I have gotten by and gone as far in the wrong way as I had come in the right? Would I have been my own "architect of fate" and made a mess of things?

I thought of John Nelson Goucher, the boy from Lime Rock, Rhode Island, who had taken life into his own hands and run away. How had he fared? Now in his mid-twenties like me, he was probably floundering through a welter of worldliness and disillusion and wishing that he could start all over again. I speculated whether our lives would ever cross again and I'd be able to help, pitying him as I plumed myself on having been spared his mistakenness. The thought of him brought memories of his wonderful mother who had had so many children, and I thanked heaven for my own family.

Then I could see the dark illuminated with a long vista of "fields whitening to the harvest," into which the Lord of Reapers was welcoming me as He had welcomed Will before me; and in a fancied fragrance of wheat and wine I felt my fingers and lips touching the chalice He proffered.

The night flew by, as wingèd as the years. Dawn was penciling a red-gold line under the drawn-down roller curtain of my room.

IV

WITH Dad gone and Annie married and three of the boys more away from home than in it, Mom had moved to a smaller tenement uptown on Watson Street, as far from Derby as she could get. And so I celebrated my first Solemn High Mass not at St. Mary's but St. James's Church.

Father McCall, the pastor, old and ill, had lain in bed for weeks; but nothing could keep him there that bright Sunday morning in June. It was graduation day, and little girls in frilly white dresses and boys in neat dark suits filled the front middle-aisle pews, their parents looking on with gleaming pride. The future of the congregation under the present gaze of the past! Standing unsteadily at the sanctuary rail, the sun making a nimbus of his sparse white hair, he did not preach but gave an informal talk; and as he praised the youngsters, his emotion was so great that he almost keeled over. "You—you're clean and beautiful," he cried, "just like your mothers and fathers before you. This is the best congregation that ever was, and I don't give a —— who says different!" Fortunately Father Gleason, the assistant, hovering near, coughed in exactly the right spot, and nobody clearly heard just what it was that the good old man didn't "give"; but all knew that he had spent himself for his flock, loving them for letting him, and that now, in the deep evening of his sojourn, he was finding their every defect, physical or spiritual, gilded with the afterglow.

He had mumbled to me while I was vesting in the sacristy, "Young man, never forget our good Irish people. We priests would be nothing without them. They're our life in the Lord." At this stage of his career he could hardly think of "other sheep not of the fold," and I doubt that he gave more than a passing thought to the fact that I had been ordained for missionary endeavor. Certainly he made no reference to the Negro apostolate in his remarks that morning. But Father James Albert, one of the most impressive of Josephites, was there to supply the lack, having come from Baltimore to deliver the sermon; and as soon as he stepped up into the pulpit and began to speak, the church was his. Eloquently he lauded the diocesan clergy, but stressed the need of outpost bands of priests to push forward the boundaries of the kingdom, since the field, according to the Gospel, was the world. Vividly he described the spiritual and corporal destitution of the colored in the South, traced the rise of the Society of St. Joseph in obedience to the wish of Rome, and recounted Father Halley's dropping a seed into the soul of an altar boy— William Aloysius Murphy—who had become the first native Salemite to devote himself to the evangelization of our Aframerican brother. In conclusion he declared, "This spirit seed already shows local growth, for a second Salemite, brother of the first, comes to you today with the oils of consecration fresh on his hands. As he is following another's example, so, please God, still others will follow his; and this storied city, deriving its name from the Hebrew word for 'peace,' may yet be celebrated as a source of great consolation to a people who have borne the cross more meekly than any other in modern times."

Father Will, having had to travel all the way from Pine Bluff, Arkansas, arrived a little late for the Mass. But his coming—at what inconvenience and sacrifice I could only guess, because it was his rule never to mention a personal hardship—doubled the sunniness of the day; and our family, all together, except for one whose very absence somehow made him even more present to us, knew the gladness of bygone years all over again.

In the simple frame house on Watson Street that noon a dinner was provided by neighbors who insisted on the "honor" of taking over and who would not let a Murphy lift a hand. Eddie Larkin, the grocer around the corner, had sent in chickens; and

Nell Lundergan, a remarkable person whose life belonged to everybody but herself, stuffed and roasted them to perfection. Nellie Cotter, Agnes's chum, mashed potatoes till they appeared and tasted like whipped cream. Etta Welch, a "living out" girl, made a batch of biscuits as light as foam and served what seemed to us the best coffee this side of Brazil. Fruit, ice cream, pop, cake; someone, strictly preserving his or her anonymity, had donated these. Roses, a wealth of them, red and white, came from Miss Emmerton. And priestly gifts! Father Will, for his ordination, had received only a very few, but for me there lay, on a table in our parlor, a generous supply of lace surplices, oilstocks, burses, stoles, and cinctures; and, dominating all, a brand-new chalice like an amber lily rose straight and symbolic in the light from the windows.

I could not understand why I'd been so well remembered and my brother comparatively forgotten, but when I expressed this perplexity to Father Albert he solved it by reminding me that, only for Will, who had lit a lamp in the community, my own ordination might have attracted much less attention.

The afternoon was given over to a reception, and every one of the five rooms of the tenement was crowded with congratulators, most of whom stayed till dusk. It was well that they finally went, because refreshments ran out and a miracle similar to the Lord's multiplication of the loaves and fishes would have had to be performed.

The last person to go was Margaret Sullivan, a teen-ager with such fresh pink cheeks, curly dark hair, and lustrous brown eyes as to have set the heart of many a youth in town palpitating, I could well believe. But her mind was not on earthly romance, and the foregleam of another world already touched her brow. "I've known your sisters for the past few years, Father," she said, standing in the doorway, "and I've often talked with them about you. I've read some of your stories in magazines, you see, and I remember especially that rather funny little one where somebody reached out of an upstairs window and received a letter from the postman in the street. It puzzled me and got me to thinking. I asked myself whether it would be any more absurd for me, away below, to reach up and—and perhaps receive a message from high above. The desire to be a Sister—I've had it off and on since childhood—returned stronger, and this morning, right after I received your blessing at the end of Mass, all hesitation seemed to—to cease. Tomorrow, the first thing, I'll go to the Notre Dame Convent and inquire about being received. Father, do pray for me."

Pray for her? I heartily promised. But many, many a time since then I've prayed *to* her, for she indeed became a nun, and after a period of oblation in which she attained a rare degree of sanctity, she quietly passed on to the realm whose ray had touched her forehead as the sun was sinking on my day of days.

The sun seemed to be sinking on the world itself in those days, and the melancholy words of Sir Edward Grey, the statesman, quoted as far back as 1914 by the American press, kept tolling in my subconsciousness: "The lights are going out all over Europe. They will never be rekindled in our time." That June of '17 the darkness had spread across the Atlantic, and American homes were being invaded by the draft. My brother Joe left us a few days after my first Mass. Jim and Tom were waiting to be called; and Frank, hardly of age, was jumping the trigger by enlisting, with Mom's reluctant but resigned consent. We saw our youngest off to Fort Devens, and were proud but saddened when he reappeared shortly afterward, manly in his khaki, still so much a kid. Thousands and thousands like him, just beginning life, had to face death. It was man's nature to do battle, but why couldn't the fight be against the common enemies of the race? Against sin with churches, ignorance with schools, disease with hospitals, instead of against fellow men with guns! When I expressed myself like this to Father Will, he smiled a little at my vehemence, though his eyes were sad. "We have many churches, schools, and hospitals," he said, "but the Devil's name is Legion."

Able to spare little time from his mission, he soon had to bid us good-by. And I spent the rest of my month's vacation re-familiarizing myself with the past and adjusting myself to the future. I saw the soft light of Cana, where water was changed to wine, in my sister Annie's eyes; and also a gleam of Nazareth, for she was now raising children of her own. Agnes, always deep and reticent, had something of the aspect of a child holding a sea shell to the ear, and I could see that she was listening for a voice less lost in silence than lent to it. Jim and Tom took the pledge from me, just as they had taken it from Father Will five years before; but the weakness was not absent from their look, and I did not flatter myself that I'd be any more successful in rehabilitating them than he had been. The matter must still be left to the Lord. And Mom, a faded figure in the twilight that her years without her mate had become, held often to her rocking chair.

I roamed the scenes of my childhood with little feeling of be-longing to them any more. They seemed to my larger vision to have shrunken like an aging face, and their miles were as so many paces. Why, this Salem that used to be an entire world was only a comparative corner! The barn where Johnnie Geary and I had whiled away our too few hours together lay in a heap of rubble from a final cave-in; and Johnnie himself, caught in a movement more compelling than the call of the missions, was already in far-off France. Father Timothy Murphy had passed away; the curates—Father Walsh and Father Dave Murphy—had other assignments; Sister Marie Concilio was imparting her mysticism, and Sister Teresa Carmel telling her holy tales of horror, to groups of children elsewhere.

I hated to leave what was left of the family, but felt eager for the great work ahead. It occurred to me, though, that the start could and should be attempted right here and now. The country was recruiting for Mars, and that was just what I ought to be doing for Christ. The campaign to which I'd invite youth would have the irresistible appeal of brightness and bloodlessness. No one in it would receive a single wound, but on the contrary, all would heal many wounds. Oh, I was sanguine those two Sundays when I preached at the children's Masses in both parishes. How I pleaded my cause! What pictures I drew, and what an effect I thought I was having as wide eyes stared straight at me and ears took in every word! Surely at least a few of the graduates would approach me afterward and ask to know more about the college in Maryland that was so ready to receive and train them. But as days went by my hope died. No one came. With big brothers marching in uniforms and parades to the beat of drums, what chance of success had the plea, "Come, follow me?"

My first appointment was to St. Barnabas Church in Baltimore, a small, rather attractive, Gothic-style structure of red brick with stone copings. It looked calm and problemless, but it wasn't. Father McCarty, the superior-general of the Josephites, had already told me that the congregation, recently flourishing, was now on the wane. The cause, a story in itself. . . .

Father Evers, the pastor and a hearty person given to indiscriminate charity, had hired a colored housemaid whose vernal name, "Mary Lily," was her only recommendation. She had just finished a period of detention in the House of the Good Shepherd, and the mother superior in charge had strongly urged him to think twice before employing her; but he was not the sort to dwell on anybody's past, for hope in human regeneration sprang eternal in his bosom, or at least as eternal as a not inexhaustible patience could permit. No sooner had Mary Lily assumed her new duties than she began acting up, and at length he felt he must dismiss her; but she protested so violently that there was nothing for him to do, short of calling the police, but thrust her bodily out the door. That aroused the very worst in her, and what she bruited throughout the neighborhood against him was enormous. Her tirades waxed so loud and livid that a bitterly anti-Catholic weekly heard of them and sent an agent to egg her on; and presently two pictures, one of Father Evers and the other of the vixen herself, appeared on the front page of one of the issues, with an article entitled "Priest and Victim." Dismayed, he broke under the strain and could give only a token attention to his work.

And now, into this non-Eden, I entered with all my callowness.

The day of my arrival, Father Evers departed for another mission, and Father Butsch, from St. Joseph's Seminary, was appointed to fill the pastorate. An old idealist, used to the orderliness of institutional life, he looked out on the blight of a parish and groaned, "God help us!" And I echoed him, for this was as different from any of my dreams as a thistle from a daisy. But we stepped right into our duties, and the battle of reclamation was on.

We restored every service, we preached and begged, we took a census which brought us even into scabrous alleys and revealed the depths to which man, created only a little below the angels, could sink. We saw disease, spiritual and physical, in most of its stages. And before any of our efforts at betterment could become really effective, the heavy winter of '17 was upon us. With no machinery for rationing set up by the Government, the shortages caused by the war were drastically increased for the "have-nots" by the grab of the "haves." It was almost impossible to get any coal, and often our little church, which we were trying so hard to fill again, was so cold that very few people attended.

On Sunday morning, on entering the vestibule, I beheld a stout old woman barging out. "But Mass is about to begin," I told her. Slashing me with a slanty look, she puffed, "And Ah'm 'bout to *end*. It's an icebox in there, that's what it is. Oughta be a law 'gin it. Can serve mah God better alive than daid."

The next day, by pulling every string, I managed to secure some fuel; only a half ton, but precious as a collection of black diamonds. Feeling myself the ransomer of St. Barnabas, I proudly watched a laborer chuting each shovelful into the church-cellar bin and came back several times to gloat over the treasure. Then night fell. By morning the bin was just as empty as before. Even more so, for thieves had entered and made off not only with the diamonds but even the dust. The cleanest sweep I ever saw! I felt that the very nadir of wretchedness had been reached.

I was wrong about that nadir. Father Butsch, worn out with worry, succumbed to a stroke and had to be removed to a hospital, leaving me to handle everything. It seemed that the whole church, like a much-cracked ceiling, was falling, and that there was nobody there but me, like Annie in the Park Street kitchen so long ago. But the thermometer went up a trifle, and our really goodhearted people, pitying one so young in the priesthood for having to assume a pastor's responsibility, started to come. Muffled to the ears, they came; and the white vapor of their breath as they sat hunched like Eskimos in the unheated pews was to me as sweetest incense from their sacrifice, or even as the very offering of their souls; and gratefully I delivered the warmest sermons of which I was capable, though my teeth sometimes clicked like castanets and my finger tips and toes felt ready to fall off.

The long winter drifted away, yielding to a mild and radiant spring, all the fairer by that contrast which Ruskin calls the microscope of the senses. In the bleak dark months I had learned the truth of Hawthorne's saying, "Angels do not toil, but let their good works grow out of them"; and my impetuosities were under better control. I found myself remembering things that brought a smile. The quaint absurdity of academic Father Butsch using his well-thumbed copy of Newman's *Idea of a University*, his second Bible, as the textbook for his Sunday-school class of eye-rolling, fidgety little boys and girls. An aged man's appraisal of Father Butsch as a preacher: "Mos' pow'rful one I ever did hear! He jus' fills every square inch of St. Barnabas with that boomy voice of his'n, an' I feels him in my feet. Shame he don't speak English." My small errand boy's denial with dewiest innocence that he had taken from the dining room the two bananas which I could see peeking right out of his pants pocket. A grandma's estimate of my own oratory, after I had delivered a Sunday scorcher on hell: "You sure knows how to console us po' sinners on a cold mawnin'!"

Oh yes, I could smile again, but the smiles no doubt were softer and wiser than once upon a time, since experience had well shown me that humor and pathos were kin. For example, how Sarah, the wizened but safe successor to Mary Lily as maid-of-all-work, had annoyed me with her habit of keeping an electric bulb going day and night in the front hallway of the rectory! As many times as I'd snap it off in order to economize, out she would pop from nowhere and, mumbling to herself, put it on. Her persistence seemed utterly senseless. But one morning when I at last succeeded in wresting an explanation from her, a lump came to my throat. It was only that, loyal to her former pastor, she believed the parish still to be his and could not accept the fact that he had left town forever. There just had to be a light to welcome him whenever he'd return.

Easter brought more than its usual resurrection of spirit. Father Conrad Rebescher, a two-fisted Josephite who had done yeoman service in the Deep South, stepped off a train in Union Station to take over St. Barnabas; and the minute I saw him, I knew that the end of trouble was assured. Just as realistic as Father Butsch wasn't, he expected problems, minimized their mastery, and proceeded calmly to solutions. Quickly the parish responded by pulsing with newness of life, and in two months' time it was again on the glory road.

My association with such efficiency being so pleasant, I hoped it would never end; but the hope was brief, for Father Pastorelli, who became superior-general in June, decided to send me in the fall to Catholic University in Washington, D.C., for advance studies that would lead to a Ph.D. Grateful but restive, I asked him why. Hadn't I been ordained for the missions, and wouldn't a doctorate qualify me only to talk over the heads of my hearers? Patiently he explained that part of the development of our society, as he saw it, should consist in bringing our college and seminary to the highest standard by staffing them with perfectly trained teachers. Appreciating this, I still wondered how a university course could fit me to teach future missionaries better than a longer and fuller apprenticeship in the missions.

My leave-taking from St. Barnabas on a Sunday morning in September was even more of a heartache than I expected. The parishioners gathered around me in the basement hall after my Mass, and their outpouring of sentiment made me think their dusky faces as beauteous as an evening sky rain-washed and star-sprinkled. From the altar I had already spoken my farewell; but that was not enough. Their pathetic devotion now forced me to over-expressiveness. "To be so far away and never see you again," I said, choking, "this is my cross for not having served you better."

The "far away" was only an hour's ride by train from Baltimore, but at the time I felt almost as if bound for the bourn whence no traveler ever returns. Off I went, bending my head and trailing my woe, and within two weeks I was right back at St. Barnabas, seeing plenty of the never-to-be-seen-again, for Catholic University, because of the Spanish influenza sweeping the country, had suddenly suspended its classes and closed its doors, and Father Pastorelli deemed it best for me to keep busy in my former location until the reopening. "God bless the Spanish influence f'r bringin' you home!" cried old Sarah, the housekeeper, when I walked in on her. And I noticed that *two* lights were burning in the dinginess of the rectory corridor.

My second leave-taking, a month later, was much less emotional than the first, because I was sobered by a sense that few things in life are so final as not to be repeated, and that repetition is pretty much of an anticlimax in the swift drama—or comedy— of one's career.

That autumn brought the hour when all was quiet on the Western Front and there fluttered up out of the thinning smoke of Armageddon the dove of peace. A puny, scrawny bird it was, but wonderful—wonderful. And nations, overjoyed, soon began to dance their way to new trouble instead of consistently seeking divine wisdom to deal with the aftermath of the old. Well, hadn't the war-to-end-all-war been fought? Weren't the weary entitled to release from grayness and grimness? Wasn't the globe safe for democracy?

As a matter of fact, the globe was not safe for anything, with the miasma of ruin still in the air, and the human race more nerve-worn than it knew, and the responsibilities of self-government too heavy for many a liberated land. Without having solved all her own problems, America was blandly trusting that peoples everywhere would welcome and adopt her principles in order to solve all theirs. She did not reckon on the passion for security that would possess whole countries and blind them to the better allure of freedom by which, with the conditions duly met, the truer security could have been achieved; nor did she appear seriously aware that in the crater of catastrophe the dragon's teeth of "isms" had been deeply sown. And so she refused to see that the war-to-end-all-war had possibly resulted in a peace-to-end-all-peace.

My first real suspicion that the new era was no better than the old, and perhaps worse, came when I was walking along North Capitol Street in Washington one afternoon. A big scowling fellow halted me. "You in that backside-to collar," he gruffed, "your racket's up. The Church—bah. It's a business! *Big* business." And thinking of the allowance of fifty dollars per year, less than fourteen cents a day, that St. Joseph's Society was at that time able to grant its ordained men for personal expenses, I had to mutter, "Mister, I have something to tell you. Brace yourself. Business is rotten." And I hastened on, wondering just how far the fungus of hate had spread or was spreading. Strange that war had united us, and that the end of it should divide.

To the strains of the popular songs of the day, whistled, quartetted, chorused on the C.U. campus by secular students, I began my postgraduate studies. We student priests swished the skirts of our cassocks from worldliness; but the pulse of the day

—and night—kept reaching us, and some of the influences too. Surprised to find scholarly Father George Johnson, a "major" in education, absorbed in F. Scott Fitzgerald, I curiously read this new author myself. And young enough, only twenty-six, to be included at least in the outer rim of the youth of the land, I was irked at Fitzgerald's idea of us as a generation grown up to find all gods dead, all wars fought, all faiths shaken. What nonsense! With a world to be rebuilt, and glorious concepts of life and living to be shared abroad and better practiced at home, how could any talented author, even one so immature as Fitzgerald, think of the future as a spent account? The struggle of good against evil, which would remain with mankind to the end, ought to be now at its height. Faith, under trial, should be reaffirmed and confirmed. As for Divinity, was it not by its very nature eternal?

There were first-rate young men in the student body of C.U., any one of whom could have given the lie to new-age tenets; but the graduate student priests were, to me, a regular galaxy. Father Haas, destined to shine in sociology and be sought by congressional brains in the parlous times ahead; Father Hart, pegging away at studies which would eventually establish him as a leader in the American Catholic Philosophical Association; Father Corcoran, bristling with new ideas for the relief of poverty and the administration of charity; Fathers Scully and O'Conner, with episcopal futures written all over their faces; Father Rolbiecki, continentally suave, Americanly vivid; Father Motry, a keen moralist; but, first and foremost, a cleric from Wisconsin. . . .

The first time I saw Fulton Sheen, I thought—and surely he would have smiled if I'd told him so—of the prophet Amos emerging from Tekoa to cry out the day of the Lord. He was walking down the pathway from Caldwell Hall, the late autumn winds riffling the folds of his cape, his chin upflung. "What a figure for a pulpit!" I said to myself. But as soon as we got talking the dramatic impression eased into a very human one, for at close range those keen, penetrating eyes of his were mild, and his physical stature seemed to diminish, though a certain something about him appeared to increase. It was a shiny something, but he wore it as a modest winner wears a medal—pinned under rather than over a lapel.

Since then I have met many other effective personalities and observed that the best have this in common: a freshness of enthusiasm, a tendency to greet each day as a privilege and adventure, an eye for the unusual sheathed in the ordinary, a habit of looking at the familiar, as Chesterton would say, until it becomes strange. And in addition to such quality, Father Sheen markedly had the virtue of reverence, a complete philosophy of life in itself. Was it not Canon Sheehan who identified reverence for God, His temples, His ministers, His service, as religion; reverence for one's fellow man, his rights and person, as justice and charity; reverence for one's self as purity?

But Sheen's reverence had no long face to it. His seriousness kept budding into smiles, and one of those buds was big the day when Father Fenlon, our Sulpician prefect of discipline in Caldwell Hall, read out to us students in the chapel a Latin meditation, the first of what promised to be a series, on the subject of "Priest and Housekeeper." The text prescribed that said housekeeper be at least forty years old, and that if she assumed any authority beyond her station, a stern rebuke be immediately given her. This would have sounded queer enough to us in straight English, since humblest Sisters, some quite young, took care of Caldwell Hall and we were as free as a breeze from domestic problems of any kind, but in Latin it was absurdity clothed with solemnity and therefore the more absurd. Sheen was kneeling beside me, and I saw his shoulders shaking as Father Fenlon read on: "*Si flet, fleat* [If she weeps, let her weep]."

At lunch a few of us discussed the singular inappropriateness of such a book for our particular needs. We became quite serious about it, and to lighten the mood someone told of a pastor who, unable to find a forty-year-old housekeeper, was simply forced to take two twenty-year-olds. But nobody smiled at this, the problem of the book remaining uppermost. None of us cared to risk the possibility of offending Father Fenlon by going to him personally, yet all agreed that something should be done.

The next day, as well as for two weeks thereafter, the book was missing. And Father Fenlon, having searched for it in vain, had to use another, which happily did not have anything to say about housekeepers. But the Saturday noon of the second week, the chapel, exceedingly still save for the low tone of his reading voice, suddenly resounded with a thud. From behind the Eighth Station of the Cross, beneath which he was kneeling, the missing volume had fallen into full view and he'd barely escaped being boxed on the ear by its abrupt descent. The mystery of the guilty party was to remain unsolved, but Father Sheen looked so very, very innocent that I admiringly felt a suspicion.

He was frank about a certain ambition of his to be not only a good but a great preacher. I reminded him that St. John Chrysostom, the greatest ever, sometimes had to speak in half-empty churches—when the circus came to town. He duly laughed at that, and went right on spending a portion of his weekly free time with a voice specialist in Washington. More than once he urged me to come along, and now I wish that I had; less for what good I might have gotten out of the course itself than for a closer association with one so amiable, interested, and interesting. But any zeal of mine for pulpit oratory was rather cooled at the time by my experience at St. Barnabas and by my having lately heard that some gentleman had donated to Cardinal Gibbons a sum of money for the simple but, as he conceived it, sublime purpose of getting the clergy taught to read the Gospel slowly, clearly, and distinctly in churches on Sunday. Father Sheen, however, was for giving his utmost not to the minimum but also to the maximum. And one night at his invitation I went to hear him preach a Holy Hour at St. Patrick's Church in the city. When I arrived, a little late, he was already in the pulpit, and I slipped into a rear pew where I could catch the reaction of the congregation much better than from up front, so as to report it to him later. To his earnest words the men strained forward, and at the beauty of them not a few women audibly sighed, causing me to realize that another Chrysostom, thank God, was really in the making.

Once started, his devotion to the orphans in a certain asylum not far from Caldwell Hall never lagged. He walked to the place each morning to say Mass, practicing his preaching on the way, with nobody to hear. And at evening he would go again, this time to gather the little ones around him and tell them stories. His supply finally ran out, because the tots were insatiable, and this was where I happened to be of some help. I had forgotten hardly any of Aesop's fables or Hans Christian Andersen's fairy tales, dear to my own childhood; so he would often make a request, "Another for tonight, Ed," and listen as eagerly to me as, afterward, he himself would be listened to.

It was a red-letter day for us both when Frank McGlynn, the star of John Drinkwater's *Abraham Lincoln*, whose son Tom was a student at the Dominican college in Brookland, visited Catholic University. We met and talked with him and were invited to attend a performance of the great play. How we admired his artistry and marveled that actors could make fiction seem just like truth, so different from many a preacher who succeeded rather in making truth seem just like fiction! And we longed to see other first-class dramatic offerings, but had to content ourselves mostly with parochial, amateur affairs. At the time, Father Hurney, an acquaintance of ours and an energetic curate at St. Patrick's in Washington, was having a great deal of success with the players' club that he had started; and once he afforded me the special pleasure of hearing a local singer, a buxom young girl with a sweet face and a personality as wholesome as new-mown hay. The songs she sang were simple things which went straight to the heart and gave it an extra beat. I felt that with opportunity she could carve out a fine career for herself, but little surmised just how fine that career was to be.

The faculty at the university were distinguished. Particularly Dr. Shanahan, whose forte was theology but whose general knowledge was so vast that students from every department sat in on his lectures for an exhilarating view of the cosmos; and Dr. Pace, whose mind was a gimlet, and who, selecting a point for himself at the beginning of a lecture, would not have swerved a fraction of an inch from it by the end but would have bored down to a well of significance. Yet much as I admired Dr. Pace's brilliance, I was astonished by what seemed a total eclipse of it one day when, out on the campus, he talked with me about the Negro. A stanch Southerner, he had some ideas which hardly jibed with those of a Josephite. He wanted to see colored people advance indeed, but he stressed their liabilities rather than their assets. When he referred enthusiastically, however, to "an organization doing incalculable good for the cause," I took heart, thinking he was paying a compliment to my own Society of St. Joseph. That is, I thought so until he made himself quite clear. "Those Pullman porters are just about the best-trained and politest servants the public has nowadays," he said. "Why, I knew one called 'George' who——"

High in the esteem of all of us ranked Dr. Kerby. His sociology lectures were not only luminous but also a literary treat, and his examinations consisted of personal chats in which, creating ease with a proffered cigar or cigarette, he found out more about one's scholarship—or lack of it—than any conventional method would have revealed. And Bishop Shahan, the rector, swayed us with a Macaulay-like eloquence, even if his handicap of deafness often resulted in his unconsciously slipping from stentorian to softest tones. (Once on a night when the Paulist choristers from New York sang for us in the university gymnasium, he gave an ardent but pianissimo speech which everyone tried especially hard to hear; but nobody quite got the thread of it until a headline appeared in a Washington paper the following morning: "Bishop Shahan Says Troubled World Needs Ear for Music.") And Dr. Ignatius Smith, my favorite! It was under the guidance of this foremost Dominican that I worked out a thesis on the "Political Theories of St. Thomas Aquinas and

Democracy," which won for me a doctorate and brought my university days to a satisfactory close.

He was amused when I told him what had happened to the two hundred copies of that dissertation which I had proudly sent to Baltimore for the St. Joseph's Seminary library just as soon as they were off the press. They arrived on a blazing hot day, and Ross, our good but unthinking old janitor, shoved them into the closet under a stairway where he kept masses of oil-soaked rags for floor polishing. The place had an uncurtained window through which the sun, outshining my scholastic achievement, poured intensely. The result, that day, was a case of spontaneous combustion in which all the copies were consumed and the seminary itself nearly destroyed. "Most dissertations don't cause even a spark," said Dr. Smith, "but yours seems to have created a holocaust."

While I was a student at the university, Father Pastorelli, my superior, had wisely kept me from being lost in *academica* by sending me up to New England each summer to try to secure vocations for our work, and then down to the missions to render some service for our Fathers and acquire experience. My eyes widened at the conditions I met in the South. The fields of my dreams! There they lay, truly whitening to the harvest; but the boll weevils of sinister circumstance were eating through the crop. I had been told from the start that the laborers were few, but not how very few; and the enemies of their efforts seemed so many. Prejudice, exploitation, peonage, poverty, ignorance, indifference, despair. Not yet having learned the Negro adage, "Countin' the stumps won't clear the land," I asked one of the pastors how he could possibly deal with all this, and smiling a bit, he said, "By thinking beyond it. Here is only the pioneer phase. Come back ten years from now and you'll be agreeably surprised." His shedlike house of worship on stilts in a rice field looked as if it could scarcely last another week, and he was planning a decade ahead!

The whole system seemed wrong to me, young in the priesthood as I still was. Why didn't the Church, so well organized, effect a better distribution of men and means? Why should some portions of the kingdom have everything and others nothing? In wartime, strategy demanded that supplies be rushed to the front: why, in the continual battle for souls, should they be kept so largely to the rear? Had I then known as much as I later learned about Church Extension, the Propagation of the Faith, and the Students' Mission Crusade, I'd have kept silent, but as it was I sat down one night, under a leaky roof in Tennessee, and wrote a jeremiad which appeared in an ecclesiastical magazine a few months after and caused some brow lifting among my fellow priests. "Patience," advised Father Will in a letter of comment. "It takes more than a peeve to make an improvement."

In one of our missions I found our Father Wareing bolstering his shabby little congregation's spirit, and doubtless his own, by preaching at Sunday Mass the worth and dignity of toil. " 'I must work whilst it is day: the night cometh when no man can work,' " he quoted from Holy Scripture; and, from some poem, he added, " 'This is the gospel of labor—ring it, ye bells of the kirk! Heaven is blest with eternal rest, but the blessing of earth is work.' " I was moved by his earnestness, and more than moved, the next morning, by his example, for he put on an old pair of overalls and started painting the outside of his house. Together with a few gaping Negroes, I watched him and soon felt impelled to help, but just then a white woman, in a floppy sun hat tied with blue streamers under her two chins going on three, waddled along and paused to inspect the work. She squinted shrewdly and asked him, "How much would you charge me if I let you do *my* house, sir?" As if slapped in the face, he put down his paint can and brush and entered the rectory; and, following, I saw him slumping in the nearest chair and covering his face with his hands.

When in Norfolk to assist Father Warren, I went on the first colored trolley ride the town ever saw. Much in need, Father had thought up this means of raising some money for his school; and the people, tired of routine socials and entertainments, responded well, as he'd expected, to something different. But he appeared to have misgivings the night we boarded the chartered car with the parish group, and I asked why. "We must pass through the center of the city," he said, "and the whites may not like it." I asked airily, "What can *they* do?" To which he replied, "I'd rather pray than think." At a street corner, as the excursion rolled merrily along, fistfuls of mud and gravel suddenly came sailing in on us, dirtying the bright dresses of the girls, causing the men to curse under their breath, spoiling everything. A whizzing piece of brick barely missed my right temple, and I might have yelled my indignation at the hooligans only that my amazement at their meanness gagged me. "Well, that's over," exhaled Father Warren when we got back to the rectory. "I had to make a start, and there'll be less trouble the next time. People get used to things."

Along the Gulf Coast, I saw enough to indicate that the Negro problem was too deep-rooted, too ramified, ever to be solved. But one night, back in Washington and riding on a street car, I was jockeyed from pessimism quite unexpectedly. The trolley slipped, and the car, filled with white and colored, was flooded with darkness in which every face disappeared. For seconds there was silence. Then a rich old Negro voice could be heard in words as simple, inoffensive, and reassuring as a baby's smile; and a general laugh, almost better than light, sounded from the hearers, for the words were, "Cheer up, everybody, an' praise the Lord. We is all alike—now."

My summer services in the South were too tentative and scattered for any appreciable results, but my search for vocations in New England proved gratifying. Johnnie Geary, who had returned from France as an officer, unlike so many of the burlier Salem boys who'd emerged only as buck privates, helped me by spreading the good word. If he could not be a missionary himself, he said, he could at least try to stimulate others. And John Carroll, too, gave me support. Soon there were, all told, over thirty boys from my home town and vicinity studying at Epiphany College in Baltimore; and my fellow Josephites were beginning to call me "Pied Piper of Hamlin" and "King of the Junior Crusade."

Because my stake in Epiphany was important now, Father Pastorelli appointed me, after my university course, to teach there; and for the same reason Father Timothy Maroney, then rector of Epiphany, assigned me to the classes in which my own particular group were enrolled. So, with all my higher education, I found myself bogged down in elementary Latin and Greek. But I liked those starry-eyed pupils of mine and adapted myself to their needs, gradually forgetting the appeal of Aristotle and Aquinas and relinquishing the idea of following up my doctorate dissertation with study, research, and possibly a book. Here around me was vital material to be molded into apostolic shape; and how much better it would be to express myself this way than in writing! Hence I sought to get close to the youngsters, the better to affect them, by conning scout manuals, organizing baseball and football teams, collecting a little fund for uniforms and equipment through a mothers' club which I had just organized by mail, providing campfires and community "sings," all of which I rather detested. But also I primed myself on the spiritualities, in order that every strand of endeavor might be woven into "the one thing necessary." Oh, I was helping to bring a golden age to little Epiphany, I thought. Optimism seemed so justified. My fellow priest-professors were the best: Father Brunner, a disciplinarian adept at making youth understand, accept, and even approve discipline; Father Maroney, second only to Father Saint-Laurent as a scholar; Father Casserly, just ordained and all aglow; and Father Goudreault, a model of precision and finesse. The student body was bigger than ever before and still increasing; new subjects were added to the curriculum, and all were better taught; and the future looked as full of sprout as spring itself. But then—ah, then a change began to creep in for me.

I scarcely noticed the difference at first, given as I was to a special interest in my New England charges, which seemed necessitated by my responsibility to their parents and by the way they looked to me for advice and direction; and I was unaware that the rest of the community was suspecting the formation of a clique. Mild hints came to me from the Fathers about "favoritism," "overdoing," and "the need of unity," but I was too absorbed to listen.

One evening when some of the Salemites and I were sitting down by the brook at the far end of the grounds, watching the awaking stars and talking about Derby Wharf and the Willows, we failed to hear the bell which sounded the end of recreation and a summons to night study, and I led them back ten minutes late. Father Brunner, standing on the front porch, saw us coming in and shook his head. I paused to explain our mistake to him and, expecting his usual smile of understanding, was disappointed to see a tightening around his mouth.

The next day, Tommy Murther, one of my vocations, got into a fistic argument with a Philadelphian and was backed up by his confrères from Salem. I stepped into the clash, stopped it, and accepted Tommy's assertion that the Philadelphian had started it, for I knew that whatever faults Tommy had, he was honest. But the boy from the City of Brotherly Love, resenting my having taken another's part, brought the matter to higher authority, and at a faculty meeting that night Father Maroney, also a Pennsylvanian, did not hint but frankly declared that a college within a college was not ideal, and that we leaders—his eye on me—must stand together or see the student body fall asunder. My hackles rose at that, and though I said nothing I probably looked plenty.

One of the motions made at the meeting and carried unanimously except for me, was that young Murther be put on a month's trial and if he did not manifest improvement within that period be then expelled. At the end of the month the faculty convened again, and this time it was decided that, though the boy had undeniably improved, he had not improved enough and therefore must go. This I could not accept with grace, but my all-out protest won only a cool stare from the rector, and the following morning I accompanied Murther, my first vocational casualty, to Union Station. He looked at me as he got on the train and said good-by, his whole expression seeming to ask how one who had effectively led him to seek the priesthood should now be so ineffectual as to let him drift away. And feeling as hurt as he, I returned to the college alone.

With this beginning, annoyances increased. Another of my boys soon got into trouble. I caught him smoking a cigarette in violation of a strict rule, and after rebuking him, I took him aside for a talk. "But what can be so wrong, Father, in such a little thing as a cigarette?" he asked. I told him that whatever he could not say no to was bigger than himself, and stressed the fire hazard of tossed matches and butts in a wooden building like ours. He listened docilely, apologized, and made such an earnest promise to abstain that I patted him on the shoulder and gave him a St. Joseph medal as a constant reminder. But one of the other Fathers had seen the smoking and now, passing by as the boy stood in the open doorway of my room, noticed the pat and the medal. He must have felt it his duty to make a report to the rector, because that night another faculty meeting was called. This time the deliberation turned not to fisticuffs but cigarettes. "It is bad enough," said Father Maroney, "that a student should break the rule against smoking, but that one of our own priests should comfort and reward him for it—ahem—seems outrageous."

My Irish was up again, but I kept silent. Perhaps a bit of contempt for human judgment—Voltaire?—was in me. Though speech had not served me well in Tommy Murther's case, a few words here and now might have been just the thing, for the rector was plainly unhappy about the whole matter and might have welcomed any sort of explanation. "But what's the use?" I thought. "We Josephites are so sensitive to the prejudice of white against black, and yet white can be just as prejudiced against white!" It was hard to swallow this, and I had a sleepless night. The next morning I accompanied my second "failure" to the train, and on the way back I stopped in at St. Joseph's Seminary for an understanding with Father Pastorelli, the superior-general.

"The society really wants vocations, doesn't it?" I began.

"Of course," he said. "That is why I sent you to find some for us. God has blessed your search."

"Two of my boys have been expelled!" I paused to let the enormity sink deep. "It's like throwing God's blessing back into His face. They were good boys."

"Our subjects must be better than just 'good,' " he said quietly, easing me to a chair. "The missions are hard and exacting."

"Not nearly so hard and exacting as some who sit in judgment. Father Maroney, the rector, who himself never brought us a vocation——"

He waved his hand silencingly and said, "Father Maroney has many personal cares and worries at present, about which you do not know. Maybe his decision looks severe, but it was the best he could make under the circumstances, and it wasn't his alone. Moreover, you yourself in your zeal have not been without fault. All our students must be treated equally. You've given special attention and consideration to a particular group and to that extent have not been quite just to the others. It appears as if you think that you yourself, rather than Epiphany, must do the molding of the boys you've brought us, and your brother priests are hardly flattered by an attitude that eliminates them. If they appear against you, isn't the reason plain enough?"

I scarcely heard his further remarks, for I was thinking, and my thoughts evoked the memory of a distant vacation in Rhode Island—John Nelson Goucher's quote, "All are architects of fate," to which I had answered at the time, "Unless the Lord build the house, they labour in vain that build it." Hadn't I been wiser in my early days? Had a little God-given success made me proud instead of humble? Asking myself these questions, I left the seminary, and by the time I reached the college my mood was chastened.

That night a frank conversation with Father Maroney, the kind that should have taken place the night previous, restored fraternal relations. And from then on everything went well enough. But the fact that a pair of my young hopefuls were gone beyond recall was still a stab in the chest, and my spirit waned.

To offset the waning I took up my pen again and during the long winter nights worked on a couple of juvenile stories, with a vague purpose of reaching beyond Epiphany toward a wider field where my efforts would be less impeded and more appreciated. My lingering hurt—those boy-scout manuals . . .

By spring I had achieved a heap of manuscript and had interested the O'Donovan Brothers, who ran a stationery and church-goods store in town and were branching out into the field of publication. They accepted the material with all the alacrity of novices and made me very happy. Now, appearing in book form with a brace of stories respectively entitled "Tale of Two Brothers" and "Just Jack," I'd be beautifully affecting young readers in hundreds of places. Like Father Finn, the Jesuit author of juveniles! And my optimism increased until, all of a sudden, it was entirely extinguished by a gust of fear when Jerry O'Donovan, chief executive of the firm, called me up. "I know Henry L. Mencken, the big literary critic of our Baltimore *Sun*," he said, "and I'm going to talk him into reviewing 'Brothers' and 'Jack.' With him behind them, they'll sell like hot cakes." *Mencken*. Had Jerry gone insane? Why, it would be like throwing baby rabbits to a Bengal tiger! Sweating bullets and mixing metaphors, I begged that my tender mental offspring be kept out of the range of this—this mental steam roller, and taking pity on me, Jerry promised. So a possible classic of Menckenana —what a job H.L. could have done on stuff absolutely perfect for his particular type of massacre!—was aborted.

My sisters and a few loyal friends declared that they loved the two stories, but, to my chagrin, the youth of the land seemed quite reserved. Somehow the O'Donovans never did get around to giving me a report on the sales, if any, and my only royalty was a five-pound box of chocolates which they sent me for Christmas and which the boys at Epiphany consumed. And even a letter from Father Finn himself, who had seen and read "Brothers" and "Jack," did not afford me much of an uplift. "They are very good," he wrote. "But, just between us, a word of advice. Next time, eliminate the rhetoric—youth likes its literature plain and straight. And watch your sweetness and light. *I* know."

The students had become so numerous that the college could hardly contain them, and Father Pastorelli, always looking to the future, laid plans for a new Epiphany. This second one would be located not in Maryland but nearer to a larger source of vocational supply. He chose in New York State a site on a hill just beyond the Hudson River town of Newburgh and directly opposite Storm King and Bear Mountain.

But we priests of Epiphany did not respond any too well to a change, much as we knew it was needed. We cherished the cradle of our ministry; and when at last the fresh structure up North was ready to receive us and we had to make ready to move, how we idealized the dear old days and forgot the bad old plumbing! Our final morning in Maryland, as I took a solitary stroll around the grounds, I could see in my mind's eye the boy I had been, curled up with a book in an alcove window, wearing a Blessed De Montford chain that chafed, playing pranks, sighing for things supernal. Was the man much of an improvement on the boy? I doubted it. Quite a degree of merit should have been mine by now, yet what progress had I really made? Perhaps the trouble was, as Father Pastorelli had indicated when I brought him a grievance, too much dependence on self. A large fault for one who had begun the higher course in all humility. I must fully re-submit, I warned myself, to the Supreme Architect, or else, for all the graces of Holy Orders, I'd be no better off than John Nelson Goucher, who ran away from home to build a life according to his own ideas.

There were some drawbacks awaiting us when we got to Newburgh. The tapestry-brick building, constructed along Tudor-Gothic lines and crowned with a gracile turret, was perfect exteriorly, but somewhat less than that inside. Though Father Pastorelli had worked hard to have everything just right for us, postwar labor troubles and shortages had intervened, and certain defects, concealed at first, soon began to show. Hardly were we settled when the insufficiently seasoned wood of a floor or two started to buckle; some doors would not open, while others would not close. One night a section of ceiling fell in the dormitory, as if to impress the boys that even if they now dwelt in a comparative palace they must not forget holy poverty. And worse than temperamental windows and doors and plaster work came the effect of a simple little deed which Mike McCormick, one of the students, committed.

Hoping to catch a squirrel, Mike set a trap on the premises, and that evening the whole house was assailed with as villainous a stench as one could conceive. No squirrel had been caught, but a *skunk*. We gasped for the air we dared not breathe, and might have murdered Mike only that the law of God and man seemed strangely against it. But we did insist that he personally release his awful catch, no matter what the consequences to himself. He complied, and his clothes, reeking with musk, had to be buried and he himself temporarily debarred from the community. Yet, finished with the skunk, we found that the skunk was not finished with us. Like the Devil cast out in the Gospel, the creature must have decided to return with others worse than itself, for a much thicker blanket of odor smothered us the following night, and we felt that the only thing left for us was to wire Father Pastorelli in Baltimore that we were through. But the pungent animals themselves, after getting a close-up of humankind, also seemed disposed to decamp; and this they suddenly, unanimously, and positively did, leaving, along with their trail of vicious essence, a clear insinuation of their opinion that, as roses, we too inspired no sonnets.

Winter blew in fierce that year, and by early December we were snowbound. There was sufficient coal, but because the basement bin had not been made large enough, the bulk of it lay outside the building and under rock-hard layers of ice; and what good was a sufficiency if one could not get at it? When our indoor supply gave out, we had to wear overcoats to chapel, refectory, and classrooms. Water pipes burst, the veins in our bodies felt ready to follow suit, and the ghost of the old Epiphany taunted us with memories of relative heat and coziness down below the Mason-Dixon line. But desperation brought its own solution. Braving the blast and bite on the hill, the doughtiest among us grabbed what axes were available and chopped away at what trees were accessible.

At a late hour one night, to the howling of winds around the hill, Death itself struck at the wing that sheltered our good nuns. No electric bell had as yet been installed between their quarters and ours, and the telephone system in town was deranged by the storm; so when the mother superior knocked on the walls and cried as loudly as her meekness dared in order to arouse us to the fact that Sister Hartia, suddenly stricken ill, needed spiritual and medical care, none of us heard. Thus a saint passed without sedative or sacrament into eternity.

The following morning when the body was laid out in the college chapel we venerated it with our very souls. How small it looked, but how great the love that had dwelt in it! The last time I'd seen Sister Hartia in life she was on her knees, scrubbing away the stains of mud and sleet which the boys had tracked into the main corridor; and surely she was still thinking of us from beyond, for those pale hands, callused by long service and folded on a drained bosom, were proof of an immortal concern.

January was bad—bad. February, no better. But March came mild enough—all praise to St. Patrick!—to let nature do a bit of "wearin' o' the green" in the form of a few nascent buds. And soon after that, spring tiptoed in earnest through the Hudson Valley, touching her wand to pear and apple trees, awakening them to glory. Filled with a feeling that after such a winter we could live through practically anything, our spirits blossomed with the season and we discovered how good the core of trial had been. The months of isolation from the world and our efforts at mutual assistance had brought us closer together than ever before, and never had our morale, even in the best time of the old Epiphany, been so good. Gazing at the rippling, sparkling river by day, or the moon-burnished, star-sown heavens by night, we could ignore the memory of our many sighs for Maryland. This was the place! this the life! Still, the strangeness had not quite worn away. . . .

One evening in May I strolled with a group of students toward the end of our acres, where somber evergreens massed their shades as if to say, "So far shall you go and no farther." Absorbed in my own thoughts, I hardly heard the conversation around me until we paused at the impasse. " 'This is the forest primeval,' " recited a youngster from Boston, " 'the murmuring pines and the hemlocks, bearded with moss, and in garments green, indistinct in the twilight, stand like Druids of eld, with voices sad and prophetic.' " And a boy from Brooklyn cried, "Cut that out, Longfellow! It gives me the willies. Say, isn't something moving in—in there?" He pointed. "Can't be just the breeze. Look. It— it has eyes."

We did sense an indistinguishable something staring. Only a fluttery old owl, I thought; but anything can be other than itself in the dark, and the youngest of the boys edged closer to me. Just then the bell rang and the sound seemed warningly weird. Turning away, we hurried back to the college.

Though I did not know it just then, a highly emotional trend had begun. Or perhaps the beginning went farther back. Most of our students were familiar with Washington Irving's *Legend of Sleepy Hollow*, and certainly we were living not very far from the region of "the headless horseman." Too, a rather morbid feeling had lingered with the boys since the day, a week before, when a whey-faced man, hatless, disheveled, gripping a revolver, appeared on the front steps of the college and squatted there, staring glassily into space until the Newburgh police patrol arrived to arrest him for having shot somebody in a quarrel down the road.

The rule of absolute silence in the dormitory was broken that night by much whispering. Father Schmutz, our new prefect of discipline, recently ordained and wholly devoted to duty, came to my room to share his concern. "The boys are so restless," he said, "and all I can get out of them is that some have 'seen things.'" I smiled and predicted that by morning they'd remember nothing. But the next day the whispering continued and increased, and the "seen things" had congealed into "that thing." Detailed descriptions of "it" circulated. One witness went so far as to attest to a long snipe nose with a hairy wart on the left nostril. Another stoutly held that there was no nose at all but the aspect of a skeleton, except for two great eyes terrible with hell fire. Yet another, possibly having in mind a picture of the revolver clutched by the man who had been taken from our front steps by the law, swore that "it" was armed. By sunset the pitch of excitement was so high that something had to happen. And something did.

Mr. Mark Callahan, one of our younger professors, with a B.A. from Holy Cross and a liking for theatrics from away back, borrowed my long clerical cloak, a thrice-precious gift from my pastor in Salem, and stole off into the eerie shadows of the grove at the rim of the estate. There he secreted himself and waited; and when, after supper, the boys went to see what they could, they were grimly rewarded. From beneath low-sweeping, twisted branches a mantled, muffled figure slowly rose and moaned, "I am Death. Your college is accursed. The head of it is doomed." Then the apparition melted back into the arboreal gloom, still moaning; and the boys, scared stiff, but not too stiff to find their legs, scrabbled back over the campus.

Father Kane, our new rector, mellowed by many years on the missions, laughed heartily when Callahan and I told him all, and pounding his fist into his palm, he declared, "Since it's doomed I am, I'll have to get ready for the end." A Tipperary twinkle lit his eye. "I'm getting old and maybe I do feel like dying— somewhat. Besides, here's an opportunity to find out just what the boys think of me." He sucked his lip. "Tomorrow night, in the pale o' the moon, I'll go with them to meet my fate; and you shall be there, Callahan, to deal it out to me. Get Luke, the janitor, to loan you the gun he uses for shooting hare. But fill it with blank cartridges. This is to be a strictly harmless killing, mind you. On that I insist! And you, Father Murphy, shall be near me when I fall. Don't let me hit the ground hard. I bruise easily."

The next evening after supper he announced to the community, with a very straight face, that having heard about some strange prowler, he intended personally to investigate and that anyone wishing to accompany him would be welcome. "I can't believe there's any danger out there," he said, "but we'll see."

The boys crowded around and begged him not to expose himself but to keep to his room and turn the key tight in the lock. Magnificently he silenced them by asserting, "A Kane never hides or cringes!" And off he and I strode, most of the boys following. The faculty, whom he had secretly put wise, did not come. "Hold up the background," he'd told them.

The moon had not quite unveiled itself, and the campus unrolled a seemingly endless dark gray carpet before us. The rector's pace and ours quickened, and soon we all were standing close to the outpost trees weaving their curtain of black. He put his hand to the side of his mouth and hallooed, eliciting only a lonely echo from space. He hallooed again, shrugging. Then, turning slightly to the jitterers, he said, "You see. There's nobody. All is as silent as the tomb."

At the fatal word "tomb" one of the boys let out a cry, the initial note of a chorus of terror. The lower foliage of the nearest evergreens had begun to tremble. And now, out of the gloom, there came a spit of fire and a loud report. Father Kane reeled, one hand extending, the other planting itself on his chest. I caught him before he could thump the ground, and had difficulty in keeping him and myself from being crushed by the boys. Gasping and groaning in a manner that might have stripped the laurels from an old-time actor's brow, he leaned heavily against me. "Have them lift me with—with care," he begged. "The— pain——"

We bore him back to the college, his body tense, his eyes closed, his hand still on his heart, clutching the wound that wasn't there. In the horror and grief of it all, nobody noticed the absence of blood. Everybody thought he was dying, and became convinced when he maundered, "Father Murphy, tell them that—that——" He strangled, shook, and went as stiff as a marble slab.

When we deposited the corpse on the bed in an upstairs room, a sly wink and kick from it bade me get rid of the funereal crew. And as I thrust them through the doorway I noticed two distinct reactions arising in them. Some made straight for the chapel, piously—and safely—to plead for the soul of the dear departed. Others, able to reason that only a real person could have fired a real shot, dashed back toward the far reaches of the campus to catch, at whatever peril to themselves, the killer. Significantly, the activists, in years to come, would prove to be the better missionaries.

The room having been cleared, the corpse now sat up and spoke to me. "Close the door tight. There. We can be ourselves. Did you ever see anything so touching? They *do* rather like me. They *are* loyal." Then came a sobering. "But this thing has gone far enough. Perhaps too far. May the Lord forgive me for so loving a joke! There's one more gesture though that I can't and maybe shouldn't resist. It will bring this night of nonsense, like spring brought the winter, to a good close. Ring the bell, Father, and gather the lads together at the foot of the stairs. I'll freshen up so as to be ready to step down to them spick and span. They'll rub their eyes and rejoice, and I'll give them a little talk about the wisdom of not believing all they see; or, better still, something on the text, 'Blessed are they that have not seen and have believed.' Oh, I'll turn it all to moral profit. Depend on that."

I did as he said, but somebody else acted on his own. Gene Rebescher, the somebody, was a bright youngster from Buffalo. He did not go to the chapel or the campus. As we should too soon learn, he went directly to the downstairs business office, the door of which was locked, and getting in by climbing through the transom, he grabbed the telephone.

Meanwhile, out on the grounds the searchers caught Callahan sneaking back, and identifying him as the killer because he had a gun on him, they would not listen to his expostulations but delivered a terrific walloping, in the midst of which the bell rang.

When all the students were assembled in the corridor at the foot of the stairs, Father Kane bloomed on their astonished vision and smilingly launched into his little address of reassurance. Just then, however, the rear door of the college burst open and a squad of bluecoats appeared, holding up, like a sack of meal, poor Callahan, whom they had found asprawl on the campus. The chief of police himself was in the lead.

Startled more than anybody else had been that night, Father Kane looked lost and beaten, but pulling himself together, he turned on his Hibernian charm, of which he had a lot, and signaled the invaders to come upstairs. I followed. There in the privacy of his suite he distributed cigars, baring the hoax in brief but from beginning to end, and turning to me for corroboration. He begged the men not to tell the press, lest the college seem ridiculous in the eyes of the town. And they laughed much, promising nothing.

Not until we searched the Newburgh papers the following day and found exactly what had been promised, did we experience any relief. But what an access of it!

"There'll be no more shenanigans around here," declared Father Kane to me briskly and sternly in his office. "I'm really

ashamed of you for not having headed off the whole business!"
But as I asked, "And not of yourself for having headed into it?"
he wiped a sudden grin from his lips with the back of his hand
and said, "Well, everybody got fooled, and nobody was harmed."
Whereupon Callahan opened the door and limped in, threatening
to quit the college and slap a suit on it.

Only by granting a raise in salary could Kane calm the man
and make him see the light. Then *I*, knowing Kane's Scottish
thrift as well as his Hibernian charm, wiped a grin from my own
lips; and I certainly did not put it on again when Callahan, turning to me, announced, "Sorry I can't restore your cloak, Father.
The boys tore it to shreds when they got me down."

V

BECAUSE our new college involved much expense, it was not enough for us priests to teach. Every penny counted. We were sent out on week ends by the rector to various churches for the purpose of rendering supplementary service and earning stipends.

To me fell the duty of going down each Saturday noon to St. Malachy's, celebrated as the Catholic Actors' Chapel, on West Forty-ninth Street in New York City. And there the touch of the theater that my boyhood had known became a real contact. The only performer who had ever spoken to me before was the little Louise of *The Two Orphans*, who from a backstage window of the Mechanic Hall in Salem had startled my boyhood with a suggestive remark. And here I now stood, set by circumstances in the very center of theaterdom, meeting hundreds of the talented people—not nearly so grand as when behind footlights, but even more attractive in the roles of ordinary churchgoers. It was at this time that I happened to read in a religious magazine about Eve Lavallière, a Parisian star, as brilliant in comedy as Sarah Bernhardt in tragedy, leaving the orbit of fame to seek spiritual betterment in obscurity; and here at St. Malachy's I could see the elements of her story repetitively at work—the divine leaven in lives, the groping through tinsel to truth, a homesickness for heaven. So it seemed to me that there were many Lavallières in show business, and that Broadway had its own peculiar link with Bethlehem.

Father Leonard, the pastor of St. Malachy's, was an ideal shepherd for his highly specialized flock, knowing their every throb, temptation, and trial, and having a place in his heart for the failures as well as the successful. I believe he loved the least the most, but he was equally kind to all. He never preached formally but always naturally. "Elocution is out," he warned me in one of our very first chats. "Actors admire acting on the stage but not off it, and if a preacher should try to impress them with himself rather than the Gospel, he might just as well spare himself the effort, no matter how eloquent his sermons or perfect his tones and gestures. The theater is their living, not their life."

My esteem for him increased as I saw more of his methods. His white head shining in the sun, he would meet and greet the brethren at the church door, tipping the candle flame of his personality to the wicks of theirs, causing countenances to light up. He had sympathy and suggestions for those who did not know whence their next engagements were coming, counsel for such as were treading the dizzy heights, enthusiasm for everybody. And he spoke their language. "One doesn't address French people in German or Germans in French," he said to me with a smile, "and Broadway has a medium of its own." Casually he mentioned things which brought a strange realm into sharper focus; that Earl Carroll, much in the limelight because of a Prohibition-defying party of his during which a pretty chorus girl regaled the guests by bathing in a tub of champagne, tried to make St. Malachy's a liberal donation; that Texas Guinan, current queen of nightclubs, never missed Sunday Mass; that there was a patron saint, named Genesius, for actors; that schedules of church services were regularly posted backstage; that show people, with their readiness to appear in benefits for charitable causes, were the only ones who gave away the sole thing they had to sell.

Over coffee in the rectory one Saturday night, he was talking about the importance of George M. Cohan to the profession; and when, in his whimsical way, he remarked, "George the Great comes from Rhode Island, by act of Providence," I mentioned that John Nelson Goucher, a boyhood friend of mine who depended less on Providence than on himself, used to live in Lime Rock, Rhode Island. He blinked reflectively and murmured, "Goucher—John Nelson. I know an actor by that name. From

Lime Rock too. He now calls himself Dowling. Eddie Dowling. His mother's maiden name was Dowling and the Eddie could have come from anywhere."

Excited, I burst into questions, for it seemed to me at the moment that more than anything else in the world I wanted an up-to-the-minute report on the young would-be "architect of fate" with whom I long ago swam and ate huckleberries. But Father Leonard, rising, said that we'd have to slip over to the chapel for confessions. "There'll be many," he added, "because tomorrow the Holy Name men go to Communion." He paused. "Dowling often comes around, even if he does prefer St. Patrick's, the rascal! Maybe he'll be along tonight. If I see him, I'll tell him you're here."

Three hours later, when the last penitent had been heard and the janitor was making ready to close the church, I went from the confessional box to the Blessed Mother's altar for a goodnight prayer and noticed a man kneeling there. He returned my look and, in the ruddy glow of the votive lights burning before the shrine, smiled as only John Nelson Goucher himself could smile. It was a sunburst of a smile, and over a span of fifteen years our hands clasped.

In the reception room of the rectory we sat till midnight, rolling back time. He made me tell about myself first, but I got through quickly and settled back to hear his own story, insisting on detail. When I'd last seen him, his face had only the soft blankness of pre-teen age tinged with the pink of ambition, but now the imprint of life and living was on it, and even without a single word from him I'd have read much.

He disclosed that his wanderings had begun on the rear end of a Mack truck bound for Boston, and with a vague intention of getting to Salem where he could perhaps persuade me to join his gypsying. But in the Hub he felt like a fly in a jug of molasses and could not get any farther for a while. Moving along Washington Street, he saw and approached an exceptionally pleasant-faced man standing in the doorway of a music store, and put on a pathetic act for him. Sucking in his cheeks to make himself look half starved, he moaned, "Mister, I ain't had anything to eat for a year—least that's how I feel"; and the man quizzed him, readily finding out about the family of seventeen that it was so hard to feed, and the perfect mother who loved to "laff," and a boy's dream of building for her a good house with plenty of windows, and the parish show in which a certain song, "Lac St. Pierre," had won a prize. In this way the young fellow talked himself into a job of rendering ballads for the customers in the music shop, sweeping the floor, and running errands. His singing satisfied, but in other respects he did not do so well, because of a persistent tendency to brush dust into convenient corners and loiter agape at city scenes when he was sent anywhere.

Soon he was discharged, but knowing his way around by now, he stepped right into work as a cabin boy on the Fall River line and increased his small salary by blending his soprano with the moonlight for romantic couples on deck. One night the boat ran into a storm off Point Judith and he was almost tossed into the sea. Instead of extinguishing his spirit, the adventure only whetted it, and he then went in for working his way back and forth between continents, on the *Mauretania* and the *Lusitania*. During one of the voyages he sang at a concert, and Sir Harry Lauder's manager, hearing him, declared that he ought to go on the stage. But while shore-leaving in London he joined the boys' choir of St. Paul's Cathedral and gave forth so appealingly that he became a soloist; and before long he embarked with the organization on a world tour in which he met such celebrities as Joseph Conrad and Jack London and fell under their spell. All went well for him till his voice changed and the St. Paul Choir decided that he was through. Then, back in the U.S.A., with memories galore but without a cent, he felt lucky to find a berth on a fishing schooner off Gloucester. Now the desire for the stage, which Sir Harry Lauder's manager had engendered in him, started to assert itself, and after accumulating a few dollars he left the schooner for a tryout in a stock company in Haverhill,

Massachusetts; but a little later, in my home town of Salem, he really got going, for there and then he acted a variety of roles and even experimented with a vaudeville sketch of his own.

At this point in the narrative I asked why he hadn't looked up my family in Salem, and he answered, "It would have made me too lonesome for my own family in Lime Rock. I was a pretty homesick kid by then, but I hated like the deuce to bother anybody. Besides, I sort of lost interest when I heard from one of the priests at St. Mary's that you'd gone South to study."

From Salem, he drifted down to Brooklyn, by-passing Rhode Island because not yet, after all his wanderings and beginnings, was he able to build for his mother that many-windowed house which still seemed to be his objective. There in Brooklyn he was lucky enough to be engaged for the opening program of Marcus Loew's first theater; and Abe Erlanger, talent-scouting, caught, liked, and recommended the little act to Flo Ziegfeld, sultan of musicals. This led to Broadway and appearance in such productions as *The Follies* and *The Girl in the Spotlight*. Next, after a series of tours over the country, came *The Velvet Lady*, which brought him into association and even collaboration with the great Victor Herbert and made it look for a while as if he was really heading for the top. But now——

"I'm in a show that's going to fold next Saturday night," he said, "and just at a time when I need success the most! I've met the best little girl in the world—Ray Dooley, and something tells me she'd say yes if I'd ask her. But I can't—not as a failure. Wish I were in a business where a guy gets to eat more regularly. Been hungry from here to New Orleans and back. Time is starting to feel and I've nothing to show. It's been like—well, like writing on water."

"Why don't you write on paper?" I suggested. "It seems more sensible."

"Write what?"

"A play. You've already done a vaudeville sketch."

"It wasn't too good. No schooling."

At that I became very wise, echoing something I'd read. "Schools can teach one to speak but not what to say. Only life does that. You've been living a story since you ran away from home. You've just told it to me. Why not tell it to the public? Dramatize it."

"Say——"

I did not see him again until three weeks later. I had pictured him all alone in a third-rate boardinghouse room in the throes of composition, spattered with ink and tearing out his hair. But when he next appeared in St. Malachy's rectory he was dressed in a natty new suit and looked as fresh as a boutonniere right out of a good florist's window. "How about the play?" I promptly asked. "The Shuberts gave me an advance," he announced brightly. "So I proposed to Ray Dooley and she's accepted me. I've told her all about you and she's keen to have you tie the knot."

His breeziness swept me off my feet, but I got back to the play. "How hard you must have worked on the script, and how fast!"

"Oh, there's no script yet. Only an idea."

"Then what in heaven's name did you sell?"

He dumped a cigarette from a pack and grinned. "The *idea*."

All arrangements were made for the marriage, and one morning Eddie Dowling—it had taken me some time to get used to calling him that—drove up to Newburgh with Ray Dooley and two friends in a borrowed car. A little girl with a treasure of quiet character, Ray seemed as remote from the footlights that day as a violet from a jewel case; and as she knelt with Eddie in the sanctuary of our little hilltop chapel, her earnestness and sincerity increased his, and their faces shone. Here, I knew, was a union that would last.

After the ceremony they had me come along to Storm King Inn for a wedding feast, and over the flow of time I can still see them just the way they looked that crystal-clear noontide, standing hand in hand at the door of the castle-like retreat, gazing down on the Hudson. Too, I can still hear Eddie murmuring, "Anything's possible now." And I believed him, feeling that, through Ray, the Supreme Architect was at last really taking over.

In many ways Broadway had grown postwar brazen. Nudeness and lewdness were keynotes of several shows; but when Dowling's offering opened at the Casino, it proved to be as clean as Lime Rock and as stimulating as a plunge into that pool where he and I first met. Basically it represented his struggle with poverty and his search for success, but aglow with his love for Ray, he had filled it with wholesomely pretty girls, sprinkled it with songs, and named it *Sally, Irene, and Mary*. And what a hit! It ran through the season, making him a star and bringing the patronage of politicoes, Wall-Streeters, and the public. Best of all, it enabled him to build for his mother the house of his boyhood's dream, one as white as the dream itself, and with green blinds and lots—lots—of windows. And as Sister Marie Concilio in Salem had said to me when I won a scholarship years before, I now said to him, "You didn't do it, but God." His eye glinted impishly at that, in indication of some bright earthy retort coming, but his expression immediately sobered and he admitted, "You're right."

Sally, Irene, and Mary pleased the road as much as Broadway, and Dowling's next splurge was already being planned. He did not have to seek the Shuberts; this time Erlanger, the producer, sought him. "He'll loosen the purse strings for the best talent in town," Eddie told me, "but—want to know something? I'd like to give newcomers a chance. Keep thinking how much a good break meant to me and what it would mean to others who've been eating out their hearts, waiting."

As he said this to me in St. Malachy's rectory, Father Fulton Sheen came to mind. I had received a letter from him just that day, bringing me up to date on his career. From Catholic

University he had gone to Louvain in Belgium on a shoestring and had finished his postgraduate work under Cardinal Mercier, whose fame and scholarship were attracting students from all lands. The United States was helping to restore the library there, damaged by German shells, and Americans were as welcome as sons of a great benefactor should be. So in ideal circumstances Sheen had completed a dissertation on *"God and Intelligence,"* for which no less a luminary than Gilbert K. Chesterton himself gladly wrote an introduction. Now, heavy with such honors as a Ph.D. from Louvain, a D.D. from Rome, and the coveted Mercier Award, he was back in the United States to teach at C.U.; but still with a predilection for preaching, he was seeking pulpits, and in his letter had asked me about New York, no doubt feeling that by now I must have become well acquainted with pastors and churches. Hence, Eddie's reference to talent, causing me to think of Sheen's, made me remember also a certain person I had heard sing when Sheen and I were classmates.

"There's a girl in Washington," I told Eddie, "with a voice like a choir of birds, and personality plus. Father Hurney at St. Patrick's down there knows her."

"I know Father Hurney," he replied. "Met him once or twice. Come to think of it, he did mention a girl with a great voice. Must be the same one. I'm playing D.C. next week, and I'll make it a point to see him and hear this 'choir of birds.' "

When rehearsals for *Honeymoon Lane*, the new show, were well under way, he phoned Epiphany to urge me to attend one or two. "You direct entertainments for the boys up there," he said, "and it would be right in your line to see how professionals operate. You may even be able to do some of your missionary work in my company, because I'm having a trio of Negro dancers—floor burners!—that I found in Harlem. Besides, I have a surprise for you."

The rector granted me permission, and when the next weekly holiday rolled around, there I was, sitting in the back row of the

Knickerbocker Theatre. Dowling and Erlanger were standing in the middle aisle and I could hear them chaffering about technicalities. I had not yet been told the "surprise," but I could wait, since it seemed novelty enough just to be here viewing a production before Broadway itself should have the privilege. Al Sexton, one of the actors, was keeping me company until he'd be needed.

The stage setting was a country railroad station in an orange sunset, with a prop train just about ready to pull out; and a stoop-shouldered old man was most earnestly going through the business of a last-minute examination of the wheels of this Honeymoon Express. "That has-been used to be considerable shakes in the sticks," whispered Sexton to me, pointing. "He's made Broadway at last, thanks to Eddie. His part would fit into an eye dropper, but *is* he grateful!" There seemed to be something vaguely familiar about the "has-been" and I asked the name. Sexton's answer shocked me by revealing how little and illusory the pot of gold at the end of the theatrical rainbow could be. Here was Jere McAuliffe, one of the handsome upstanding matinee idols whom, as a boy, I had watched atingle from my ten-cent gallery perch in the Mechanic Hall in Salem! And now I was beholding him as hardly more than a "super," still giving his all to what had turned out to be practically nothing.

Then onto the stage traipsed a score of girls, all so lovely that it would have been difficult to pick the best. "Why, they're fresh from the hand of God," I said to Sexton. He gave me a sidewise, rather comical look. "Fresh is right, Father," he said, "but their beauty comes as much from the nearest drugstore as anywhere else." He laughed quietly, then pointed again. "*There's* someone, though, who's what I'd call really fresh and—refreshing."

A plump female, with a step so light that she seemed not to be walking but wafting, had joined the bevy. Contrast with the slenderness of the others made her look even bigger than she was; and the aliveness of her, like a risen breeze, almost blew away the varieties of charm all around. I gasped delightedly as recognition dawned. This was Eddie's "surprise." The girl from Washington!

Mr. Erlanger's voice impinged on my ear, for he was asking sharply, "Who's that?"

"A discovery," I heard Eddie reply. "She sings—*dances*——"

"Like the frisking of an elephant, I bet. Sings, eh? How distinctive! Warblers come a plugged nickel a gross."

"This is one in a million."

"Looks to me like a million in one," said Erlanger. "Good advertisement for a restaurant but not a theater."

"Listen, please. She has hardly more to do than a walk-on in Act I——"

"Make it a walk-out."

"—but I'm giving her a real spot in Act II where the show sags. She'll build it right up."

Erlanger cleared his throat and clicked his teeth. "We don't need her. She'd sag it worse. She'll have to go."

This conversation, reminding me of my own early experience of being driven from the Mechanic Hall in Salem and the possibility of a stage appearance, made me squirm. I knew just how the girl would feel.

The rehearsal continued. And when I got Dowling to myself for a second, I murmured what a shame it was that he—the author, star, and director of the show—could not have his own way. His jaw set and his eyes snapped. "I'm having it!" he said.

The Broadway première of *Honeymoon Lane* occurred some weeks later, and Eddie phoned to me in Newburgh. "George M. Cohan and Al Smith came backstage to congratulate us," he declared, all enthusiasm. "Jimmy Walker made a speech from one of the boxes—told the audience that he'd been elected mayor of New York because he looked like Dowling. Think of that! Flo Ziegfeld and George Jean Nathan stayed right through. All gorgeous reviews this morning!—and those critics can be murder when they're in the mood. Man, what I've escaped! And say, guess who was the hit of the show." He waited, whetting my curiosity. "The big little girl from Washington! *Kate Smith.*"

Shortly after, my joy at Eddie's second success was heightened by a letter from Marguerite Zender, the titian-haired beauty who had been his second leading lady in *Sally, Irene, and Mary*. Somehow she regarded me as a dispenser of wedded bliss and wanted me to perform the ceremony for her and a certain wealthy Emmanuel Margolies. So, securing papers and authorization, I went ahead.

Never was there a fairer bride, I'm sure, than Marguerite; never a more devoted bridegroom than "Manny." But while the candle glow from the altar added luster to her clear big eyes during the ceremony, his—not big or clear, and a trifle shifty—seemed to me to be in shade, and I began to wonder whether he was really worthy of her.

Several months passed. The couple toured Europe, and Marguerite sent me pictures of churches and shrines, but "Manny's" postcards were scenes of Parisian and Lido gaiety. "He's too worldly," I thought. However, I chided myself for uncharitableness, hoped for the best, and mailed him a St. Joseph's medal. Then one night in midwinter I received a phone call at the college from Marguerite in Newark, and the sweet voice that had set audiences humming "Time Will Tell," the hit tune of *Sally, Irene, and Mary*, was now almost inarticulate. "Manny" had crashed to his death in his private airplane near Miami.

The next day the rector gave me leave to pay Marguerite a visit of sympathy. In Grand Central Station I bought a newspaper to read on the way to Newark, but one of the front-page headlines caught my eye and riveted my interest. The write-up revealed the life that Margolies was now being said to have covertly lived, an amazing series of mulctings and frauds. If all this was true, what chance, with an ending so sudden and unblessed, could there possibly have been for his soul? Had I said my Mass for him that morning in vain? Sick at heart for having had any part in uniting so good a girl as Marguerite to so dubious a character, I lost not a moment's time in getting to her.

The body of the deceased had been flown up from Florida, and there in Newark, at a specified funeral parlor, I found the young widow. Pale and tense, but dignified in her bereavement, she thanked me for coming and led me toward the casket. Halfway there, she paused. "I mustn't look, Father," she said. "I want to remember him living. And I do believe he is now more alive—spiritually alive—than ever before. The medal you sent him—remember? He always wore it. They found it when he was being removed from the wreck, and they brought him to a Catholic hospital. Under stimulants, he revived just long enough to make his peace with God and receive the last sacraments. I'd not known of any shadiness in his past. He never told me. But my mind was not always at ease, and I prayed and prayed for him."

I went to the coffin, which the mortician now opened for me, and gazed on the pitiful features over which he must have worked for hours to achieve a faint degree of naturalness; and I was moved by the fact that some lives are safe only in death, as well as by the faith enabling a lonely young wife to accept such a fact with meekness.

It was my intention to linger for the funeral, but as the hour drew near and mourners were assembling, an attendant tapped me on the shoulder and whispered, "Newburgh, New York, is calling you, Father." At the phone in an anteroom I was informed by the rector of Epiphany that a telegram from Salem had just come for me. "Perhaps it's important," he said, "and if you wish, I'll open and read it to you." It was very important. *Mom sinking fast. Come at once. Annie.*

I explained the situation to Marguerite, and she merged her own grief in mine. Then I left the mortuary, but the process of getting beyond it was not easy. Outside, victims of the dead man's alleged schemes had gathered and were closing in; and several reporters surrounded me, popping questions. "Your name and station, Reverend?" "A friend of Margolies?" "How long have you known him?" "Did you recognize the body?" "What assets has he left?" "Any chance of the losers being compensated?" My brain whirled. I told the men that I had never been aware of any shady activity on the part of the deceased, and requested that they keep my name out of any of their accounts of the funeral.

There wasn't nearly enough money in my pocket for a train ticket to Boston, but a phone call to Father Leonard from the Newark station attended to that. He met me at the information booth in Grand Central Station and supplied my need.

When I arrived in Salem late that night, I found Agnes, Annie and her husband, and all my brothers except Father Will, standing around Mom's bed. But Mom was not dying. On the contrary, she was sitting up and dominating the scene, having earlier received Extreme Unction, the sacrament that not only prepares one for the end but sometimes restores enough health for a rebeginning. And I thought of Mamie Blake—a colored woman in Baltimore whom I'd anointed on no less than four occasions when her doctor solemnly assured me that she was "nearly gone," and who had bounced back each time like a rubber ball from a wall. Indeed, the recurrent convalescences of Mamie, victim of an acute kidney ailment, had won for me, my first year in the priesthood, a smack of reputation as a wonder-worker, which must have extended, however incredibly, as far as Chicago, for a scribbled message reached me from someone up there, "I hear you cure kidneys. Enclose fine twenty-five cents, which is all I can afford at presence to cure mine." And the memory of that absurdity now danced like a sunbeam in my relieved mind as I saw what an anointing had done for Mom.

"Sure, it's grand to have you, Father Ed," she said, extending her thin arms, "but you shouldn'ta come just for me. And Annie —that one!—would've sent for Father Will too if I didn't stop her. Why can't we be leavin' everything to the Lord? I'll go when my time's up, and not a whit sooner or later." But I could see her gaze turning wistfully to Jim, Tom, and Joe, the weak ones who needed her even more than when they were children; and I knew that, though counseling absolute submission to Providence, she had sought to be spared for their sake.

We were happy to be together that night in our own little circle. The world was asleep. But as soon as I lay my head gratefully on a pillow, the telephone rang. It was a long-distance call for me from some enterprising reporter, doubtless one of those with whom I'd talked that day. Late hours meant nothing in his profession. He had gotten in touch with Epiphany College and been referred here. His purpose was to follow up a hunch that the body buried in Newark was a decoy and that Margolies himself had absconded to South America or Canada to enjoy his gains beyond the grip of the law; and it appeared to him that I, as a clergyman and the only person who, except the undertaker, had had a good look at the corpse, could give very credible testimony if I would. "How about it, Rev.?" he urged. Exasperated at the plea and worn out with the worry the day had brought, I had to bite my tongue.

I remained awake until dawn, thinking the old thought that had haunted my boyhood: the nearness of death to life. And I mulled over Shakespeare's concept of existence as a stage, speculating whether, in the long run, there were more tragedies than comedies, or more comedies than tragedies, acted out on it. Why had the Lord allowed the repertoire of sadness and silliness, uplift and down-beat, dignity and indignity, to continue for ages? At best, the performances of most of us were so bad, and the appearances of all so brief! But on and on went the show, each part of it dovetailing into others. If it hadn't been for *Sally, Irene and Mary*, I'd never have met Marguerite; and if it hadn't been for her, I'd not have given Margolies that medal which brought him the last sacraments.

It was good that I had gotten home, for I was needed. The problems of my brothers were coming to a head. I had confidence that our youngest would be all right, because having returned in fine fettle from the war, he had met a sensible girl and was planning to settle down. But Joe, who had been in a number of major battles and drifted back to his former habits, looked spent; and Tom, through personal neglect, had contracted a chronic cold which our family doctor was now pronouncing tubercular; and Jim, still donating his singing and piano playing to any and every cause, and plied with stimulants by the grateful but thoughtless, seemed far from well. So I laid down the law to Joe, feeling like a cad for talking that way to a veteran who had served his country nobly. Tom I got into a hospital for treatment. As for Jim, it occurred to me that, with his talent and kindliness, he could fill the role of a lay assistant in the missions; and communicating with Father Will by long-distance, I found him most receptive to the idea. He promptly scraped together some money—how, a mystery—and sent for him.

Jim went down to St. Anthony's Church in Memphis, where Will was pastoring; and he took to the new life like a tired wanderer to cool calm waters. Away from old associations, his native goodness at last throve unimpeded. He found good Dixie friends to help him. Colored children flocked around, and he big-brothered them beautifully. Re-studying and teaching the catechism, cherishing the sanctuary that he was now privileged to live so near, singing his songs into the hearts of old folks, retrieving every mistake, he was proving—wrote Father Will—that if he had received the call in early life, he might have made a perfect priest.

Tom's opportunity for spiritual rehabilitation was different. It had to be through gloom and pain, for his long months in the hospital brought no physical improvement. Agnes, always the angel, gave him every minute she could spare from her daily work and certainly helped to prolong the little life that was left. But one night when rain was pattering the windows of the hospital, just as at the time Dad died, the end came. It was a quiet passing, and the touch of peace on Tom's face smoothed away all the marks of the wasted years. And Mom said brokenly but thankfully, "He's young again."

Joe took the loss hard, because he and Tom had been very close. "I've got to get out of town," he told me on the day of the funeral. "I'd only be causing more worry for Mom here. But I don't know just where to turn." My suggestion was that he take a trip to Memphis to visit Jim and Father Will, who had not been able to come on because of the expense, and that he let me provide the fare by borrowing from Charlie Murphy, a cousin of ours. He feared that he was not fit for such a journey, but when I mentioned that the Travelers Aid would make everything easy for him, he took courage, and next day he bade the family good-by. I accompanied him to Boston, and should have gone as far as New York only that there still were matters to be settled at home. Too well I recall the uneasiness that kept me awake that night, the self-questioning, the foreboding. Toward morning, the telephone, jangling, woke me from a doze and brought word from the Travelers Aid in Manhattan that veteran Murphy, having taken sick on the train, was being given medical attention.

I found him that evening in a hospital on Kingsbridge Road in the Bronx. "Exhausted from shell shock" was the diagnosis, and the doctors would not approve his removal. Childlike in his helplessness, he fixed his dark eyes on me and mumbled so faintly that, bending, I had to hold my ear to his lips to hear. "It's no use," he said. "I'll never get to Memphis or see Salem again. But I think there's a little compensation due me for—for being a soldier. Spend it all on Mom and try to make her happy again, like I never did." He could say no more.

For months he lingered, mostly in a semicomatose state. It was on the eve of St. Joseph's feast day that he passed away, and the following morning when I sang his requiem Mass in New York, I was comforted to find that, over the altar, a niched statue of the patron of happy deaths was shedding a smile of seeming assurance that one more soul was saved. There were other signs too, things that have ever since puzzled and consoled me. I knew that Mom had been praying to St. Teresa, the Little Flower, for Joe; and as the boxed casket, draped with the American flag, was being borne onto the train in Grand Central Station a scent of roses was wafted through the air, though I looked in all directions and could not see the source. And just before sunset that evening, when the casket arrived in St. Mary's Cemetery in Salem and was being briefly opened for Mom's last look at her son, I noticed a rose lying fresh and dewy near his cheek, apparently placed by no mortal hand, since I myself had been the last to view the remains at the start of the long journey home and could testify that it had not been there then. Mom's fingers trembled toward that flower to take and treasure it, but her impulse changed and she left it untouched. The memory of it, ameliorating her loss, would remain unwithered. And my thoughts on leaving the new grave beside Tom's were of Father Will, far South with Jim but present in spirit, who the morning of his first Mass years ago so simply expressed to me his trust that, because he and I had been called to farther fields, the Lord himself would take our brothers in hand.

Eddie Dowling's warmhearted mother now began to mean much to the remnant of my family. She had not only her many-windowed house but also a big automobile. She frequently rode up to Salem from Lime Rock, with one of her several grandchildren chauffeuring, and always the back of the car was filled with fruit and vegetables, for living and giving were the same thing to her. She and Mom became fast friends, and the relation greatly helped Mom, for such a woman as Bridget Dowling Goucher, who had brought so many children into the world, was a veritable transfusion of life. In their exchange of recollections the two relived the past, with the light of an unfading future already upon them.

Anxious to do for Mom what Eddie had done for his mother, I was pleased to find myself at least partly able. Joe's compensation had to be spent according to his last wishes; and would he not have wanted Mom, who had always had so little, to be given a good home? There was a house on Loring Avenue in Salem that had long attracted me with its quaint and distinctive charm; and I now learned from Charlie Murphy's wife Mary that Mr. John Deery, the owner, intended to meet the needs of his growing family by moving to larger quarters and that therefore this little dream place would soon be up for sale. But Joe's "estate," of which I had been appointed administrator, was very small, and I had to surrender the extravagant notion of a purchase. When somebody told me, though, that the original owner of this property had belonged to the stiff old Yankee school, and that during his tenure sons or daughters of Erin had been permitted to enter only by the back door and as menials, I wished my wish all over again. It became almost an obsession during my visits to Salem, and I'd go out of the way to stroll Loring Avenue and feast my eyes.

One day as I was passing my magnet, Mr. Deery came out. He tipped his hat to me, and there and then we became acquainted. His cordiality invited confidence, and before I knew it, I'd told him my reason for being in the neighborhood. "If a cat can look at a king, why not a Murphy at a mansion?" I said, shrugging. "It's not a mansion but it could be more than a look," he returned with a smile. "I know of your mother, and I'd like to have her living in this home that's meant so much happiness to me and mine. We'd be leaving it in the best of hands. Wish I could sign it over outright, but I'm not that wealthy yet. What down payment do you think you could make?" I mentioned the modest sum of Joe's allotment. "That would be just about enough to buy one of the two bathrooms, exclusive of fixtures," he said. "But" —he stroked his chin—"mortgages could be arranged, and if your mother wouldn't mind taking in a few roomers from the normal school right near, there'd be an income for interest and upkeep."

And, soon after, we Murphys came to occupy the house, one of the most comfortable and attractive in Salem, the kind that both hugs the landscape and seems to grow up out of it, rambling like a vine. It had a sun parlor, fireplaces, french doors, nooks, an oriel window in front, and a red-tiled patio leading in the rear to a terraced garden. The Deerys generously left us some of their furniture, and Annie and Agnes made our old things into new with varnish, enamel, energy, and a touch of unsuspected genius. It was easy to rent out three of the rooms to teachers, who gave no trouble at all and paid well, and the fact that we owned hardly more than one of the bathrooms (exclusive of fixtures) did not bother us in the least.

That was the summer Eddie Dowling and Ray, after a strenuous theatrical season, took a much-needed vacation in Europe. They returned in the fall, full of vigor and reminiscences. I particularly recall Eddie's account of one incident.

When he and Murray Hulburt, acting mayor of New York, were strolling a Paris street one evening, *sans* their wives, who preferred to relax at the Ritz-Carlton, a mam'selle slithered over to them out of blue shadows. "*Avez-vous une cigarette, messieurs?*" she wheedled, hand on hip. They saw in the light of a street lamp that she was young, frail, and heavily rouged. With what little French they could command, they gave her some advice against the life she was living. More, they slipped money into her palm. She inhaled deeply as her fingers curled over the francs—the saving difference between virtue and vice for a night, they thought; and with the misty glow of a couple of boy scouts who had just done their good deed for the day, they watched her depart. She did not go far, only across the sidewalk and into her house. While they stood under the lamp discussing her, a slight noise of shutters opening overhead caused them to raise their eyes. Framed in a second-story window, she was again visible. Catching their gaze, she spat at them and flung down the francs. In astonishment, they went their way.

When Eddie told me this, he added, "I'm still puzzled that after Hulburt and I treated her so well she turned so bitter and contemptuous." But it did not seem puzzling to me. Though I

knew nothing about the twists and turns of French psychology,
I could at least infer how a streetwalker must have felt when a
pair of well-heeled *Américains* seemingly insulted her. Had they
given her no money at all but simply the word that their wives
were waiting for them, she most probably would not have been
made to feel repulsive. Well I realized, from the first year of my
priesthood spent largely in the slums of Baltimore, that even the
lowliest want to be wanted. And during my few summer visits to
the Deep South I had heard some good people say, in effect, "But
we treat our colored well. We give them schools, direction, opportunities, and ask only that they keep in their place. Queer
that there's a growing spirit of thanklessness and resentment
among them." Queer?

With two big successes to his credit, Eddie now reached out
for a third. This time he conceived a show to promote the coming presidential candidacy of his friend Al Smith, and to star
Ray. He called it *Sidewalks of New York*. It opened with éclat
at the Knickerbocker, and Ray covered herself with glory. That
season was the biggest yet for the Dowlings, with Eddie touring
prosperously in *Honeymoon Lane,* and *Sidewalks* attracting a
steady stream of customers on Broadway, and a New York daily
revealing by a poll of its readers that Eddie and Ray were cur-
rently the most popular of players.

They put some of their savings into an estate in Bayside, Long
Island; and occasionally, when my weekly stint at St. Malachy's
was over, I'd spend a Sunday afternoon there. It was always not
only a rest but an experience. W. C. Fields, who had rented
Norma Talmadge's nearby bungalow, was quite apt to show up,
hamburger nose, beer-barrel torso, humor and all; and the public,
I wager, never saw him more Dickensian than I did. Philip Barry
the budding playwright, Jack Donohue the double-jointed
dancer whose feet cracked jokes, Marilyn Miller so Aprilesque,
Charles Dillingham the producer—such were the visitors I met.
And if Eddie's mother happened to be down from Lime Rock,

the gathering would be complete. Artists were as amateurs in the presence of her naturalness. They hung on her every word and probably learned to become better artists just by listening.

I like to recall her retort to a svelte, glittering actress, twice married and still childless, who earnestly wanted to know why any woman should consider babies more important than bliss in wedded life. "Because there's not much bliss without thim, and it's so much better to have'm on y'r lap than on y'r conscience," she said. And though W. C. Fields nearly burst with mirth at that retort, he nodded his admiration the time she spoke of the faith of old Ireland and cited, as an example, the case of a certain "great man entirely" that she had known in her girlhood over there. "A saint of God he was!" she declared. "Faith he worked twenty-four hours a day, visitin' the sick, helpin' the poor, comfortin' the sorrerful. The people kissed the ground he walked on an' blissed the day he was born. An' even whin he'd fall drunk in the gutter—because the Divvil, mindja, sometimes does be gettin' the better of the best, God help us!—they'd ginuflect to him."

Each brief interlude at the Dowlings always brightened the college week in Newburgh for me. And that meant much, since teaching did not come too easy at times to one like myself who yearned for the missions. It consisted mostly of planting seeds, and immediate effects could not be seen. Only the future could tell whether there'd be a crop, and it was hard to have to wait. Moreover, the routine of institutional life, after the taste of parochial service that St. Malachy's afforded me, seemed monotonous. One day in spring I expressed this feeling to Father Hugh Duffy, a zestful individual who had been ordained only a year and who had been appointed to Epiphany, and he hit me with as extreme a suggestion as I'd ever heard. "Let's go to Europe this summer," he said, "and be different—like everybody else."

Before I could recover, he had maneuvered me into the college Ford and was driving down the road toward Newburgh. "Europe?" I gasped, the absurdity fascinating me almost to acceptance. "But where are we going right now?"

He grinned. "Where we can get the money. There's a lot of it, they say, at the bank."

In those days loans came as readily as refusals today. Penniless Father Duffy and I were received at the bank like magnates, and no questions were asked, the cloth being its own recommendation. With a fine flourish of pen, he signed my note for five hundred dollars, and I signed his for the same amount. Simple as that. Then, still mad with the ease of it all, we went to a travel agency and made reservations, third class, on a boat scheduled to sail June 29. The *Leviathan*.

"How are you ever going to pay the money back?" I asked him, a glimmer of sanity returning as we rode home. "Same as yourself," he smiled. "Now you tell me."

When I told Eddie Dowling the following Sunday about the plan and the method of financing it, he shook with glee. "If you can get to Europe on nothing, just imagine how much farther you could get on *something*," he said. "But I'll take care of everything. You must let me. Been intending right along to do something for you for splicing me and Ray. Treat yourself to a real Cook's tour—London, Dublin, Paris, Venice, Rome. It'll make you a better missionary for knowing what a big place the world is, and perhaps you won't be so worried about Negroes when you get to see what a tough time the poor everywhere are having in this great era of plenty. By the way, Billy Linn, the chief steward of the *Leviathan*, is a personal friend of mine. I'll have him give you the glad hand."

Fortunately, the superior-general of the Josephites made no objection to the trip. In fact, he quite approved, because of a certain circumstance. The Maryland Academy of Science had just prepared a gift for Pope Pius XI and was looking for a responsible party to convey it to him. It was a rosary of strange crystals known to the ancients as "fairies' tears" and molded by nature in the form of Celtic crosses. The scientists of the academy had sifted through twenty-five thousand specimens to secure a perfect matching and provided for the token an exquisite plush casket of white and gold, the papal colors. To present this unique testimonial of esteem to His Holiness would be a signal privilege for the bearer or bearers, and as soon as Father Duffy, a Marylander himself, read all about it in the Baltimore *Catholic Review*, which his sister Alice sent him weekly, he phoned an influential acquaintance of his who was connected with the academy, and secured the honor for himself and me.

Free from all financial involvement myself, because of Eddie's generosity, I now could not but feel a fresh worry for Duffy. "How can you *ever* pay that note of yours?" I repeated. "If I can't," he replied, "well, your signature's on it. Remember? But don't be too disturbed." Assuming a serious, sad expression, he went on, "I've a well-to-do old relative whose health is very poor. The doctors say that before the leaves fall she must go. How I'll miss her! But she has to leave her money to somebody, and I'm a favorite."

VI

THE morning the *Leviathan* was ready to sail with many hundreds of passengers there were apparently twice as many spectators down at the pier. "Aren't we popular!" said Father Duffy.

Just about to go on board, he and I were halted by a demand that we show our passports. Having put mine in a money belt next to my skin, I had to go through a process that felt like disrobing under the eyes of New York, and Father Duffy laughed at my predicament until he suddenly froze with a realization that his own passport was similarly cached.

As we walked up the gangplank at last, I resolved to thrust everything unpleasant behind me, forgetting what a nimble imp unpleasantness could be and how prone to hop ahead. When Father and I were on board and looking around for someone to direct us through the confusion to our stateroom, we overheard a macaw-like woman talking to a chinless man. "Hebrews, Hebrews, Hebrews," she complained. "Why, land alive, this boat is ca-rawling with them!"

Father Duffy gave me a nudge. "Fancy meeting old Mr. and Mrs. Prejudice here," he whispered. "They do get around, don't they! If they hate Jews, they certainly don't love colored people and Catholics. Let's jump overboard."

I did not answer, feeling as if a little seasick already, thinking. Whimsical remarks, especially when they came from Duffy, sometimes had a way of setting me serious, and this was one of those times. *Prejudice.* I thought of the K.K.K. (Koons, Kikes, Katholics, according to the humorists), and Al Smith's debarment from the presidency largely because of his faith, and the placards spread around during his campaign ("High money,

High Mass; low money, Low Mass; no money, no Mass"). And I wondered whether the land of the free would ever be quite liberated from a nonsense worse than ignorance. But then I remembered that I was embarked on a refreshing ocean voyage; so, exhaling, I snapped at Father Duffy, "Can't you think of *anything* pleasant?"

We found our third-class stateroom 'way below the water level, and we also found that it was not just ours. Two men were there to share it, though it was hardly large enough for one, besides being as hot as a fryingpan. Under the circumstances, we four became acquainted very quickly and not too cordially.

A scribble of notes about that crossing is still among my papers. Details, impressions. The Turkish bath that first night in the stateroom, before we could get used to it, turned out to be . . . Father Duffy, no paragon of grace, lumbering into and out of his upper berth and causing the wooden guard piece to slip and crash to the floor each time . . . The two nuns on board, succumbing as naturally as anybody else to the informality of life at sea and charming everyone with their blend of humanness and holiness . . . Prohibition reigning on the Yankee-run *Leviathan* but not preventing our roommates from treating a case of "near beer" with grain alcohol which they had brought along for the purpose . . . Loud and ribald nocturnal conversations of the pair, whom we now knew to be a lawyer and a doctor, and who had no intention whatsoever of letting the clergy cramp their style. "Listen, padres," said the medico, "I believe in trying everything once." "Even suicide?" I asked innocently. He laughed and went on, "I'd even join the Church, only there're so many knuckleheads in it." And Father Duffy drily advised, "Don't let that stop you. We can always squeeze in one —or two—more, and you'd feel right at home." . . . Moods of the sea. Steel-gray sobriety; bright-blue, gold-shot gaiety; purple pensiveness . . . The gangly, pimply youth sidling up to us on deck with the momentous information that he had visited Paris the previous year just to find out "what things to do," and that he was now returning to do them, and that in Montmartre he had been "solicited" fifteen times . . . Morning Mass, with the sun pouring its amber light through portholes on immaculate corporal and polished paten and chalice . . . Jacqueline Marie. A tot of five. Flaxen hair filagreed with gold. Soft little heart-shaped face. Big hazel eyes, dark-lashed, lustrous. Loving, clinging disposition. I carried her all over deck, her elbow tight around my neck. She liked to be jounced in the air, and was quite fearless when perched on the ship railing, with the ocean achurn beneath and the wind ready to blow her like a leaf into space; for everyone near—and she knew it—kept watch over her. A much-traveled mite, she; her divorced parents lived on different continents and a nurse regularly brought her back and forth.

Father and I were the recipients of many cordial attentions from Mr. Billy Linn, the chief steward, because of Eddie Dowling. He personally conducted us on a tour through the bowels of the boat. Jonah, swallowed by the whale, could have experienced nothing more astonishing in interiors. Temperatures Hades-hot and arctic-cold by turns. Giant turbines, endless levers, utter complexity, perfect unison. The section we inspected was vast, yet only one of three. Should a compartment fail, either of the other two offered instant availability. A repair shop worthy of Vulcan kept going day and night. If only the mechanism of men's lives, I thought, were but half so well conceived, geared, and assured! And why couldn't it be? So much genius in a machine age had been applied to less important things. With the same amount finally given to the vastly more important, what a world we'd see!

Five and a half days spirited us on to our first sight of France. "Did you ever behold such a sky?" I exclaimed to Father Duffy, envisaging Deity embracing "the eldest daughter of the Church," as we sailed into Cherbourg harbor. "Of course," he answered abstractedly, fondling Jacqueline Marie. "The day we left New York, and just about every day since. A sky is a sky, is a sky, is a sky."

We were lightered off the *Leviathan* and hurried to the customhouse on the dock. It seemed, in the crush of business there, that our turn to have our baggage inspected would never come and that we'd miss the train for Paris. While we were waiting impatiently, I noticed signs on the walls, which specified that it was a punishable offense to try to secure special consideration with a bribe. Calling Father Duffy's attention to them for want of something better to do, I effected no caution in him. On the contrary, he immediately removed a dollar from his billfold and brandished it so that the nearest inspector could see. Down came the latter's left eyelid; out went his palm; quick was the transfer; and in no time we were on the train. "But you broke a law!" I chided Father Duffy when we were seated. "With such excellent co-operation from an official, would you call it a violation?" he replied, waving out the open window at Jacqueline Marie.

The train started and France began to unfold. Storybook houses, some whose thatched roofs were Easter-hat-like with flowers that must have sprung from wind-blown seeds. Poppy-swept fields. Farms that seemed to have few toilers and yet gave evidence of tilling thoroughly done. Wayside crucifixes. Peasants out of a Millet painting. Villas tucked away in trim landscapes. Violet-gray towns seemingly built from dream mist. I turned to Father Duffy in order to share my enthusiasm and found him sound asleep. When I shook him, he muttered, " 'S'time to eat?" And I marveled that a man of God could have come so far for so little. But the word "eat" reminded me that in the excitement of landing neither of us had had breakfast, and resignedly, even alertly, I accompanied him to the dining car.

Whether the meal was good or bad, we scarcely knew, for each time we glanced out the window or became absorbed in conversation, our agile waiter totally removed a course. "They don't serve food on French trains," observed Father Duffy. "They just tease you with it. 'Thrift, Horatio, thrift!' "

After a six-hour ride, climaxed with a zoom through a tunnel, we reached the city to which, as Oscar Wilde would have it, all good Americans go when they die and, according to travel agencies, all wise ones come when they're living. From the very start of our ten-day stay the nonsensical and the sublime were our companions. Scorning guides, we set out to discover Paris for ourselves, and lost as much time as we gained experience.

Father Duffy soon expressed his opinion that Paris would be much better off with fewer foreigners, but by "foreigners" he seemed to signify the French themselves. And he complained about the language, as if it had been invented mostly as a means of annoying and baffling Americans. I almost agreed with him, for neither of us knew just how to get a really good meal in this city so famous for cuisine. There was special irony in my case, because during my pursuit of a doctor's degree I had acquired a good reading knowledge of French and German and, later, had even taught both. But now I recognized only too well the chasm between the academic and the practical, able as I was to quote Corneille and Maritain in the original but not to order a corned-beef sandwich in the Café de la Paix. In truth, Father Duffy did better with his forefinger than I with all my grammar and syntax.

But he was at a complete loss one noon when we availed ourselves of the facilities of a certain lavatory on a boulevard. An efficient establishment, that lavatory, with many *compartiments* over each of which a clock ticked away. A dessicated little woman, suggestive of *Grimm's Fairy Tales*, was in charge, keeping her eye on every timepiece. Readily I caught the significance —pay as you leave, according to the length of your tarry. But not Duffy. When he had done with his ablutions, he stepped gingerly forth, without giving the woman a glance, to join me at the door where, finished before him, I was waiting. And immediately she was at him, waving three gnarled fingers and screaming, *"Payez-vous, Monsieur l'Abbé. Trois minutes. Dix centimes."* Not comprehending her in the least and thinking she was crazy, he quickened his pace. She quickened hers. Out the entrance and down the boulevard they flew, creating something queerer than a Keystone comedy. Doubled up with mirth, I merely looked on. All

I could hear was *"Payez-vous! payez-vous!"* And all I could see was the incredible: a Roman-collared clergyman pursued by a broomless witch.

Fortunately the pair encountered a good-natured gendarme who must have understood English—and American—a little. To Duffy's evident plea for protection and the woman's demand for compensation, he plainly made an adjustment, for my fellow priest handed over some money, and the woman grabbed it with not only fist but fervor. Then she returned to her be-clocked business, her wrinkled face shiny with triumph. And when I caught up with Father Duffy he grumbled, "Paris has as much conscience as a—a turnip. She makes you pay even for being chased by a loon."

At our hotel, the Montréal, he changed his opinion of the town the night a *garçon* came to our room with a bottle of ginger ale on a neatly napkined tray and proclaimed in broken English the compliments of the house. Happily we tipped him more than the beverage was worth and toasted the hospitality of *la belle France*. But when we received our bill at the end of the week we discovered the ginger ale coyly tucked away in the itemization, and from then on Duffy really fought conscienceless Paris at every turn. The morning we were leaving the Montréal for good, the *maître d'hôtel* looked relieved.

But in the meantime we had done things that made our visit very worth while. We went to the old Carmelite convent on the rue Vaugirard where, one sad Sunday in 1792, so many priests were butchered during the Revolution; and there on a glass-covered section of a wall were still to be seen some of the bloodstains of the tragedy, reminding us of the spirit that every "other Christ" must preserve to the end. We lingered in the Chapelle-Expiatoire where Marie Antoinette, daughter of the Caesars, had been buried at a cost of six livres for a bier, fifteen for a grave, and thirty-five for diggers, an outlay of about ten dollars and a commentary on the cheap and dusty passing of glamour. We prayed in the students' chapel of Saint-Sulpice and heard the little

organ on which Mozart himself used to play; and the music of
another era, another world, seemed ours. In Notre Dame our
imagination burned brighter than the vigil lights at the shrines,
and we saw great events of the past as if they were flowing before our very eyes, so that our sense of time was lost in timelessness. We roamed the jeweled chamber of Sainte-Chapelle and met
the mild ghost of good Louis IX, who erected it as a repository
for the Master's own crown. We studied the macabre souvenirs
of the Reign of Terror in the Carnavalet Museum, and pondered
with perplexity that man, created for heaven, is so adept at raising hell. We stood on the heights of Sacré-Cœur, looking down
like God on the fabulous highways of two thousand years. And
I knew that Father Duffy was as much affected by these and
other such experiences as myself. Perhaps more so, because he
was one of those individuals who usually keep their finer emotions to themselves. Children, with their intuitiveness, came to
him spontaneously, and whenever we sat in the Luxemburg or
the Tuileries gardens, some little Jeans and Jeannes would be
sure to cluster around. Then his lack of any knowledge of their
language was by no means a handicap, for he could and did talk
to them with his eyes and hands and the *Esperanto* of the heart,
and their attention was something to see.

From Paris we entrained to Rome and had our audience with
the Pope, a special audience because of the important gift we
bore. That gift—the rosary of crystals—now rests among the
treasures of the Vatican Museum, but the chaplet of blessings
that His Holiness gave us is still in our personal treasury. Leaving the Vatican, we were silent, and felt as if trailing some of
those clouds of glory sung about by Wordsworth in his "Ode on
the Intimations of Immortality"; and part of my abundant sentiment was gratitude to a Broadwayite who, out of the profits of
his song-and-dance shows, which most folk would have considered a far cry from sanctities, had enabled me to gaze on the
Vicar of Christ.

Our first night in Rome we visited the Colosseum, and in a mingling of starlight and shade imagined a kneeling group of those early martyrs from whose blood—the seed—Christianity rose. Father Duffy was so moved that as usual he had to cover up, and he did it characteristically. "Ever hear the one about the small boy whose parent showed him a picture of Christians in the arena with lions ready to devour them?" he asked me. Yes, I'd heard it. What priest hadn't! But I didn't stop him. Who could! So he proceeded to describe the child bursting into tears not for the poor humans but because it looked as if a certain tiny lion in the background wasn't "gonna get none."

During the next few days we toured the city, and one of our first sights was the church of the Capuchins, where the body of Crespin Viterbo has lain for almost three centuries. The preservation awed me, but not so much as the schoolmarmish woman at my elbow, who looked less fresh than Crespin himself. "Just another miracle," she sniffed.

We went down into the strangest of crypts beneath the church, where in soil brought from the Holy Land whole generations of religious had been buried. Space was so limited that innumerable exhumations had necessarily been made at intervals throughout the years, and skulls, tibias, femurs, etc., were everywhere, ingeniously arranged as decorations. At each corner stood a skeleton clad in a snuff-brown habit; as did also, near the doorway, an unmistakably live monk, holding a plate with which to receive whatever donations might be induced for the poor. "Disgusting!" pronounced a well-upholstered, thin-nosed gentleman. But Father Duffy and I could see only that these Capuchins so little feared death as to be able to play with the very symbols of it; and we could find nothing unseemly in alms being elicited with a vision of the dead to buy food with which to help keep flesh on the bones of the living.

In the Sistine Chapel of the Vatican we should have been lifted up out of this world by Michelangelo's genius, only that many of his frescoes were painted on the ceiling and we were distracted from the contemplation of them by cricks in our necks. An Italian guide slipped over to us with a hand mirror in which we might effortlessly view the splendor above; but this relief failed, because he stood close to us to explain everything and his breath was so heavy that we almost swooned like Victorian lassies. Not even the grandeur of the greatest artist of the Renaissance could compete with ordinary garlic.

We heard Mussolini delivering one of his typical balcony speeches, and were told by the English-speaking proprietor of our hotel that his young son Luigi burned candles in his bedroom every night to this new god who had come to save Italy and possibly the world. We learned also that the Duce required that his photograph be placed above the crucifix in each classroom, and knew that fate was already cooking the new god's goose. And when we found in the heart of the city a weird pit into which stray, starving cats were thrown, we witnessed, even if we did not realize it at the time, a kind of prefigurement of the snarling, famished state into which a sunny, singing people were being led.

In the dark, deep catacombs, while we were soul-shakenly meditating the death and resurrection of pristine Christianity, we were startled to hear a sweet-sixteeny voice with a Boston accent expressing a discovery, "What a perfect place, Keith, for pitching woo!" And "Keith's" reply came as brisk as nauseous, "You said it, babe. Let's."

We rode the Appian Way and tarried at the chapel of Quo Vadis, commemorative of the apparition of Christ to Peter during the sanguinary reign of Nero; and Sienkiewicz's novel which had captivated my boyhood again unreeled its scenes for me. But the mood was dispelled when our guide indicated a stone with an enormous imprint on it and solemnly explained, "The footmark of the Lord!" Duffy threw me a glance, his lips beginning to pucker. "The Lord must have very big feet," he said. "Why not?" puffed the guide. "Isn't He infinite!"

We went up the Scala Santa, reputedly the very same steps,

brought to Rome by St. Helena, that the Savior ascended in Jerusalem to Pilate's tribunal and descended to His death. And again Father Duffy was so affected that when I later probed his feelings, he put me off by lightly remarking, "I understand that Martin Luther once did those stairs on his knees, just like us, and came down with his faith twisted. Must have got a Charley horse in his soul. I don't feel any too chipper myself, from all that climbing. Who was it that said the Protestant religion's a good one to live in but the Catholic is better to die in?"

Our Roman stay lasted only a few days, but centuries were compressed into them, and we were very sober and thoughtful as we left. Never had Masses meant more to us than those we celebrated in St. Peter's, and never had our appreciation of the Church we loved and lived to serve been greater than when we strolled the streets trodden by so many saints and glorified by their examples. The smiles that the Eternal City had given us were as superficial as the stirrings profound.

Our next stop was Venice. On arriving at the railroad station there, we boarded a gondola and sailed a canal to our hotel. The air was bland that evening; the sky, velvety-blue and pinned with stars; the crescent moon, a visible sonnet; and the glossy black waters dimpled with jewels at each dip of the gondolier's long oar. Poetry, poetry. But then—prose. "You little bloodsucker!" cried a college-boy tourist in front of us, slapping to death a mosquito on his wrist. "Ah, Venezia," burbled a fat female who, seated alone, was balancing the boat rather well with her middle-aged spread, "to be with you is to be twenty-one again and in love!" Father Duffy, a hater of wincing, winced. "It's people that spoil places," he hissed to me. And for once—or maybe the thousandth time—I agreed with him.

Three things were to stand out even more vividly in our memory than all the glories of the queen city of the Adriatic, except St. Mark's. First, our small hotel room. It had a big bed with a netting which enclosed it entirely and reached up to the ceiling. As soon as I saw that netting I protested to Father Duffy the impossibility of anybody sleeping in a stuffy cubic space under a hot thing like that. "Oh, I don't know," he said. "It's sort of interesting, like a snowstorm in equatorial Africa, what?" So I suggested that he take the bed, netting and all. The floor would be mine, provided that he'd make the small concession of letting me have the mattress. He agreed. But neither of us rested much that night. And when he got up in the morning, the side on which he had lain resembled a waffle iron, what with the indentures the bare bedspring had made. As for me, I'd been punished for my shrewd bargain by being insect-bitten into a wreck barnacled with lumps.

The second experience was an open-air event which we attended one night in St. Mark's Square—*Cavalleria Rusticana,* with Mascagni himself conducting! His spark-tipped baton opened up a realm of peerless color and sound, and only a stone, I was sure, could have been insensate to such perfection. But I was wrong. Turning to Duffy beside me to share my rapture, I discovered that, just as on the train ride from Cherbourg to Paris, during which the scenic beauty of France had so breathtakingly unrolled, he was sound asleep. And, much worse, he emitted a healthy snore which superfluously proved it. Some folk twisted their necks around to look indignantly at him, and I edged away from his soullessness, fearing that I'd be identified with it. Closing my eyes tight, I restored myself to the sonic spell, but presently felt a jab in my arm and heard a voice which surely was not in the opera. Coming to with a start, I amazedly realized that I too must have fallen asleep, because Father Duffy, now wide awake, was rebuking me: "Haven't you any shame? Snoring before all these people who've come to hear the music—not you!"

The third episode, really a series, occurred on the day set for our departure. We had committed all arrangements to the Thomas Cook Agency, whose motto was—and is—"Travel without Trouble." The man in charge there had warned that we must abide strictly by the schedule made out for us, and that to be even a minute late would constitute a species of crime. I was duly impressed, but not Father Duffy. He said his Mass more slowly than usual at St. Mark's that morning, dawdled over his coffee and rolls at the hotel, decided to write a raft of postcards, and deferred his packing. "We have lots of time," he said. "I'm taking a lesson from these *Italianos* who siphon a lot more out of life than we do. They don't believe in trying to get a house painted before the paint gives out." Only a knock on our door and a voice announcing that if we were seriously concerned about leaving on time it might interest us to know that we had just twenty minutes in which to reach the station and catch the eleven-o'clock train stirred him to action. Finally checked out of the hotel, we hailed not a gondola but a naphtha launch; and great was my relief that we were actually on our way. But we weren't —quite. In the course of our glide over the waters Duffy fingered his inside pocket and found that he had left his passport at the hotel; so back we had to turn to get it, losing five or six of our precious minutes. My heart renewed its pounding, and when once more we were moving along, I tipped the boatman ten lire to sail it faster. He did. And my watch indicated eleven exactly, as we drew up to our destination. Out of the launch and into the station we ran, bag and baggage, lickety-split, only to learn that we were not a second too late but an hour too early. Our train was delayed in Padua.

"You and your pep!" said Father Duffy. "This is Italy, and all that stuff about *il Duce* getting things to run on the dot is *il bunko*. Don't say I didn't tell you. Come on, let's stroll around. We have sixty minutes—to kill." With no comment available, I merely watched him placing my luggage with his own in the center of the station. Then, going outside, we spied three olive-skinned urchins. He had only to smile, and they came to us forthwith. I stood studying him at his old trick of expressing the wonders of America with gestures, and them, bug-eyed, absorbing the pantomime so well, especially when he quickened their wits by handing over all his loose change. They looked ready to die on the spot with delight and devotion; and, much interested, I hardly noticed the passing of time until I chanced to glance once more at my watch. *Madre mia.* The hour was practically up.

Dragging Duffy away, I leapt back into the station. It was strangely deserted. Our luggage stood just where it had been put, but all the iron gates to platforms were closed and not a single passenger was waiting at any of them. Noticing a uniformed Cook man over in a far corner, we hurried to him and asked about the Simplon-Orient Express for which we had our reservations. "Came and went a quarter of an hour ago," he said, causing us almost to collapse. Sympathetically he advised, "You must have your tickets canceled without delay. There will be a refund, but not for the full amount, because, after all, the mistake is yours, not the railroad's or ours. You can leave on the evening train for Paris if you care to." *If.* Our funds were now low enough to need budgeting. Even a little loss would be large, and though Eddie Dowling had said that I should cable him in any emergency, I was determined to keep within bounds.

At the ticket window we were politely informed that since the Cook office in Venice had made all arrangements for us, it was there we must go for satisfaction and any further service. Burning under our collars, we confronted the agent hovering near and demanded that he get our money back for us right here and now. This, he regretted, was impossible, for he was only an ordinary employee and there were certain formalities to be observed. The best he could do, he said, was to put us on a gondola which would take us again into town. "Who's going to pay our fare on the gondola?" asked Father Duffy. "You reverend gentlemen yourselves," came the reply. "No, sir!" rasped my now purple fellow priest. "We've already paid enough to be taken out of Venice and we won't give a cent more to have to stay in!" His voice rose, and the Cook man himself began to look angry. Miserable, I just stood and stared.

Then the three urchins stuck their curly black polls in at the door of the station and, seeing that we were in some sort of trouble, hurried to defend us. Stanch little demons, they went right to work on our supposed enemy with their hands and feet, shaking off our attempts to restrain them. People gathered, and these seemed to draw others. Father Duffy and I quickly became a center of Latin excitement. Struggling, we got out of the group but seemed to drag it along to the canal, where somehow we got into a gondola just taking off. And, looking back, we beheld the mussed-up agent flapping his wrist in a gesture of good-riddance-to-bad-rubbish at us. Our trio of little champions, in the grip of adults, were still spitting fire at him.

When we reached the Cook office in St. Mark's Square, the doors were locked, the shutters down, and flies buzzed lazily in the intense sun. *Siesta.* So we'd have to wait for four o'clock when, as a passer-by told us, the place would reopen. "Let's take this like Christians," said Father Duffy with a snarl. And we went to the nearest hotel, downed a ravioli lunch, and engaged a room in which we hoped it would be possible to snooze off some of our wrath until the time came to talk turkey with good old travel-without-trouble Cook.

At long last the whole stupid affair seemed to end when, at 6:45 that night, we boarded the next train for Paris. But trouble was still fond of us. En route we became ill from a combination of nerves and badly digested ravioli. And, too depressed for prudence, we hung our clothes near the unscreened open window of our compartment when retiring, with the consequence that next morning two important items were missing. Somewhere, possibly onto an alp in Switzerland, my shirt and Duffy's pants had been blown. (They were our best, but fortunately not our only.)

In no mood to enjoy a return to the city on the Seine, we tarried there only long enough to take a plane to London. Then, as true sons of Irishmen, we could not leave England fast enough, with the charms of old Erin, sung into our souls since childhood, calling, calling.

Finally stepping into the Royal Hibernian Hotel in Dublin, I breathed, "This is——" But Duffy, interrupting, finished the sentence for me. "—it!"

"It" did not exclude certain peculiarities. After registering we betook ourselves to our room on the second floor, and I sighed a home-at-last sigh as I turned the key in the lock; but when I tried the knob of the door, off it came and fell at my feet. "Gently, gently," said Duffy, smiling. "It mistook you for one of those English grabbers, that's all." And picking up the sensitive thing with much display of respect, he adjusted it so that it worked perfectly. But a few moments later when he was whistlingly engaged in washing his face at the little porcelain basin in a corner of the room, he struck his head against the bottom of the marble shelf beneath the mirror, and something which probably could not have been done with an ax was easily effected without one. The shelf broke in two. "Sabotage! Darn thing must've been made in London!" he exploded. And to my "Gently, gently," he snorted a vibrant "Phoo."

The first church we found had a bronze tablet which we did not take the trouble to inspect. One blessed word, "Patrick," sprang out from it as if to welcome us, and that seemed enough. But what was our consternation, on entering, to discover no Roman Catholic insignia at all! And there we were, heads uncovered, in a fine old Protestant cathedral.

Our first restaurant had a French menu and a Bavarian waiter, and an awful feeling crept over us that Dublin was less Irish than New York, or that maybe we weren't in Dublin at all. But soon we were taken under the wings of the angels who, according to Broadway's Tin-Pan Alley, had found a little bit of heaven fallen from the skies one day, and sprinkled it with stardust just to make the shamrocks grow, and called it Ireland. Then our dreams began to assume reality. True, we saw poverty beyond belief in Gardner Street, but also, even there, belief beyond poverty. Life could be, as long it had been, a trial for the Irish; but a sense of resurrection and glory to come had sustained and was still sustaining them. As a people they evidently looked for no lasting city here below; and we glimpsed, or imagined, a reflection of eternity in almost every face. Nor was our impression dispelled when we heard an old shawled woman near Nelson's monument blessing a man for giving her an alms and then blasting him because the amount was so meager. The benison, "May the Lord's grace iver follow ye!" The curse, "But niver overtake ye!"

And neither were we at all disillusioned by the chip on many a shoulder or the itch in many a fist. Here was a race with a pride that had withstood the humiliation of centuries and become the prouder; a people whose very wounds seemed to goad them to fight the more, notwithstanding a compassionate desire to bind up all wounds. Our natural liking for them blurred out their faults and made their virtues doubly clear.

So many mystic wells and stones in County Wicklow! Links between longing and fulfillment. Such clean, fresh scenery!— wild, sweet, and a little sad even in sunlight, as Thackeray used to say. On one of our side trips we scaled the steep rocks leading to the cave where St. Kevin had cultivated his soul, and we looked down on a lake into which a single misstep would have plunged us. " 'Tis no bottom it has entirely," warned our guide, pressing a finger to his nose and shedding a humorous gleam from his cool blue eye, "as you can see f'r yourselves." And he added, "Iveryone who comes here can make three wishes. And, bedad, who's to stop'm? Without wishes we'd be havin' no hearts atall atall." So I made a triple appeal to the great Kevin that I might descend in safety and be given enough brains never to climb such giddy heights again. And, like all honest sighs to the right party in Ireland, it was granted—in a way.

An excursion of ours to Avoca included, little to its improvement, some loud-mouthed Americans who had equipped themselves with several bottles of Guinness's stout, the famed dark ale of Dublin. Thinking of the poet Moore, who had roamed here and found such inspiration, I said to Father Duffy, "We are on holy ground. This is the vale where 'the three rivers meet.' " But he only jerked his head toward the tourists pouring a stream of liquor into themselves. "There goes the fourth and biggest," he observed.

We wanted to remain in Ireland indefinitely and visit the Lakes of Killarney. But before we'd taken in a fraction of the beauty around Dublin our time was up and our exchequer almost empty. Back to England we had to speed, there to catch the *Leviathan* at Southampton.

About to go on board, we met Bishop Toolen of Mobile, so pink, portly, and benevolent that just to be near him was to be happy. He lingered on the dock to talk with us, because, as a native Baltimorean, he knew Father Duffy well and, as a former student of St. Mary's Seminary, had a warm regard for companionate St. Joseph's. His work in the Propagation of the Faith having been one of his many well-known recommendations to an episcopate, we could speak to him freely about things nearest our missionary hearts. "Now that your diocese is in the Deep South, Your Excellency, how about the Negro?" I asked eagerly. He smiled. "Why not give me a little time to be a bishop?" he said. "I've only recently been installed in Dixie, and the Negro has been there a long while. Before settling anything, I myself must get settled." But already, looking at him, I could see fresh blessings for the colored along the Gulf Coast and longed to be sent there to assist in the bestowal.

He invited Father and me to a testimonial dinner which the captain of the *Leviathan* was to give him, and promised to arrange permission for us to pass from third to first class for the event. And two nights later, far out at sea, Father Duffy and I sat at the captain's table. We ate with such obvious relish, because soon we'd be back to college hash and plain boiled potatoes, that a lady in a décolleté gown raised her lorgnette, and a distinguished-looking gentleman smirked. Superlative food! And to think that only for the circumstance of a prelate's kindness we could not have gotten even a whiff of it, to say nothing of admittance to the splendid salon where it was served!

Yet further were the humble to be exalted. When we reached the United States, we were written up in the New York *Journal* because of "the million-year-old rosary" that we had presented in the name of the Maryland Academy of Science to His Holiness; and also, by some marvel of misinformation, we were mentioned in several other papers as having been honored by the captain of the *Leviathan* with a brilliant banquet at which many notables were present, including Bishop Toolen.

VII

W<small>HEN</small> I saw Eddie Dowling and described the trip to him, he said, "Would you like to go again? I'll be well able to give you another vacation if you pull some more strings with heaven for me. Y'see——"

And he told me that while out on the Coast he had written and starred in a talkie, *The Rainbow Man,* the première of which was to be held at the Astor Theatre a few weeks hence. Would I pray hard for its success? What a question! With all my heart I wanted to see him shine in this fresh venture, this new medium of screen sound that had been thrilling the country since Warner Brothers and Al Jolson demonstrated the possibilities of it with *The Jazz Singer* and *The Singing Fool.* It could mean a second and perhaps greater career for him.

He made me promise to attend that première. And the rector of Epiphany, appreciating how much I owed such a benefactor, was pleased to let me go. Came the gala night, and there I was, worming my way through a crowd outside the Astor. Hollywood was doing itself proud on Broadway. Limousines rolled up to the curb, disgorging the bon ton into a sea of light which set every jewel asparkle. But suddenly, as I gazed, I saw only one person and stared. Could this be, by jingo, Eddie's mother? No —yes, yes.

To give her such an appearance, Eddie and Ray must have had the services of the best couturier and coiffeur in New York. She was gowned in black velvet and cream-colored lace and corseted almost to an hour-glass mold. Her slippers were French-heeled and silver-buckled. A fluffy light fur lay casually on her shoulders, diamond pendants peeked from under her soft-crimped

white hair, and an orchid caressed her bosom. Her plump cheeks
the tint of rose petals, her eyes a couple of stars, she won a gasp
of admiration as her identity became known, and she stole the
show. But she might have stolen it just as readily, I thought, if
she could have been seen as I had so often seen her, in the calico
that best suited her simplicity and with little grandchildren tug-
ging at her skirts. I knew right well that she'd have much preferred to be at home, cooking a meal or darning a sock. But she
certainly was not going to let that famous boy of hers down, and
brushing escorts aside, she swept independently, royally, into the
flower-banked foyer.

The crowd milled after her, and it was only with great difficulty that I myself entered, losing my breath and ticket in the
crush but, as a clergyman, being admitted anyhow by the very
Hibernian doorman. Standing in the orchestra rear, I now saw
her seated away up front. There was an empty aisle chair beside
her, and it occurred to me that I might occupy it briefly and
whisper my congratulations; so I stepped forward, no usher inter-
vening. And the instant she saw me, up she sprang to wring my
hands. "Father Ed Murphy, me darlin' praste!" she cried, either
unaware that her voice carried or forgetting to care. "You sit
right down here an' help me be meself. Heaven sent you! Eddie
and Ray are backstage and 'tis lost I am in all this ter-do. Didja
iver see the beat of it, an' the way they've done me up to be
lookin' like an acthress? The feet're killin' me. I'll bust somethin'
if I so much as brathe."

I took the vacant chair eagerly but uneasily and chatted with
her. Two or three minutes passed, and then a tall fine-looking
man with steel-gray hair loomed in the aisle, bending just a trifle
as he touched my shoulder. "Pardon me, Father," he said quietly,
"but there must be a mistake." He showed a ticket stub.

She bristled. "You stay right where you are," she ordered me.
"God's praste comes first ivery time!" And she turned on the
obtruder. "Git y'rself another seat."

He smiled good-naturedly.

I murmured an apology to him, thanked her, and managed to release myself. When back again in the orchestra rear, I asked an usher about the gentleman now sitting beside Mr. Dowling's mother. Who was he? "Oh, the Wall Street millionaire," he replied. "Mr. Mike Meehan."

The Rainbow Man, one of the best and clearest of those early talkies, was a real hit. The audience remained to cheer, and Eddie came out on the stage to deliver a witty, folksy speech and introduce his ma. She stood up and had to take so many bows, the millionaire leading the applause, that at last she flapped her wrist as much as to say, and I could almost hear her saying it, "Yerra stop it now. It's the boy, not me, thit's iverything." And I knew that not only her feet but her happiness and pride were "killin'" her. She seemed as much a hit as the picture itself. And Kate Smith, gracing the occasion, perfected it by singing from a box, at Eddie's request, some of her best songs.

When I saw Eddie afterward for a minute, he thanked me for coming and, winking, added, "You surely must have prayed hard for me. Start thinking about that next trip abroad. It's yours."

In another June off I sailed once more with the blessing of my superior who realized that such opportunities were too great to be foregone.

It was now the summer of '29, and an electric something was in the air. A hectic or a hopeful sign? I could not tell. Having seen Europe on the road to recovery, I'd quite discounted Sir Edward Grey's prophecy that the lights over there would never be rekindled in our time. And the beacon of prosperity in America had never burned brighter. What powers of recuperation from war this modern world possessed! Yet there was a phony, artificial note which could not but be sensed or at least suspected in the revival, as if civilization were living on borrowed time and capital and trying either to forget or to be gay about it.

All crossings to Europe were popular that summer, and each liner was laden with youth, from sixteen to sixty, in search of some equivalent of old Jason's golden fleece. The argosy on which I sailed was not the *Leviathan* but the *Bremen*, and liquor flowed. One moonlit night I joined a slightly alcoholic and very collegiate group on deck. Perhaps it was a rash thing to do, but, taking this trip all alone, I was a little lonely. The boys accepted me as casually as, I dare say, they would have accepted anybody, from the Lord Chancellor of England to a regular Bowery bum. The topic under discussion happened to be freedom of speech, "the foundation of all other freedoms," one of them stressed, "because if a man can't say whatever he pleases, he's not a man but a clod, a chattel, a thing." Well, well. I focused my hearing and simply had to part my lips. Soberly I distinguished between saying what one pleased and being pleased to say what one should, and asserted that nobody had a right to speak what was certainly, consciously, and clearly wrong, else all cases of libel, for instance, would have to be ruled out of court and the liar would enjoy equal standing before the law with the honest man. "Everyone is a liar. Should all be muzzled?" muttered a rather tense fellow; and another came right at me too, dragging along my old inimical friend Voltaire. "Sir, no matter what you think," he cried, "I'll string along with the Frenchman who said, 'I don't believe a word you say but I'll defend with my life your right to say it.' That's democracy! That's America!"

"But doesn't America acknowledge," I asked, "that certain abuses of speech are crimes, and attach penalties to them when proven? No government, nor even God himself, can grant anybody the right to say or do wrong. True liberty consists in being unimpeded in living and expressing what is reasonable and good. Would you call this un-American or commonsensical?" A hiss stung my ear. Unruffled, I continued, appreciating the opportunity and attention. "Can't you see that if the Frenchman really made the remark just quoted, he must have had this tongue in his cheek? Would he have defended with his life anybody's 'right' to call him, say, an embezzler, a sodomist, or a murderer? Wouldn't he have summoned the police or hauled off with a fist?" Silence fell and lasted a few seconds. It was not a resentful silence, and I knew that I was winning an adherent or two.

We met on deck or in the lounge frequently after that, and they plied me with questions; and giving answers mostly from the catechism, I was somewhat admired for my apparent originality. Their teachers, it seemed to me, had informed them neither that the very old could be very new nor that simplicity might have a subtlety of its own, for orthodoxy came to these students with all the freshness of a surprise. And how I wished that they could have been given a course in scholasticism to discipline their thinking! Their desire for truth was like fire out of a furnace rather than in it, and I feared for America if they and so many like them were not better directed in time. But time was running out, and the Jazz Age was at its height. "I like to discuss important things," said a Harvardite to me, "but I prefer to shoot the breeze with a blonde, brunette, or anybody who wears Gertie garters and bobby pins. Can you blame me?" No, not exactly. I inclined to blame the modern substitutes for Aristotle and Aquinas in schools of higher learning which had largely turned philosophy into psychology and interpreted thinking as a "gut" condition rather than an intellectual process. Until the beauty and unity of truth were again as manifest as in the Age of Faith, what chance did youth's mental quests have, in competition with physical excitement? What did they amount to but "bull sessions"?—notwithstanding that Will Durant with his *Story of Philosophy*, and H. G. Wells with his outline of more history than he had ever read, were bending every effort to render knowledge attractive, quick, and painless.

That summer I made my tour of Europe different from the first, concentrating on peoples rather than places. Having brushed up on colloquial French, German, and Italian, I got around a great deal better; and Paris, Heidelberg, Cologne, Genoa, Florence, Naples, and Rome came humanly alive for me. I saw the deeper scars in men's spirits and felt the fierce yearning for security in the too swift flux of national and international events. The Rock of Ages was still there to be clung to, but materialism, like a great dust storm, was swirling minds away from it and blinding them.

I returned to America that fall in a very serious frame of mind. Eddie Dowling had thought that after seeing the greater problems in Europe I'd not be so sensitive to the lesser ones at home, but my sensitivity seemed to have increased. The Negro was more in my mind than ever, because I now considered him a test of the worth of American leadership which lands overseas so badly needed. We had tendered material assistance, but our moral example, so long as any of our own citizens remained underprivileged, appeared pharisaical. What an asset to Americanism the colored could be, if accorded their rights not just Constitutionally but also actually! Otherwise, the old cynicism, "Physician, heal thyself," would have to be hurled at us from abroad, and to that extent our influence would decline. The patriot as well as the missionary in me was moved.

Then came the Wall Street crash, moving everything, everybody. Rich men went poor, poor men desperate, and social welfare weak. Most charitable organizations necessarily trimmed their sails, but I kept hearing about a certain project that was braving all uncertainties and progressing toward completion under the inspiration and auspices of probably the most remarkable nun in America, Mother Katherine Drexel, known as the angel of the Negro and Indian missions. She feared no depression, having adopted self-denial as a mode of life, and made herself poor for the poor. Her Philadelphia banker father had left her and her sister the income of a fortune, from which she had built a series of schools; and now she was busy with her greatest project, a colored university that would help to develop a people from within by supplying them with leaders of their own.

Deeply interested, I discussed the noble plan with Father Pastorelli, my superior, during one of his many visits to Epiphany. "We owe Mother Katherine more than we can ever repay, because of the help she has given our work for decades," he said. "And when her latest institution is ready, it will be only fitting that the services of one or two of our Fathers be donated her in partial return for her goodness. We don't have nearly enough Josephites, and it's hard for me to encroach on my faculty here, but nothing is too hard to do for such a friend. Would you like to be sent to Xavier?" My heart leapt. Here at last was the opening for which, broadened by the effect of two summers in Europe, I had prayed. As with Moses and his approach to the Promised Land, I had neared New Orleans in my past brief southern interludes, but never entered it. With all the appeal of the unknown, it beckoned me like paradise.

Remembering my first pastor's devotion to Newman's *Idea of a University*, I promptly secured a copy of that classic and not only read but absorbed it. What heavenly blueprints I'd bear to the Crescent Bend and the Negro apostolate! What results I'd see!

When I saw Eddie Dowling at St. Malachy's and told him where I was to go, he said, "Why don't you stay around here and help me discover some more Kate Smiths? Broadway needs them worse than ever these blue days. Well, when the time comes for you to run out on me, and it won't be long now, we can at least keep in touch. I'm still banking on your pull with God, and if any very interesting playscripts turn up, I'd like to send them on to you and get your opinion. Yeah, I have a yen to be a producer. Every actor has, after a hit or two."

I assured him that I'd rejoice in being of assistance anytime and anywhere; and thanking me, he went on to talk about New Orleans. "You're going to a great town—one of the most picturesque in the whole U.S.A.," he said. "It's over ten years since I last saw it, but it might have been just an hour ago, the way everything stands out so clear. Canal Street, Royal, Jackson Square, St. Charles Avenue, Lake Pontchartrain, and those French restaurants!—Antoine's, Galatoire's, Arnaud's. See, I even remember the names. But I never had a meal in any of them. Just couldn't afford it on my salary in those days. Had to fill up on poor-boy sandwiches or an occasional oyster loaf. By the way, there's a fellow down there—when he's not in Washington—who's great guns in politics. He's the kind that don't wait for things to happen but makes them. Pal of mine. I'll give you a letter to him when you get going. Name's Huey P. Long."

My family might have been dismayed at the distance that soon would separate me from them only that Father Will had been just as far off since his ordination and they had learned to be satisfied with a moral union here below in preparation for the lasting one above. Mom wanted and expected little from the life that was left her, and she felt awkward and unworthy about having what she deemed to be so much. With regard to the house on Loring Avenue she had said, "I'm so thankful to be here, Father Ed! But it's like putting me that's been used to a wrapper into a stiff stylish gown. Don't feel bad if I tell you that I'd like the other kind of home better. We're gettin' along good, but it all must seem too showy to our old friends, and it's a care; grounds to be kept up, and that newfangled oil-heat system to be watched. There's nothin' like an old-fashioned coal stove, the kind you all used to gather 'round in the Derby Street kitchen when you were little and—and needed me. The heat that comes from a contraption hidden in a cellar—it don't seem real. Am I talkin' sense?"

Wise Mom! Just before the start of the depression she had persuaded me to sell the house; and it was most fortunate that she did, for, shortly after, a purchaser willing to pay a fair price would have been very hard to find, with families doubling up to save expenses and property values falling to nothing. Salvaging what money I had put into it for her, I found a modest little place on Ocean Avenue, from the back windows of which she could have the comfort of viewing the steeple of a church on Castle Hill. "I've lived in a mansion," she said with a contented sigh, "but this is home. Thanks, Son." And there she spent her last few days.

One night in December Annie phoned me at Epiphany in Newburgh to come quickly to Salem, and I knew without asking what she meant. This time, Extreme Unction was not prolonging a life but solely preparing it for departure.

From Memphis, Father Will came too; and at last he and I could kneel to Mom as when she first taught us our prayers. The peaceful smile on her lips seemed to be a final request that we rejoice with her rather than grieve after her, since she was merely joining those of our family who had already gone ahead, and would be awaiting with them the rest of us. She had ever tried to practice resignation, and we felt that we must try to imitate her example.

But Eddie Dowling's mother, arriving from Lime Rock for the wake, manifested no restraint. As soon as she entered our crowded parlor that night and gazed down into the casket, she filled the air with a keening the like of which I had never heard, as if the body of her, which had given so much life, could not at all endure the sense of death. Yet when she had shed every tear and tone, and therefore perfectly done what she must have conceived to be one's duty, she turned her attention wholly to another. Led by my ever young and sprightly Aunt Aggie, she made her way to the mourners in the kitchen, and soon strange new sounds were audible. I scarcely believed my ears at first. Laughter? Yes, that. Warm, healthy, human, it flowed through the dining room into the parlor and wreathed itself around the casket, and as I looked at Mom's pale face almost apologetically, her lingering smile appeared to harmonize with the merriment and approve it. And apology melted into gratitude, for I realized that Mom's true friend was doing just what Mom would have had her do. She was driving out gloom by means of the same good humor with which she had so endowed her son Eddie that he had become a Broadway star. She was supplying a need of the living as fully as she had brought her tribute of grief to the dead.

The wake was to be voted the most unusual but the best the neighborhood ever knew, and all because of one who believed and exemplified the text, "Blessed are they that mourn, for they shall be comforted." "God love her!" said Father Will, and my "Amen" was fervent.

My brother Jim had accompanied Father Will from Memphis but did not return with him. Mom's passing affected him the most. He thought constantly of the things he might have done for her, and our attempts to bolster his spirit by reminding him that his good work in Memphis had been a great solace to her were not too successful. He spent his days largely between the church and the cemetery, growing more and more silent, regarding himself a failure of failures. His health deteriorating, I induced him to leave home for a change-and-rest cure in a certain Maryland retreat which I remembered from my student days. And from there, one morning, the nuns in charge sent us word that, solaced with the sacraments, he had passed away.

We buried him in Salem. And as I read the ritual prayers at his grave, I thought of that old white iron bed in which four brothers had once been so snug and secure; and of what Mom had said when we were laying Tom to rest, "At last he's young again." Too, I thought of the pleasure Jim had given so many people with his humble talents. Failure? His life, a spring meandering through muddied grasses but regaining a crystal purity in its flow, had afforded refreshment for other lives along the way. Was my own doing half so much or nearly so well?

Agnes wanted to stay on by herself in the house where Mom breathed her last; and Father Will and I were glad to have her do so, because the place was a kind of shrine to us and she would be the perfect custodian. Like Will, I'd be visiting home less and less as duties in the Deep South claimed me; but the fact of a New England haven ever waiting with a welcome would be a priceless consolation.

In August of 1932 Xavier University in New Orleans reached completion and readiness for its autumn opening, and I had to be off. My possessions at Epiphany were few, and "packing" was nothing at all. I smiled to myself at a remark that, years before in Baltimore, I'd overheard a colored man make to a fellow Knight of Peter Claver who was about to go to Chicago to attend a convention: "Jus' button yer coat, Pete, an' you're all packed."

But I did have some books and a collection of notes on behaviorism, the psychology popularized by John B. Watson in the twenties, and on the lives of the saints, which I had found most helpful in teaching religion to my classes. Twenty-five of the books were copies of my doctorate dissertation, "St. Thomas's Political Theories and Democracy," which I once considered so important, especially when it was given an excellent appraisal in the *Ecclesiastical Review;* but apparently few besides myself and the Board of Examiners at Catholic University in Washington had ever really read it. Riffling the pages of one of the copies, I clucked my tongue. Such early erudition, so brave and proud. Such futility. With security the great aim, who cared at all that modern liberty was traceable to medieval principles? So I brought twenty-four of the relics to a kiln on the college grounds and burned them, and watching the smoke spiraling up, I hoped that if the urge to write should ever rise in me again it would be exercised only in simplicity, practicality, and humility.

Our janitor could send on to New Orleans the remainder of my little library. Memories, absurd or significant, such as the skunk assault, the mighty snows, Sister Hartia's lonely decease, the "ghost" with a gun, meditations under the cedars and the stars, and the Claverhood to which I'd tried to lead young lives—these would be my personal, imponderable luggage.

Just before leaving, I visited our little chapel where I had united Eddie Dowling and Ray Dooley in holy matrimony one spring morning; and I prayed for them as I thought of the vistas that their grateful generosity had opened up to prepare me for a larger life by affording me a fuller realization that "the field is the world."

My last look at Epiphany was given to the statue that had

stirred my emotions the day I arrived as a boy in Baltimore to begin my missionary training. It had been removed to Newburgh and re-erected on the college grounds. The inscription, "Go to Joseph," originally carved on the pedestal, was no longer to be seen, but it had remained within me and in the light of it I now saw the past only as a prelude to what really mattered—the future. Now I would indeed be going to Joseph, the master carpenter whose foster Son had built a moral temple in which the worshipers were neither Jews nor Gentiles, bond nor free, but only children of the Father. How, under such a patronage, identical with the Lord's own will and way, could I fail?

VIII

THE August morning I stepped off the train in New Orleans the temperature was so high that I could almost believe what one of our Fathers had written me: "Down on the Crescent Bend you'll see something new under the summer sun. Dogs chase cats in slow motion." My heart skipped, but my feet dragged.

With my copy of Newman's *Idea of a University* in one hand and a valise in the other, I made straight for the washroom to remove my high-collared clerical vest and substitute a simple lightweight rabat. Yet as soon as I ventured forth again into the torridity, I had to turn back to take off my shirt, which was clinging to my skin like a wet rag. And still no relief! So I doffed even my undershirt and wriggled into my coat, buttoning up tight against the possibility of any exposure, sighing to myself at the loss of what I had intended to be so dignified an appearance on my entering so important an assignment. I felt as awkward as the day I had to get at my money belt to produce a passport when Father Duffy and I were about to board the *Leviathan*.

The arrangement that Father Pastorelli had made for me was twofold. First, I should present myself at St. Joan of Arc Church as pastor and, later on, at Xavier University as spiritual adviser and teacher. How eager I was to start! So I took a taxi instead of a trolley, and the mounting of the meter appalled me as I rode away up Canal Street and then down Carrollton Avenue; but I tried to calm myself with a realization that henceforth I'd not have to watch pennies so much, since the annual allowance which each Josephite was given for personal expenses had recently been raised by the society from fifty dollars to a hundred; and surely, as pastor of an already established mission, I'd not find the financial going too rough.

Father Pastorelli had briefed me on the history of the place to which I was speeding. The property had been bought from a white congregation about twenty-five years before and opened to the colored by Father Lebeau, a pioneer Josephite who'd trailed the Gospel along the bayous and been so esteemed that a town upstate was named after him. The first piece of furniture in his rectory was a fruit crate; but soon his zeal recruited a following and attracted an income, and all went well until a hurricane smote his church, which, built on crawfish land at the foot of a levee, had invited its own destruction. He had to begin all over again; but then his strength waned, for he was getting on in years. Father Wareing, sent to replace him, was not a well man either. In fact, he had undergone so many operations that only a section of his digestive tract remained; nevertheless, he forced himself to his duties until he, too, had to give up; and, only half alive, he set forth on a voyage to his native England to die. It was not the end for him, however. With World War I raging at the time, he was blown up by a German submarine in mid-sea and— got all better. At any rate, he passed a physical examination in London and became a military chaplain; and presently, in the hell of combat across the Channel, he made a vow to the Maid of Orleans that if she should bring him through and restore him to his beloved flock in New Orleans, which Father Saint-Laurent, once the rector of Epiphany College, was temporarily leading, he would build a brand-new church for her. Back he came, with several more years of life in his skeletal frame; and up went the pledged structure in the name of his great patroness. It was made of brick, and any future high wind would have a hard time shaking it down; but it had to stand on the same old unstable ground as the old one, and before long showed jagged cracks in its plaster walls. Part of my work, now that Father Wareing had gone on to other fields requiring his remarkable energy, and his successor Father Neifert was likewise leaving, would be to make repairs.

The rectory, a cottage with a broad front porch, looked quite inviting that morning of my arrival, but the church itself much more so. My first visit was to the sanctuary, and finding vestments laid out and chalice and cruets ready, I said Mass. Nobody was there to assist at it, but the sun shone bright through the stained-glass windows, and a suggestion of the celestial permeated the interior, and I breathed the words of Peter, James, and John on Thabor, "Lord, it is good to be here." Enchanted, I scarcely noticed the cracks in the walls.

When I presented myself after thanksgiving at the door of the rectory, expecting a welcome from at least a small delegation of parishioners, I had to ring and ring the bell before the sound of a shuffling footstep evinced any life at all inside. Finally the portal opened to me, and I almost wished that it had remained shut. There was no friendliness in the face of the little yellow-brown woman standing there, only a sharp resentful look from eyes glinting like two small black buttons.

"I'm Father Murphy, the new pastor."

"I'm Alice Murray," said she, her tone implying that she had seen pastors come and go and was capable of surviving yet another.

A colored woman with a name as Irish as my own! And why was she so antagonistic? I should have remembered the enigmatic old Sarah of my days at St. Barnabas Church in Baltimore, but at the moment I didn't.

"Where is Father Neifert?"

"He ain't in!" she snapped. "He's asleep."

Asleep at nine o'clock in the morning? No wonder the church building, and doubtless the congregation too, needed repairs. Well, I'd be taking over now and things would be entirely different.

"Tell him I am here," I ordered, a crackle in my own tone.

"He ain't t'be disturbed. But you kin come in an' wait."

"How very generous of you! Well, let me tell you, Mistress Murray, you're no longer in charge around here. Get your things together and go."

There. It was a trifle early, perhaps, for an official act, but out of my memory had sprung the lesson of that meditation which Father Fenlon had read to the student body in Catholic University chapel so long ago, the counsel about housekeepers in ecclesiastical ménages, and their illusions of grandeur, and the necessity of dealing swiftly and sternly with them. It had once seemed silly, but now how pertinent it was proving to be! *Si flet, fleat.* "If she weeps, let her weep."

This one did not shed a single tear. On the contrary, she slapped her palms to her hips, threw back her gray frizzled head, and—I couldn't believe it—smirked at me. "Neither you n'r anybody else kin fire me," she said.

Taken aback, I plunged forward, commanding loftily, "Step aside. If you're not out of this house in ten minutes——"

Just then Father Neifert came down the hall stairway. He was in his undershirt, and I should have been distinctly shocked only for a sudden realization that I wasn't in mine. "Hello, Father," he said, blinking. "Been expecting you and was up nearly all night, trying to balance the ledger. After Mass and breakfast I fell into a snooze. The heat——"

"I've just discharged this person," I interrupted injuredly, throwing a thumb at La Murray.

His nose crinkled and his jaw sagged. "But you can't discharge her."

Indignantly I demanded why not, and indicated that no housekeeper, particularly this sort, was indispensable.

"Now, now," he tried to soothe. "Alice is not a housekeeper."

I could well believe it. She seemed more like a general drawback. "Then why——"

"She comes here to work for absolutely nothing," he explained. "Takes care of the altar and sacristy and keeps the church clean. A treasure! Wise as an owl. Salt of the earth."

"Oh."

No doubt salt had a right to be salty. But I had a duty to be ashamed, and ashamed I was, not only at my misreading of this woman but also at my lack of self-control. Would I ever be a fitting instrument of the Lord? "Sorry," I murmured.

He then conducted me through the place. "There're two regular housekeepers here," he mentioned as he opened the door of a kitchen which needed sweeping and had a pile of dirty dishes in the sink. "Two?" I exclaimed. "I don't see any."

"Oh, one of them is at home for a few days, with the misery in her back. The other's visiting some relatives in the country."

"But that leaves nobody except Alice Murray."

He hoisted his belt. "She's better than three. Always around when she's needed. Turns her hand to anything."

She had already turned her back and disappeared. And I exclaimed again, "*Two* housekeepers! How can you afford them?"

He shrugged. "They work for the salary of one."

"But that's injustice."

He smiled. "It's charity—in these days of depression. Like food and shelter, jobs have to be shared. The women are friends and like the arrangement. They split the six dollars a week I've been paying."

Only six dollars a week? Worse and worse. I spouted something about the encyclicals of Leo XIII and Pius XI and a just wage, and resolved that I'd raise the wretched sum to at least ten.

That night Father Neifert boarded the train for his new station in Clayton, Delaware, and I was left alone to deal with the Murray problem so present and the two underpaid housekeepers who weren't there, as well as with a certain cash—or rather cashless—situation. To round out his fare North, Father Neifert had had to borrow what little money I possessed.

I slept badly that night, tossing and turning in the mosquito-infested heat. How could I possibly make anything out of this chaos of mismanagement called a mission? How—how? But toward morning an old text and thought returned to me: "Unless the Lord build the house . . ." And I reflected that He who had brought order from confusion in the beginning was ever ready to repeat the performance. Why should I, His servant, be worrying like a disbeliever—an atheist? Wasn't an atheist definable as one who had no invisible means of support? Faith, faith! I must hope and trust more intensely than ever before. I'd better, and promptly, else my future down here would certainly be a blank.

Morning brought both inner and outer light, and I began to see that Father Neifert's economics had been less crazy than Christian. He'd spent nothing on himself but everything for the needs of others. A close examination of his bookkeeping proved that. As for me, why had I been so rash as to look for a welcome from parishioners losing a shepherd whom they rightly held dear? I had not yet put in any service at all for them, and he had given so much. Last night, at a farewell gathering in the rectory, I'd seen testimony in their tears and gratitude. So at Mass I asked the Lord to forgive me—a fool.

Alice Murray prepared breakfast for me. The coffee was bitter, the toast burned, and the dish of fried eggs greasy. But, very hungry, I did not wholly disrelish the meal, and as she was removing my plate I said to her quietly, "You mustn't mind about yesterday. I understand a lot better today and know how you and the people feel. It will probably be impossible for me to make up for the loss of so good a pastor as Father Neifert, but I'll do my best. Pray for me." Pursing her lips, she left the dining room without a word; but lunch, served promptly at twelve, was neat and appetizing, and her scowl was gone. It appeared that, before long, I'd be having a real friend—my first in town.

Sunday came. Counting the collection, I winced. On an income like this, exactly $12.53, how could I pay two housekeepers ten dollars a week? *Ten?* I couldn't pay them even six! And if I gave them nothing at all, I'd still be living beyond my means.

Another probing of Father Neifert's account of parish receipts showed me that such a small collection, despite the depression, was quite unusual. Hence the indication seemed clear that the people were purposely holding back. Why? I scratched my head. Was it all because of my displacing him? No. The record further revealed that his own initial collection, notwithstanding his having succeeded the revered Father Wareing only a year ago, had been relatively generous. Then, questioning Alice Murray, I learned something. The congregation believed, she told me, that since I was to teach at Xavier, I'd be only a part-time pastor to them; and that with "the big salary" I'd be "agettin'" from Xavier, I'd not be "aneedin'" any support.

Steadying myself, I assured her that priestly service for Joan of Arc would in no wise suffer, for an assistant was to be sent me by my superior, and that my "big salary" at Xavier would amount precisely to a rimless zero. With a pleased look, she promised to "put them stoopid p'rishioners wise to jus' what's what." And she must have kept that promise, for the following Sunday the offerings noticeably improved. And I breathed again.

Breath came rather faintly at first, with everything still strange. So near was my church to the Mississippi that there, at the foot of the levee, I could feel the Father of Many Waters over my head; and my silent prayer was identical with the title of a popular song of the day, "River, Stay 'Way from My Door." Trees— palm, banana, fig, pecan; flatness of land, in sharp contrast with the hilliness up North; odd blooms, especially magnolias, like blobs of moonlight lost in shadowy leaves; sudden and frequent rainfalls that often left the air warmer rather than cooler; all such details made me feel as the first settlers from far-off lands must have felt. The books about the Deep South that I had skimmed and from which I'd jotted down some notes during my few visits to the New York Public Library, had largely unprepared me for actual, close-up impressions. Charles Dudley Warner, for example, had written that, in old N'Orleans, "everybody carries roses and wears roses, and houses overflow with them"; but not one rose-toting person or rose-crammed corner did I see during that sweltering August. And the assertions, quoted by

Charles Gayarré, that the climate guaranteed an infinitely varied wealth of vegetables all the year round, that soft banks of crystal streams met the gaze at every turn, that dust and mud were wholly excluded, that birds darted everywhere with bright ribbons of song atwirl from their beaks, that even the poor dined royally on ducks, venison, snipes and woodcocks! If all this were so, I'd have had to conclude that I was going blind, for such happy "facts" I could not find. Nor did I observe, as Thomas Asche claimed he did, the whole town promenading the levee or reposing under orange trees. Neither was I quite able to share the ecstasy of Lafcadio Hearn at what he assumed to be the uniqueness of Louisiana's skies: "The mind asks itself if what it beholds is not the Pneuma indeed, the Infinite Breath, the Divine Ghost, the Great Blue Soul of the Unknown."

That there was an abundance of natural beauty hereabouts, I could well admit; but the degree of it seemed to me to have been grossly exaggerated, since fortune had not yet set a pair of pink spectacles on my nose. Those spectacles would never be mine so long as the congregation, for whose liking I longed, remained remote and to be won. And Alice Murray kept saying, "How d'you know what the jelly tastes like till you opens the jar?" Because the jar appeared out of reach, I was downcast and could see myself only as a rank outsider, and repeatedly thought of something I'd already heard down here about the difference between a Yankee and Durnyankee being that the former knew enough to stay where he belonged.

Most of the parishioners lived at a distance; some so far that they had to come by bus. Noticing, on the third Sunday, that the attendance was larger than on the previous two, I sought the cause from Alice Murray, who knew just about everything. She interested me much with the information that I could expect occasional increases according to the way "a 'ticular one of them white pastors" happened to feel and speak. The Sunday before, she said, this " 'ticular" one hadn't been feeling so good and "took it out on the Joanavarkers" who were in the habit of going to his church for convenience. She mimicked him roaring from the pulpit that they should stick to their own church and support it, that their nickels and pennies weren't needed by him, and that a church belonged to those who built it. Did it not belong rather to the Lord to whom the builders presumably had given it, and didn't the Lord welcome all His children anywhere? Glad to have more of my sheep around me, but indignant that any of them should have been hurt, I let Alice Murray know my intention of approaching this pastor and telling him just what I thought.

"Wouldn't do that, Father, if I wuz you," she said, shaking a finger at me. "It wuz swellin' that bust the poutin' pigeon. He talks biggety when his high blood pressure's aworkin' up; but he don't hate us colored, an' many's the good thing he's done f'r us on the sly. We sniff out what's inside a pusson." Her nostrils enlarged and quivered. "We've been doin' it a long time, an' hadta, 'cuz most of us sure want t'get along smooth when we kin. Them that likes eggs has t'keep watch on the hen. Whites—we know'm better'n they know us. We keeps astudyin' them while they keep athinkin' we ain't got a brain under our kink. Love that ole man o' God!—even if he do blow up once in a while an' make us sore. Better leave him be."

I took her advice, but not to the extent of discarding my intention of having a talk with him. When I went, he did not frown me out. On the contrary, he seated me in the softer of the two chairs in his reception room. His blood pressure must have been down to normal that day, and I was determined not to let mine rise. We communed without the least clash. "It worries me," he said, "when I see Negroes crowding the back pews of my church, because I can't help feeling how much they're wanted in the front ones of their own. It's not ideal to have separate congregations, but until the South changes, what can we do? White and black are brothers, but so were Cain and Abel. If these two Biblical boys had lived more apart, so that the one didn't get on the nerves of the other, murder might have been averted." He sucked his lip and changed the subject. "I used to send Father Neifert little donations from time to time to help him out; the sums, as near as I could gauge them, that his parishioners put in my baskets. And I'd like to continue the practice with you. May I?" Gratefully I acquiesced, though I did not approve some of his expressed feelings on other matters. Would the South ever change so long as the *status quo* in race relations continued to be regarded as unchangeable? And was it separation rather than understanding that might have served to prevent the first slaying recorded in Bible history? But later I'd find opportunity to express myself along these lines. Meanwhile, instead of an enemy, I was making, thanks to Alice Murray, a friend. My second.

My third was Archbishop Shaw. In the main room of his residence, as informal as my mother's kitchen in Salem used to be, he directed me mildly. "New down here, and devoted to the Negro, you'll probably be worked up over some of the things you'll see and hear," he said, his old eyes moist, his long thin fingers locking and unlocking; "but don't let yourself slip into a belief that the South is a solid conspiracy to keep the colored miserable." And he drew for me a picture of Dixie problems as he saw them, specifying and commending such agencies as were interested in solutions. He ended by expressing his gratification that Xavier University would now be contributing its light. "Mother Katherine Drexel, the foundress, is a rare soul," he said, "and it's a rare privilege you'll be having, Father, in an association with her."

My first sight of Xavier surpassed my expectation. The handsome Indiana-limestone structure indicated that Mother Katherine deemed charity too beautiful a virtue to be rendered unbeautifully and that she was giving her best to a people who so often received the opposite from others. And the motto cut into the cornerstone soon to be laid was perfect. "God's masterpiece on earth is man. Man's master art is the leading of men to God."

In an office on the second floor, I met Sister Madeleine Sophie, the dean. Every inch an executive, she inspired a faith that this institution would have a healthy and vigorous start and growth. And while we were conversing, Mother Agatha, the president, entered. She was small of stature and gentle as a dove, but so evidently strong with the wisdom that only a blending of experience, dedication, and humility could give. I'd been told by my superior about her innumerable and arduous journeys with Mother Katherine through the missions of the West and South, and could see in her the selflessness of an ideal servant of the Lord. My surmise was that the motto on the cornerstone had been her own personal selection, and I thought of the phrase applied by the angel Gabriel to Mary, "full of grace."

She and Sister Madeleine Sophie led me from the administration building to the convent, and there at last I beheld Mother Katherine Drexel herself. Garbed exactly the same as any of her daughters, she was down on her knees, absorbed in the homely task of measuring a floor for a carpet. And instantly I knew that she considered nothing too small or unimportant to be done earnestly and completely for the Lord. As she rose, her amazingly clear eyes focused on me, and from the depths of them came a gleaming like a lamp in Nazareth. A privilege to be associated with her, as Archbishop Shaw had said? Rather I felt that, next to my priesthood, it was the greatest honor of my life.

Friends. More and more of them! The people of my parish had sniffed, as Alice Murray put it, my yearning to be acceptable to them and my resolution to emulate Father Neifert. They began to gather around me and offer their assistance, and I was getting to know them as I should, not only by sight but, better, by insight. Their economic attitude, despite hard times, included little complaint. As one man said to me, seeming to voice many, "We've lived in a depression since our forefathers were brought over here, and we've learned to manage. Anyhow, we've outlasted the Indians." And I noticed that a few of the more thrifty owned property, some of which was rented even to whites; that white and colored could be found living side by side in some neighborhoods; that certain Negroes had good automobiles, dressed well, and bore themselves with an air. The homes I visited were mostly trim and neat; several, quite attractive, as if from serving and observing the finer families in New Orleans the occupants had acquired much of the art of gracious living. Pianos, radios, and various up-to-date conveniences appeared here and there; and I discovered what seemed to me at the time an astonishing thing, that the underprivileged had their social levels— high, middle, low—just like the privileged. The high spoke quite grammatically and without the least trace of dialect, read the latest books, played bridge, and planned the debuts of their daughters. It did seem to me that they could and should have done more to lift up their many, many far less fortunate brethren, but no doubt the maintenance of their living standards taxed their interest and resources to the limit.

Soon came autumn, and my parish school, an old elongated wooden building on brick stilts, threw open its doors to let in bright-eyed youngsters whose complexions ranged from black to gold. Five Sisters of the Holy Family, a colored order, were there to receive and teach them. The physical condition of the school was bad: shaky piazza, interior beaverboard partitions, shabby desks and benches. But when I apologized to Sister Gilbert, the principal, she smiled and said, "It's Bethlehem. Thabor will come."

From their mother house away down in the French Quarter, my five little nuns daily journeyed, rain or shine, to Joan of Arc by trolley. They did not have to pay carefare, because New Orleans prized all Sisterhoods and granted them special courtesies; but the inconvenience of this back-and-forth routine was considerable, and I longed to build a small convent near the church. They brought their own lunch every day, and though I urged them to use the rectory at noon, they gently declined, preferring a small anteroom in the school and holding to it.

Their "salaries"! Someday somebody will write a treatise on livelihood as exemplified by missionary Sisters, and startle the bigwigs in Washington with the Sermon on the Mount. "Behold the birds of the air, for they neither sow, nor do they reap, nor gather into barns: and your heavenly Father feedeth them." These Holy Family daughters received from my parish only twenty-five dollars per person a month, though the loving zeal that they put into their labor was priceless; but, with the Lord their shepherd, they did not want, and they found in simplicity and frugality the green pastures that "planned economy" has yet to provide.

To raise a trifle of extra money for "a special purpose," they humbly asked permission to sell candy during recess to the children; and they jotted down in a neat notebook every single penny they made. Never mindful of themselves, they were thinking very much of "Father's feast day," which arrived on October the thirteenth, a date that I was never to forget.

At three o'clock that afternoon (or "evening," as they say in the South) when the school bell signaled the close of classes and I was reading my breviary on the rectory porch, a delegation of six boys, their shoes and faces highly polished, came as a guard of honor to escort me across the yard. Entering the school building, I found the hinged beaverboard partitions folded back and the classrooms changed to an auditorium. An audience of pupils and parents were seated and waiting. At a clap from Sister Gilbert, they all rose and broke into a song of greeting, "Happy feast day to you, happy feast day to you, happy feast day, dear Father Murphy"—some of the smaller children pronounced the name "Mercy"—"happy feast day to you-hoo."

Filled with appreciation, I scanned the pleasant scene and spied, to my surprise, a throne up front. An old armchair, which had been borrowed from the rectory that morning, it was now bedecked with colorful twisters and a canopy of crepe paper, and posited on a dais composed of four carpet-covered boxes. My guardians led me to it, each bowing from the waist as I ascended. How different from the day when I'd been shooed out of the Mechanic Hall in Salem! Here I was Monarch Murphy, no less.

The entertainment promptly began and proved to be mostly a

well-prepared series of laudatory little speeches. One small ora-
tor's stocking kept falling down as he delivered a description of
my "wunnerful" efforts to "hold up" (*sic*) the parish. A tiny girl,
staring straight into space with eyes bigger than herself, recited a
poem, "The Beautiful Hands of a Priest." A frail, pretty, sweet-
voiced child in a white veil which was probably intended to suggest the mists of morning or evening, sang a song, "Gently Falls
the Dew"; but the rendition was somewhat marred by the fact
that a head cold caused the tip of her nose slightly but obviously
to illustrate her theme. Then gifts, nicely wrapped in tissue paper,
were presented to me. Heavy with gratitude, I sank back, which
was just the thing I should not have done, for the empty boxes
supporting my grandeur were queasy. Suddenly one of them
collapsed, causing me and the throne to do the same. Down I
went. And as I lay sprawled on the floor in a swirl of crepe paper
and presents, nobody dared laugh.

To relieve the tension, I myself laughed; and immediately
everyone, except Sister Gilbert, at least smiled. Only my dignity,
already lost more than once since my coming to New Orleans,
was hurt.

Helped up by many hands, I thanked everybody for everything and thought the affair was over. But it wasn't. There was
another novelty, more striking even than my downfall. It came in
a final ensemble serenade consisting of the choruses of two well-
known songs, "That Old Irish Mother of Mine" and "Mother
Macree," for which, two weeks before, I had expressed to Sister
Gilbert a particular fondness because my brother Jim used to sing
them so well. And now I could not believe my ears, for the songs
had been super-adapted to the occasion, and what I heard was
"That Old Irish *Father* of Ours" and "Sure I love the dear silver
that shines in your hair, and the brow that's all furrowed and
wrinkled with care. I kiss the dear fingers so toil worn for me-hee.
Oh, God bless you and keep you, Father Murph-ee."

IX

THE big event of that autumn was the dedication of Xavier University. Cardinal Dougherty came down from Philadelphia to preside; many bishops attended; and the whole affair went so well that, as master of ceremonies, I felt fully happy, especially when Mother Katherine Drexel whispered to me her praise and thanks. But that evening when the last guest had gone and the moon was silvering the façade of the new institution committed to the art of leading men to God, joy was driven out of me by a remark which I overheard while standing on a corner to await a bus for home. "That college called Xavier," said a sharp-faced woman who, with another like her, was also waiting, "is a shame. Higher education for Negroes! Robbing us of our servants— that's what I call it."

To open my mouth would have been to blaze at her; so I compressed my lips and edged away, wondering how, with even the least glimmer of common sense, anybody could think for one moment that the local domestic supply was at all threatened by Xavier's enrollment of a mere fistful of students out of a colored population of over a hundred and seventy-five thousand. And why wasn't it evident even to the dimmest wit that the betterment of some Negro minds and hearts could not possibly be a disservice to the community? Ah, the South. . . .

But a fortnight later an expression of thought, or rather thoughtlessness, came likewise from the North. It was a write-up about Xavier in one of those magazines that rate entertainment above truth, and it breezily alleged that these mornings in New Orleans white folk were rubbing their eyes at the spectacle of colored boys and girls on their way with textbooks to cultural heights, and cocking up their ears at wisps of such "typical" conversation as, "Has you-all done yo' Greek yet?"

Vastly unamused, I promptly sat down at the battered typewriter in my rectory and thumped out a letter of complaint to the editor. And soon came his reply, a very polite apology for having offended *my* sensibilities.

I now ached to have the truth safeguarded from nonsense. Really known, Xavier's work could not but be widely appreciated. If others were brought to see what I was daily seeing!— the pathos of decent Negroes struggling upward for a little extra light and air in a land of liberty; the help, like a clasp from the hand of Christ, that Mother Katherine and her Sisters of the Blessed Sacrament were giving, and the example they were setting; the Gospel really being lived. And I wanted to shout from the housetops but chose rather to become acquainted with some of the religious leaders of the white laity in town, so as to share a lesson with them. What could they do after the sharing? At least, I thought, they could tell their followers the facts and inspire some Christian courtesy. Until good morals should prevail in race relations, good manners might suffice; yes, and even before long induce a degree of charity and justice. How boorish to look down on any human creatures instead of sympathetically helping them to rise! How inferiorly the superior class acted, in flaunting their status! True superiority implied breeding, and breeding, to be proved, required politeness. The Dixie dogma that the Negro must be kept in his place took it for granted that the place was under the white man's heel; that the brotherhood of men, alluring as a principle, was impossible as a practice; and that simple Christianity, under certain circumstances, was social peril. Oh, I was long on emotion in those first days of my enterprise, and short on a knowledge of the finer elements in the South. I sensed the color line vividly, but not so well the tendrils of natural kindliness that crept over it in spite of everything. I was determined to establish a standard, as if no one besides

Mother Katherine and a few missionary Fathers and Sisters had ever thought of doing so before.

Miss Elsie Vulliet, a very intelligent and active sodalist who, I later learned, had been helping the poor since her childhood days, was one of my best listeners, and she promised to do what she could toward promoting my courtesy program. Miss Patricia Toye, a whole-souled person, stirred her family to great interest. Soon many others visited Xavier, studied the life there, became friends with our faculty and students, and went forth to spread a goodly enthusiasm. The miniature movement caused me to think in terms of the parable of the tiny mustard seed that became a great tree.

How badly some intercommunion was needed! Deeply religious by nature, but handicapped by segregation, Negroes had to depend mostly on their own meager resources in developing their forms of worship; and I quickly became aware of certain effects of this situation. The awareness was keen one morning when somebody phoned to inquire, "Are you the pastor of a real zigaboo church?" I acknowledged my position with pride but sternly denied that there was any such thing as that kind of church. "Oh, but there is," came the reply, "even if your voice does sound so white. I've been told by a bellhop in my hotel that the best show in town is those revival meetings, and my wife and I want to see one before we leave so we'll have something to tell the neighbors when we get back up to Chi. How about it, Parson? If there's nothing doing in your place tonight, won't you tell us where'll we find a regular coon-shouting service? We'd really appreciate it."

I banged the receiver on the hook and, turning around, tried to relieve my disgust by expressing it to Alice Murray, who was feather-dusting my office at the moment. She manifested no surprise. "Mother Catherine Seals's Church o' the Innercent Blood —that's the kind that man wants," she said.

Curious, I asked many questions and learned that "Mother Catherine Seals," lately deceased but still carrying on through a lively successor known as "Mother Rita," had had quite a story. . . .

Literally the story started with a punch, her no-account third husband beating her into a semiparalyzed state from which she tried in vain to be restored by one "Brother Isaiah," whose specialty was the laying on of hands—but only on whites!—along the levee. So she resolved to shame this highly prejudiced holy man by getting herself cured directly from above and then spreading the tidings that "this here Brother 'Saiah—him!—ain't so many." Accordingly, she lost herself in "the Lawd God Jehovia" and eventually did feel "whole" and ready for action. "I ain't like that evil wretch 'Saiah," she proclaimed, "bein' as I heals all colors."

Without a single adherent she somehow built a "manger" on a vacant lot and achieved an atmosphere of mystery by enclosing it with a high fence which, apparently designed to keep people out, fired them with an eagerness to get in. Started with nobody, the "manger" soon could boast a congregation of hundreds; and there was a good prospect of many more, because she mothered all comers "jus' like home," providing feast tables at which holy lemonade was served in hot weather, and holy coffee in winter, and a dosage of holy castor oil—"anointin' the innards," she called it—for each and every communicant whenever she felt like administering it. And most of the dosed ones had to admit that, except for first impressions, this part of the "worshipin'" did much good.

When officiating, she wore white robes, which caused her to look larger than she was and added much to her appeal; and usually she took off her shoes, expressly for the reason that "the Lawd didn't wear'm," but probably to give her flat and heavy feet some comfort. And hers was no ordinary entrance at meetings: assisted by a select number of the faithful to ascend a side ladder, she would come down through a hole in the roof of the "manger," shedding benedictions and smiles "jus' like the Holy Ghost hisself." She never preached from the Bible but only on "facts," and always so strenuously that her sermons were describable as "rockin' Jerusalem." After the oratory she would proceed majestically to the despised "Brother 'Saiah's" own ritual of the imposition of hands.

For her "cures" she asked no money, but often pointed a meaningful finger at the poor box whence she derived her support, and it was said that, on set occasions, she had the congregation come forth to pin their offerings on her—a device which automatically eliminated mere coins. Sometimes the pure white of her robes would be decorated from neck to hem with beautiful green.

Though I smiled when I heard all this from Alice Murray, I sighed too. In different circumstances, this Mother Catherine Seals might have led many of her people out of the old bog of superstition, emotionalism, and grotesquerie, instead of into it. That her natural gifts had been many and her desire to do good great seemed even clearer to me from the study I soon took the trouble to make. And, while making it, I became well acquainted with several other queer churches like hers, where the poor, hungering for the Bread of Life, were being fed with crumbs and crusts of absurdity.

Surely the remedy—and *atonement*—was more education and less isolation. And I thanked God for Mother Katherine Drexel, the Sisters of the Blessed Sacrament, the Josephite and the Holy Ghost Fathers, the Vincentians, the diocesan clergy, and all the other inducers, Protestant and Jewish as well as Catholic, of a better day and a better deal for Negroes in New Orleans.

X

ALONG with many consolations, I was incurring some difficulties in my own worthy but very human congregation. For one thing, I found that to have an especially good friend among them was to be guaranteed two or three comparative enemies. The especially good friend saw to that. It was an easy process. Proud of being close to their pastor and inclined not only to demonstrate but safeguard the distinction, he or she would contrive to keep others away, and usually a word dropped here and there sufficed. *Father doesn't like this sort of person or that*. Then Father, until he finally caught on, had to wonder why this-sort-of-person-or-that didn't like him.

Another disturbing factor lay in a tendency of every parish meeting to be two. Under the eye of authority the people were normally docile; beyond it, they easily swung into a state of being pretty much themselves. The way I saw it, suppression, as an unremitting condition, had forced them into the habit of external conformity with white will; but away from the range of that will, they were inclined to vent the passion for freedom that burns in every man, whatever his complexion. After I'd return to my rectory from a meeting and try to read my breviary, voices sounding off in the street would distract me. I'd hope against hope that the debaters would disperse and quietly go home, but I never went out to bid them do so.

Nor did my parishioners always restrain themselves in my presence. For instance, there was the night when the committee for our Fall Festival convened to lay final plans. It was decided that ten baskets of groceries be raffled off as a feature of the affair. Good enough. But then came a division of opinion, some thinking that the baskets should be purchased from a certain colored widow who, modestly in business to support her large brood, needed all the patronage she could get, and others maintaining that a certain white grocer, who had liberally contributed to many a parochial need in the past, must be favored. It was a choice between charity and gratitude, and somehow these germane virtues were being taken as opposite sides of a fence. A huge discussion arose and got hotter and hotter. Called upon by the chairman for my opinion, I cleared my throat and, more amused than dismayed at the tremendousness of a trifle, proceeded to throw oil *à la* Solomon on the troubled waters, little thinking that, in exactly no time, I'd be taking Mother Catherine Seals's estimate of Brother Isaiah—"He ain't so many"—as a fair summation of Solomon himself. Just as the famed Jewish king readily settled the dispute of two females over a child by offering to slice the little one with an impartial sword and let each have half, I now suggested that instead of buying all ten baskets from either the colored woman or the white man, an order for five apiece be placed. What could have been simpler? I smiled, believing that the dove of peace had descended. But immediately the storm broke out all over again, twice as loud. Such argumentation had never assaulted my ears before, and, beaten, I departed to await the return of calm. For at least an hour the echoes of the tumult rolled across the schoolyard to the rectory, causing me to conclude that, withheld from the right to express themselves on important concerns in the community, Negroes could not but let forth a Niagara of accumulated feeling on minor matters in their own group.

And their occasional obliqueness of attitude!—possibly the effect of their having to dodge so many blows in a society arrayed against them. Even when something was conceived solely in their interest, they were inclined to be antagonistic on the ground that something else, more suitable, could have been undertaken. I first discovered this tendency when I scraped together enough means to decorate the sanctuary of St. Joan of Arc so as to render my

congregation's Christmas bright and attractive. This would be
my gift to them, and I reveled in the anticipation of their joy.
Through the week preceding the great day I supervised and sped
the work of tinting the plain white concave wall a warm sky-blue
and powdering it with stars, and nearly broke my neck hoisting a
heavy statue of the Maid of Orleans from a corner to a glorified
position above the tabernacle. On the eve of the Nativity, I
personally heaped the high altar with flaming poinsettias, slipping
off a stool in the act and wrenching a vertebra. But when I threw
open the doors for midnight Mass, my satisfaction was supreme,
for the combination of candlelight and color showed heavenly,
and it seemed certain to me that no other church could excel ours.
How everybody would respond! How my hand would be
wrung! *Humph.* Not a single face lit up, and throughout the
services I had a feeling almost of aloneness.

As for the Christmas collection, customarily the largest of the
year, it was the smallest in the history of the parish, and I could
not conceive why until Alice Murray told me. "They think," she
said, "that what was good 'nough f'r Father Neifert is good
'nough f'r them, an' that it's a new school we're aneedin', not a
fixed-up old church. But don't pay'm no mind. If y'all did somethin' f'r the school, they'd be agrumblin' how it oughta be f'r the
church instead. They like grumblin'. Makes'm feel somebodyish."

And how easily a valued friendship could be impaired! Somehow I offended, of all people, Sister Gilbert, the principal of the
school, whose co-operation was as complete as it was comforting.
When spring came to us, preparations for Confirmation began,
and with her usual zeal and flair, she attended to the special catechism priming. Some of the boys and girls who were to be confirmed had passed on from Joan of Arc grammar to the high
school of the Blessed Sacrament nuns in another section of the
town, and she thought that since they still belonged to Joan of
Arc spiritually, they should be given their final instructions here
on the home ground. However, the principal of the high school
phoned to tell me that it would be inconvenient to release pupils

from class for Sister Gilbert's purpose and to beg me not to require this. Knowing what a fine religious training the high school afforded, I assured her that such a transfer would not be necessary, and considered the matter closed. But the following morning Sister Gilbert, quite upset, came to me with her first complaint. She had just heard, via the grapevine that flourishes in every parish, about my having made "exceptions," and wanted to know if it implied a lack of confidence in her efforts. Earnestly I told her that this was not so, but to little avail. Lips quivering, she left the room, and from that day on, though her service to Joan of Arc did not diminish, she never seemed the same.

But the joys of missionary work exceeded the sorrows. And a special consolation came to me from a group of colored nuns who lived in a little house on Apricot Street and did all the cooking and cleaning for the diocesan seminary which was Archbishop Shaw's pride. Appointed their confessor, I'd visit them every week; and my ghostly chore seemed comparable to the washing of spotless linen, for there was not a blemish in their hearts. Renewed with the grace they had never lost, they would invite me to their modest reception room and refresh me with coffee, as if just to be near them were not stimulation enough. These Marthas, winning heaven with skillet and dishrag, would sit, Mary-like, around me to receive my merest utterance as something precious, inflaming my desire to be a perfect priest with their belief that I already was. I gave them my best, but sometimes the raptness of their attention embarrassed me, because they were so far advanced in the spiritual life that I wanted rather to listen to them and learn; and then, my mind groping, my tongue faltering, I'd deliver platitudes. Always, as I left, I longed for some of their rare merit and chided myself for not having read and meditated enough to be better fitted to direct them.

One morning when I chanced to meet one of them in the vestibule of St. Louis Cathedral, her eyes shone as she said to me, "Father, I simply can't find words to thank you for the inspired conferences you give us. You said something a month ago that's buoyed me up ever since. I'll cherish it till I die." Her countenance grew yet more luminous, and I more than wanted to know just what utterance of mine had meant so much. "Tell me, please," I urged, expecting "a gem of purest ray serene" to be returned to me. With a break in her voice and an evident thrill in her being, she obliged. "You said"—she stressed each word—"that every cloud has a silver lining."

Then there was the Convent of the Holy Family on Orleans Street in the French Quarter, which affected me like a replica of Bethany. Not that it had any hint of Bethany in its background. Quite the contrary, it once fostered considerable excess, having been the scene of the Octoroon balls at which "Creole" mothers made certain unpretty "arrangements" for their pretty daughters; and tragedy was known to have loomed on the winding central stairway and hurled a man over the banister to his death. But such an inviting old stairway, for all that, with so soft an upswing as to leave the ascender less conscious of effort than ease. Extra broad it was, like the way to perdition. And now this former haunt of scandal, standing only a stone's throw from a little garden behind St. Louis Cathedral, had become a house of prayer! When, forgetting the brothel opposite St. Joseph's Seminary in Baltimore, I happened to express to a senior Orleanian priest my surprise that immorality could have ever flourished so near sacredness, he startled me by saying, "It still does. 'Wherever God erects a house of prayer, the Devil always builds a chapel there.'"

But the Holy Family Convent was a counterevidence that at the divine touch anything can turn holy, just as the soul of a great sinner, the Magdalen, became that of a great saint. And within this retreat, purged by rule and idealism, the spirit of Bethany truly reigned. From Mother Elizabeth, the superioress, to Sister Vincent, who was old and deaf and tended the door, the greater love seemed to weave a rosary of remarkable examples; and the most remarkable was Sister Rosary herself. Many a poem might have been written by a Crashaw or a Donne about this particular nun. On my very first visit to the convent I was conducted by Sister Vincent to the infirmary; and there, in the plainest of beds, the most cheerful of patients lay, peace radiating from her and shedding its blessed contagion, though Sister Vincent had whispered to me, "She's in constant pain."

Sister Rosary's story was simple. She had labored long in the Vineyard, training young vines to creep up on props of moral principle. One day, as she was hanging a holy picture, the wire broke and a corner of the frame struck her chest. Someone warned her that a picture fallen from a wall signifies death, but she only smiled. Gradually, the little injury developed into a malignant cancer nestling near the heart and reaching with tentacles toward the throat. "If it will only spare my face, Father!" she said whimsically yet seriously. "I've never been beautiful, and I don't want to be seen any worse." Strong, sensitive soul. No personal cross seemed too great for her, but to cause even the least degree of unpleasantness for others would have been unbearable. She little realized the deeper, better beauty that had come to be hers and was rendering a bedside almost as magnetic to the community as the tabernacle itself. "She's our treasure," Mother Elizabeth told me, "because she's made her affliction her jewel and she's offering it to God for all of us. St. Teresa used to say that every convent should have at least one sick Sister, in order that, caring for her, all might be schooled in charity; but Rosary is not only an occasion, she's a cause of our spiritual betterment."

Only once during her unremitting trial did a moan escape Sister Rosary's lips; and she performed a special penance, known only to the Lord and myself, in atonement for it. That moan sounded on the day when her agony, having at last victimized all her frame and most of her flesh, caused her right thigh bone to break. And even then it was less the torment in her body than the stab in her spirit that hurt, for she knew the time was near for leaving those whom she cherished more than life.

I had seen Calvary mingled with Nazareth in that infirmary

where she lay, and a gleam of Thabor from her consecration and patience will brighten my memory till the time of my own ending.

To share my joys and sorrows—and indeed to increase them—a fellow Josephite now came to assist me. His name was Conahan, but the smaller schoolchildren pronounced it "Commonham." With the freshness of his ordination still in him, he began like a bayou breeze. Just as the arrival of Father Rebescher at old St. Barnabas in Baltimore, when élan was so badly needed, changed things overnight, so did that of this young priest at Joan of Arc here in New Orleans bring verve and tone. He did not have to win the people; they clustered around him like bees on a honeycomb. And not only was he thrice welcome in the parish but also in Xavier, where, like myself, he was appointed by our superior to teach. It took me two whole weeks to discover, and even then I only suspected, that his merit was not yet infinite. The suspicion, which I strenuously tried to resist, first seized me when he declared, "We must make Xavier the Negro Notre Dame. A great football team—that's the thing!" Medieval me, thinking that "the thing" in an institution of higher learning was *higher learning!*

He taught brilliantly. At least I thought so until the day when one of the students said to me, "Father Conahan makes us laugh and laugh in philosophy!" And then I wasn't so sure, having been and still being convinced that though philosophy and fun are good, they go no better together than salt and sugar. But I said nothing and watched my assistant flourishing. There was not the slightest doubt that he had a heart of gold and warmth enough for not only one institution but two or three. Whenever he appeared on the campus, he was the center of it; and he had only to step into the auditorium to receive a salvo from any assembly. At the bedside of the sick he could and did put me to envy and shame. One night when we found a woman apparently dead, he breathed some of his own life into her until she recovered sufficiently to receive the Last Sacraments. And once I saw him as an agent of what certainly seemed a miracle. It was during a visit to the Charity Hospital, when we came upon a colored patient whose body might have been described as a huge suppurating sore. Having in his pocket a relic of Teresa Helena Higginson, which Mother Mary of Grace at Xavier had given him, he pinned it on the gown of the sufferer; and two days later, when we returned, the terrible skin had become petal-smooth and clear. After that I was disposed to venerate him; but he disliked being aureoled and missed no opportunity to indicate that he was just as ordinary as "the least of these his brethren." In fact, he carried this attitude to such an extent that I vaguely wondered whether there was a touch of pride in so much humility.

He gave to the poor every cent he could spare, which was very noble of him. But then he would also give away every cent that I couldn't spare, which was not even considerate, in as much as bills had to be paid and the depression was still making our income look as skinny as a half-starved chick. We had a custom of setting aside for charity a portion of our Sunday collections, which averaged at this time about twenty-five dollars, and I groaned at the realization that even if I handed the whole weekly amount over to him, by Monday noon it would have been gone. "God is rich," he'd say, "and we shall not want." But this did not soothe me, for it sounded less like piety than presumption, the kind that Father Duffy had demonstrated when he borrowed five hundred dollars from the bank in Newburgh and based his ability to pay it back on a confidence that his well-to-do aunt would soon be dropping her money bags and assuming wings. "If you had the responsibility of being pastor, you'd serve the poor more discriminately," I'd force myself to rebuke him. After reminding me, however, that one of the responsibilities of a pastor is the relief of the poor, and forgetting that his own largess left me little to be lavish with, he would deftly restore my good humor by bringing up a certain episode which was always good for a grin between us.

One afternoon as he and I were walking on Baronne Street a sere old beggar woman stopped us and soulfully murmured to me, "You look like the Savior." Touched deeply, I gave her all my money—two nickels and ten pennies. But a few days later, when we were in the same vicinity, she accosted us again, this time with an alcoholic haze in her eyes and a definite slump in her technique. "You," she huskily wheedled, waving a dirty hang-nailed finger under my nose, "look like Huey P. Long."

Or he would remind me glibly of yet another indication that I was a better preacher than practicer of prudence in giving. This episode occurred on a morning when I was leaving the rectory for Xavier. Out on the sidewalk an undersized Uncle Tom coz-ened up to me with a tale of woe. The night before his one-room "lean-to" on the levee had caught fire and his wife had been burned to death. He lacked all means to defray the expenses of her funeral. "Look, Father, what a fix I'm in," he tremoloed, lift-ing with a crusty hand a leg of his threadbare trousers to expose a black-red lesion through which a section of bone glistened. "I got burnt too in tryin' t' save her. It's worse in other—private—parts. Wanna see?" Abrim with horror and pity, I ran back into the house and emptied the cash box. Then, returning in a flash, I poured a stream of coins into the cup of his palms, expecting a "God bless you," but getting not even a "Thanks." "Doctors 'n funerals cost a heap," he whimpered. Almost apologetically I told him I had no more. Then suddenly I remembered that I'd put carfare in my vest pocket; so deciding to walk or thumb a ride, I let him have that too. Still no expression of appreciation came. Well, why should grief and gratitude go together? Bidding him come back around noon, and promising to find some further help in the meantime, I hurried off to my classes. Father Conahan met me brightly at Xavier; and though I hated to kill that smile of his which was so becoming, I told him all. To my surprise and disgust, he beamed. "So he rooked you too," he said. "Why, Ed, he's a professional. Been covering the town with that trumped-up gag of his for years. It's a meal ticket. The sore on his leg—it's the remains of an old disease, and he keeps it open with acid. The police know him well. One of them put me wise. They've arrested him many times, but they kind of like his spunk and always let him go with nothing worse than a don't-let-us-catch-you-again. Well, you were an easy mark for him. Me too. Let's face it, we're a couple of God's gullibles. But that's better than being the Devil's smarties, eh?"

He was so right. Yet, readily fooled by others, one readily fools one's self.

A great believer in the value of extracurricular activities for Xavier, Father Conahan soon prevailed on Sister Madeleine Sophie, the dean, to let him develop a football team according to his own plan. She had no way of conceiving how large that plan was until a brigade of huskies, wooed from all over the South with promises of paradise, broke into view. They looked like higher education in reverse; and what to do with them was an immediate problem, for they had no money and Xavier had no dormitory. But here they were; and even if we tried to send them away, they couldn't go. Like Robinson Crusoe building a boat too large to be launched, my assistant had outdone himself. His faith, however, removed from his consciousness the mountains he had created; and, as cocky as a child buying ice-cream cones for all the kids and charging it up to Pop, he leased a whole house on nothing, furnished it on less, rubbed his hands gleefully, and thought only of the "profits" that would soon be "simply rolling in" to pay for everything. There was no stopping his flow of imagination and optimism in this matter; and if it were not for Mother Katherine Drexel's quiet decision to accept the situation and make the best of it, he himself might have been removed along with his mountains.

As it was, we found ourselves holding a tiger by the tail; and, as tigers will, this one swung us every which way and got us nowhere. We lost game after game that season and won only an excellent prospect of doing the same the next. But Father Conahan did not see it this way. "We're heading for the top," he enthused. And when I presumed to inquire whether wholesale defeat indicated the top, he loftily replied, "But look at the teams that beat us. Some of the biggest and best in Negro football!"

I threw up my hands and almost ran to my copy of Newman's *Idea of a University*. But I didn't give it more than a glance. What good? Conahan's "Idea of a Football Team" was the thing.

Now committed, willy-nilly, to the quest of pigskin prestige, Xavier tried earnestly not to let this interfere with "the art of leading men to God" but rather promote it. And well I remember the day when the dean, just as the bell was ringing for assembly, requested me to address the students on the queerest of subjects, "Athletics and Spiritual Values." I had to think fast, because it was now hard, with my youth far behind me, to associate the two or even consider them associable. It seemed to me that they were as much apart in the scheme of culture as the brawn of Hercules from the brain of Plato. To be sure, physical prowess was praiseworthy and desirable, but that was all. I did not want to say this, though, to the student body.

It so happened that I didn't need to say it; for thinking hard as well as fast, I began to see that the dean's suggestion was not extreme. Weren't all saints, even the most delicate and exquisite, athletes of the Lord? What proofs! Mary with a sword of sorrow in her heart, dying a hundred deaths at the foot of the Cross; the Magdalen fighting the world, the flesh, and the Devil; Sebastian peppered with Nubian arrows; Lawrence on the white-hot gridiron, asking only to be turned over; Joan of Arc in flames; Father Jogues among the Iroquois; Father Damien in Molokai; Sister Rosary with her cancer; Mother Katherine Drexel herself, so gently reared, journeying to harsh places and becoming poorer than the poor she relieved.

With such thoughts, I spoke fervently that morning and convinced not only my audience but myself.

Because Father Conahan was attending to one phase of the life of Xavier, I now felt an urge to contribute a special effort of my own to some other. One day between classes I sat at the grand piano in the auditorium and, stroking the keys, felt pleased with a tune taking shape. Jimmy Faustina, a smart-looking freshman in a white yellow-lettered jersey, chanced to be near. "That's catchy, Father. What's it called?" he said. "Nothing—yet," I answered, smiling, "but suppose you give it a name." He closed his eyes and listened more intently, his face brightening as I struck a few notes faintly reminiscent of Debussy's "Claire de Lune." "I'd call it 'Moonlight Time in New Orleans,'" he murmured. "All right," I said. "Now think up some words for the tune." He whipped out his fountain pen and, leaning on the piano, diligently wrote in his biology notebook:

> *Moonlight time in New Orleans,*
> *Mississippi dreaming in the beams,*
> *Everything is sweetness, so it seems,*
> *In New Orleans.*
> *Banjoes strum a silvery tune,*
> *And the crickets hum a song of June,*
> *And the breezes whisper, 'Wedding soon,'*
> *In New Orleans.*
> *Ah-h, life is like wine,*
> *Ah-h, love is divine,*
> *Ah-h, Dixie eyes shine!*
> *I am yours, and you are mine.*
> *While the Mississippi flows*
> *All my love for you just grows and grows.*
> *Ask the smiling old man moon—he knows*
> *His New Orleans.*

I commented that this was not so bad as "Yes, We Have No Bananas," nor so good as "Shine On Harvest Moon." And since there was no one around, I suggested that we try it with the music.

He had a pleasant baritone. And while we were duetting, three or four students strolled in to listen. Soon their feet were tapping out a perfect rhythm to the melody, and their voices were harmonizing with Jimmy's so acceptably that I started thinking of Eddie Dowling's musicals and envisaging a stageful of Xavier performers. A revue might be easy to do, because of the potpourri nature of the thing. Any kind of talent could be used. Why not try it?

The project grew like Topsy. There was no need of my composing any more music, for Al Allegreto, a freshman like Jimmy, came forth with some original songs, every one of which seemed good, though such titles as "I See Red When I'm Blue" and "Just the Softest Push and I'd Fall Right Hard for You" gave me pause. Nor did I have to write any sketches, for I found that the boys had thought up and jotted down not a few. As for an orchestra, Xavier already boasted an energetic outfit called the Yellow Jackets. Dance numbers? There was a young man in our midst who, expert at all kinds of stepping because of his tuition-earning stints in various nightclubs, gladly offered to direct them. Costumes? The girls could use their party dresses, and the boys their best suits. Scenery? The stage of our auditorium had monk's-cloth drapes and a good lighting system, and these would be sufficient for some Elizabethan, simple effects. So in no time rehearsals were rolling along, and enthusiasm mounting; and then we posted signs all over the colored sections of the city. WATCH FOR THE NEWEST THING IN NEW ORLEANS—"THE FOOTLIGHT PARADE."

The night we opened success appeared certain from the start. The hall, filled to overflowing, broke into applause when the velvet curtains, parting to a lively yet dreamy arrangement of "Moonlight Time," revealed a group of our girls, each as pretty as a peony, and our boys—every last one of them trig and dapper. Songs, sketches, and specialties, all well arranged, fully rehearsed, and smartly delivered, kept the audience as happy as a kindergarten just let out. There was not a single real hitch in the whole affair—until the finale.

I had conceived this finale as something different from the rest of the show, a wedding scene in which the entire cast would saunter forth, with our soprano and tenor as the bridal pair, to render the lullaby from Mendelssohn's "Midsummer Night's Dream." And now the number was on. Standing backstage, mopping my brow, I heaved a sigh of relief and congratulated myself that everything had gone off perfectly, except for one of the dancers performing vigorously enough to snap his belt and have trouble with his trousers, and one of the girls throwing herself so strenuously into her part that she almost fainted. But suddenly there was a roar of laughter, instead of an expected purr of admiration. What could it mean?

Peering from the wings, I saw something which Jimmy Faustina, plainly having presumed on the leeway I'd given him throughout rehearsals because of his helpfulness, had conceived at the last minute and dared to insert without consulting me. Directly behind the bride—blond enough to pass for white—and the very dark groom, Jimmy was stalking and frowning exaggeratedly. Talcum-powdered and gray-goateed, he looked quite like a Dixie colonel, and in his right fist he was holding vertical and firm—a *shotgun*.

The satire of the thing—the very idea of a southern colonel forcing his daughter to marry a Negro—simply "made" *Footlight Parade*. But it almost "unmade" me.

Flatly I eliminated Jimmy and his weapon from all subsequent performances, of which, by popular demand, there were many. The Pittsburgh *Courier*—national Negro weekly—and the local Negro press gave the show a great rating. But I was not happy. The whole thing, I thought, seemed to miss the standards set for Xavier. In encouraging the native talents of the performers, I had perhaps imposed too little restraint and permitted too much exuberance. It seemed to me that the effect was more frothy than substantial; and now I, who in the beginning had smiled at the spiritualizing of football in Xavier, frowned on my own attempt to do the same thing for song and dance. True, I recalled that Eve Lavallière, the great Parisian actress-convert, had once said,

"It was by the way of the Devil that I came to God," but certainly it was for me, as a co-operator with Mother Katherine, to exercise scrupulous care in the training of Xavierites. Well, fortunately I'd insisted on the inclusion of two or three purely cultural features in the "Parade," and one of these, the sextette from *Lucia*, was so elegantly sung that it almost redeemed, in my estimation, the whole. And it gave Xavier an idea. Why couldn't an entire opera be produced? Sister Elise, in charge of our music department, had a glorious voice, and with her patience, skill and persistence might well bring glory out of other voices.

In that highly experimental period of Xavier's existence, any idea was apt to have a tryout; and the next thing I knew, an English version of Gounod's *Faust* was being undertaken. Sister Elise and her students struggled hard with the score, but as the date for the presentation approached, they saw that if they were to be at all ready some of it would have to be recited rather than sung. And too little time remained for polishing the acting. Hence it was a unique *Faust* that finally unfolded. Our Mephistopheles was so very Mephistophelean as he flounced his cloak of scarlet all over the stage that one child in the audience screamed with fright and another with glee. The love scenes, antiseptically coached, were as cool as a stepmother's kiss. But our Marguerite sang most sweetly, her high notes suggesting to us so many silver bubbles unsprayed by a fountain. Yet just as a poem is ruined by one touch of prose, her performance fell from grace when a character in doublet and tights—guess who!—burst too soon into her tirra-larra-ing and brought it to an abrupt close with a bald command and question, "Cease! How long has this been going on?"

An *Item* reporter, sitting beside me in the front row, pressed his knuckles to his lips. But the following day he let his mirth explode in his review, and Mother Agatha, our president, came to me to suggest that I call him up and tell him how Xavier felt. "He should not have expected perfection in our very first attempt at a work so difficult and ambitious as *Faust*," she said. As far as

I could see, he had not expected perfection; but Mother, kindness itself, was hurt because her children were hurt, and it was all too easy for me, who had dismissed the criticism with a smile, to share the attitude. So I phoned the offender and delivered a rebuke. "But, Father, be fair," he said. "You must admit that the 'Cease' in the middle of an aria was funny." Coughing, I hung up the receiver. "And what did he say?" asked Mother. "I don't think we'll have any more trouble with him," I murmured evasively, "if our next opera is *entirely* sung."

Our next was indeed entirely sung, and our next after that. *Carmen, Oberon, Mignon, Tales of Hoffman,* and another *Faust:* all were seasonally presented, and so successfully that the memory of the first offering faded to nothing, and the colored of New Orleans were proud, and the great Metropolitan up North took notice of the contribution that Xavier was making to storied song.

Our only setback came as an oblique effect of our merit. It involved us when the director of a white choral group in town visited Sister Elise with a request, since so many singers had been excellently trained by her, for a number of them to render the Ethiopian Chorus in his forthcoming production of *Aïda* at the Municipal Auditorium. The soul of co-operation, she readily agreed and lost no time in readying her selectees. However, when one of the patrons of the opera heard that "black voices" were to ring from the same stage with white, he protested and threatened to withdraw his support. The invitation to Xavier was canceled.

But Xavier, now big and strong, merely smiled, and in due course Sister Elise put on her own production of *Aïda.* Superlatively done, it was one of the neatest demonstrations of the value of turning the other cheek that I had ever seen. And when critics lavished their praise, I seized my opportunity to instill in the students a lesson that the best answer to humiliation is to use it as a stimulus to such achievement as places one beyond or above it.

Meanwhile, the head man of the Negro Associated Press, visiting New Orleans, confided to me his desire to have his wife, a noted diva, appear in a concert at the Municipal Auditorium. Upon inquiring, I learned that Negro artists might be presented there, but only under white auspices; and what white auspices could be found for Negro talent, except in the unique case of a Marian Anderson? So, as a missionary with the welfare and dignity of the colored at heart, I went to some of the civic leaders. But at the same time a colored committee, of whom I was unaware, got busy and launched an attempt to sue the city and force its hand. The suit was soon thrown out of court. Nevertheless, neither the committee's procedure nor mine quite failed, for the result was a somewhat clearer realization in town that Negro taxpayers were entitled to more consideration in the matter of tax-supported institutions. Before long they were to be provided a hall of their own, with modern décor, air-conditioning, indirect lighting, perfect acoustics, and first-rate fixtures. Same old separatism, but in an attractive guise and not without a measure of well-meaning. And, trying to appreciate any progress, however small, I wished that I could forget the cotton-field proverb which Alice Murray often muttered, "Foot ain't no good without leg t'hang it to."

Athletics and grand opera having been assimilated by Xavier into the purpose of "leading men to God," I began to think how much more assimilable a sacred play would be. The holy season of Lent was approaching, and soon the Mardi Gras gaiety of New Orleans would be giving way to ashes, introspection, and supplication. *Mea culpa, mea culpa, mea maxima culpa.* One night when the moon was misty pale, like a holy penitent's veiled face, and the wind was sighing with the very music of Francis Thompson's "Hound of Heaven," I found myself pondering something that Father Conahan and I had recently experienced, something that seemed part of the peculiar warp and woof of this old city in which vice and virtue kept weaving an intricate design.

He and I had become acquainted with a silver-pink lady who liked to visit our church and leave flowers for the altar. She invited us to her home for dinner, and we gladly accepted, because Narcisse, our cook, was not doing too well by our stomachs. The excellent meal our new friend provided appeared on such ornate dishes that we wondered somewhat, for she was a person of quiet taste, and any showiness did not seem in keeping. She urged us to come again and, if we wished, bring others. The next day while talking with a fellow priest who, as a native, knew the town and its background thoroughly, we told him about the dinner, the dishes, and the lady; he looked so strange that our curiosity was aroused. Had he met her himself? Was there anything wrong? Hesitantly he enlightened us. "Nothing's wrong—now," he said, "but there was a time when nothing was right. She's come a long way. Used to run a 'house' in the Quarter. Those fancy dishes are probably all that's left of her past." And as I listened to him, the ancient story of Mary Magdalen seemed as recurrent as dawn— as modern as tomorrow.

Sitting at my desk in Joan of Arc rectory that misty-mooned night, I recalled Bourdaloue's striking observation that the Magdalen's vice consisted in her having had many lovers and her virtue in her having loved much. Almost without realizing it, I took pen and paper and began to write. Before twelve o'clock a fairly satisfactory outline of a Lenten play lay before me. With my imagination and inventiveness exhausted, I named it simply *Mary of Magdala*.

On Passion Sunday the play was ready for its first showing at Xavier, and hopes soared. Charlotte McGaffey, a beautiful and talented sophomore, was just right for the leading role. All the members of the cast had received Holy Communion that morning and had gone down on their knees before the curtain rose that afternoon, because I'd impressed upon them that this was to be not a play with a message, but a message with a play. Perhaps I overimpressed. Nearly everyone acted his or her part to the hilt; and Archie Lescene, as Peter, threw out such a wave of grief in a post-Calvary scene that, fallen at the feet of Mother Mary, he looked as though he was unable to get up. Even for a soulful portrayal this was going too far; and impatient at his lack of restraint, I myself, staring at him from the wings, lost control. "Stop it! stop it," I hissed. The small sound must have carried to the audience, for somebody, overcome by the pathos of Peter, gave a countercommand: "Let'm go on. He's *good*." At that somebody else tittered nervously, and then came a ripple of general amusement. A pox on Peter and his paroxysm! *Mary of Magdala* was ruined.

But Archie, suffering an artistic hang-over, continued his acting even after the final curtain fell and the audience departed in a drizzle of April rain. This I could see with a weary glance from a backstage window. There he was, pacing in caged-lion fashion up and down a segment of the campus, his false beard limp, his shoulders drooped, his robe clinging damply to him. And raising the window, I called, "Come in out of there, you!" He turned his drawn face to me, shot his clenched fists dramatically up in air, and, very vibrato, declaimed, "I spoiled everything! Everything!" My impulse was to reply bitterly, "You certainly did," but I said, "If you don't hurry in from the rain, you'll spoil that costume." And two minutes later I had him to myself for a lecture in which I compared emotionalism to a flame, and drew the lesson that, properly furnaced, fire warms a house but outside of such confines destroys it. He listened docilely. And during our other performances of *Mary of Magdala* he exercised just the right degree of restraint, acquitting himself with distinction.

Today he is a very successful barrister; and when he recently delivered a baccalaureate address at Xavier, all his hearers agreed that it was as calm, complete, and effective an exposition of Negro needs and aspirations as one could wish. In response to my congratulations, he smiled and said, "Thanks, Father, to your Passion play of long ago. I've kept the old fire going, but under control. It's cooked the ham in me but hasn't burned down the house."

Archie Lescene was not the only one affected by that play. From having written it, I rediscovered in myself the desire to write other things. There was an urgency from without as well as a stimulus within. Roosevelt had impressed on the economically harried nation that the only thing to fear was fear, but for me the fearing of fear was no help, and the comforter in the White House left me quite discomfited when the first of each month came around and I had to confront my little heap of bills which seemed hill-high. How I'd tried to save, but with what poor success!

In a semitropical land of frequent rainfall the expense of even such a minor thing as keeping a roof in repair was a major matter, and the apparently deliberate inefficiency of repairers made it much worse. I'd have to call them back on the job repeatedly and pay them anew for what they hadn't done and seemed set on not doing. Leaks laughed at their brand of service, if service it might broadly have been called in those wonderful W.P.A. days when men, looking to Washington for relief, really learned to loaf. Mindful of how my father had had to slave for a pittance, I'd entered the sacred ministry with a profound pity for the workingman and a burning zeal for his interests; but now that I had to hire help and was finding it so unsatisfactory, I began to surmise that capital might have some just grievances against labor, as well as labor against capital. Dollars were so hard to get; and when one had to dole them out for nothing, it left one feeling grim.

One day I vented some of my discouragement on a few of my students at Xavier who had come late for class and were comporting themselves rather listlessly. "Soon you'll be facing life and having to earn your living," I told them, "and you'll bring into the outside world the same qualities you're showing right here and now. What employer is going to keep you if you're tardy and remiss? And when you're fired, you'll very probably say, 'Race prejudice,' instead of 'Through my fault.'" But I deeply regretted this lecture, for that noon I spied some of them, who could not afford the cafeteria, eating for lunch a few speckled apples and slices of dry bread, inferred that they had had even less for breakfast, and wondered how they found strength and idealism enough to pursue higher education at all.

But of two things I was certain: first, bills must be met; and, secondly, they could not be met without means. To be a missionary, it was necessary to be many things more: organizer, handshaker, pleader, financier, and what-not. "All things to all men," as Paul of Tarsus summarized. Therefore, in addition to my parochial and academic duties I sought and secured a literary outlet.

The archdiocese of New Orleans was defying the depression by starting a weekly called *Catholic Action of the South;* and Monsignor Wynhoven, the editor and a personality equal to any enterprise, invited me to assist. He could pay only a wage of enthusiasm and encouragement, but promised that if the paper succeeded my efforts would not be forgotten. So I had the privilege of contributing the very first article to *Catholic Action*, then serials, and even a column, "Along the Levee."

And what a friend the monsignor proved to be! He had me deliver sermons and addresses which yielded some stipends for my mission; invited me frequently to his rectory for nourishing meals; helped me to get individuals out of trouble or into jobs; arranged, at my request, some of the first radio presentations of Negro talent in New Orleans. He gave attention in *Catholic Action* to the Negro cause; but the colored disrelished some of his ideas and, instead of going to him for a clarification and explanation, made complaint to higher authority. He was hurt at this, but did not hold it against me.

His deep knowledge of human beings in general, if not of dusky ones in particular, both guided and fitted me to serve my flock better. For example, one day we were discussing a jailed Orleanian who had murdered both his wife and her mother, dismembered the corpses, and disposed, in an unprintable manner, of a hacked-off finger encircled by a wedding ring. I expressed my conviction that such obscene butcher-beasts should be death-sentenced and executed without delay, but the monsignor amazed me by saying quietly, "This one should not." And to my why he answered, "You do not know, as I know, what he had to deal with. Come along with me to the Parish Prison and I'll show you a 'butcher-beast's' soul." I went with him and found the prisoner meek, bewildered, sad. He spoke little, but his eyes were expressive with traces of the spent torture that had temporarily turned patience to the fury that caused his deed. Somehow he made me think of the good mother who, back in the time of my boyhood, had been driven to stain her hands with her own children's blood; and never since seeing him have I wittingly passed snap judgments on the frightful deeds of goaded humanity, but kept more conscious that a minor crime, if planned and deliberate, exceeds in guilt a major one that is frenzied and blind. Nor have I ever since recoiled from the morally bereft and diseased, but better remembered that a priest must be a physician of the soul.

Knowing Monsignor Wynhoven was, if not a vocation, at least an adventure. Though he could understand a murderer, he could not tolerate such "an assault on ethics"—that was what he called it—as the play *Tobacco Road*, which was now touring the South and heading for New Orleans. Vehemently he prepared for battle and called on me for support with my pen in the pages of *Catholic Action*. When the *Tobacco Road* troupe, led by "Jeeter" James Barton, arrived in town, excitement spurted high and the chance of the curtain going up went low, because the city hall had been swung Wynhovenward and the mayor decreed that permission would be granted only if, after a private unveiling, an ecclesiastical committee should approve. So to the ballroom of the St. Charles Hotel the monsignor and I and three other clergymen betook ourselves at an appointed hour for the witnessing of a sceneryless performance in mufti. It turned out to be as harmless as a well-policed lovers' lane, the nicotine having been removed from the tobacco and the refuse from the road. There was nothing for us to do but give in. I shook hands with Mr. Barton, and the following day a local tabloid ran a full-page picture of him and me under the caption "Star and Censor Amicably Talk Things Over." To be absolutely sure that no tricks were pulled, however, we committeemen planted our dignity in five front seats at the St. Charles Theatre that night, no doubt looking like so many black crows ready to pounce on any inserted grains of poisoned corn. Purity again disarmed us by prevailing, and the company was necessarily accorded *carte blanche* to fulfill its half-week engagement, Wednesday matinee included. But into the next performances, which we did not attend, for we really could not spend our lives tobacco-roading, the nicotine was slyly re-injected and the dirt reshoveled, and by Saturday night the shocker was going full blast. Yes, Saturday night; because, by dint of all the free advertising, the show was held over and had a solid and extremely profitable week's run. Those who wanted sapolio had gotten it, and those who preferred spice had gotten that too. Everybody was satisfied—except the committee, most of whom have taken a rather dim view of certain methods of censorship ever since.

Aside from a helpful and exciting association with Monsignor Wynhoven, I still needed more material support for my work, and the second opportunity that came my way seemed very good. Father Harold Purcell, of the Passionist Order, was at the time very successfully editing a national monthly, *The Sign;* and remembering some of my early efforts at authorship and having been stimulated to much interest in the Negro missions by Father John Clarke, a Josephite of saintliest mold, he invited me from his editorial office in New York to contribute a regular feature. Accepting promptly, for the pay would mean the equivalent of an extra Sunday collection each month, I pegged away a couple of midnights each week at exemplifying, under the pseudonym Ig Nikilis (little flame), my idea of what a feature should be. My page went well as a novelty in *The Sign* and won a following. Better still, it developed a warm relationship between Father Purcell and me, and I like to think that our several communications helped to increase his already fervid regard for the

Negro apostolate, since eventually he relinquished his editorship to labor among the colored and reared in Alabama the beauteous, now famous, mission city of St. Jude.

Though the monthly sum of thirty-five dollars from *The Sign* was appreciable, it still left me pauperish, what with my reverend assistant's charities and my own trend in the same direction. Rummaging one day through my very few possessions, I not only found my old notes on behaviorism and the lives of the saints, but again conceived the notion of amplifying them into books. By sitting up late many, many more nights, I finished a treatise which the title *New Psychology and Old Religion* seemed to fit. Then I wrote to Fulton Sheen, whose name was already one to conjure with, and probably in return for the slight service I had rendered him long ago when he lacked stories for his little orphans, he readily did me the large favor of furnishing a formal introduction in which he stated: "The type of psychology which Dr. Murphy has here set down will not help one to appreciate critically the 'sublimial self' of a Meyers, or the 'sciousness' of a James, or the 'sexualism' of a Freud and an Ellis, or the 'collective consciousness' of a Jung, or the 'instincts' of a McDowell; but it will help one to save his soul, and because Dr. Murphy believes in a soul and salvation, I believe he knows more about psychology than any of them."

This sent my flag up. Benziger Brothers of Barclay Street, New York, immediately accepted my manuscript and made such earnest plans for bringing it out that I began to think my financial trials a thing of the past. But, unfamiliar with the strict budget within which a business concern must operate so as to keep its head above water, I made the mistake of blue-penciling the galleys unlimitedly and even overhauling some of the chapters, and the sum of money that had been earmarked for advertising the book now had to be expended on the embodiment of those costly changes of mine in the final text. As a result, the profits from the little publicized venture were very modest, though the reviews were excellent, and afterward a learned Benedictine included *New Psychology and Old Religion* in a revised-for-Catholics version of Mortimer Adler's list of great books.

Hardly richer but still sanguine, I whipped up yet another work, this time a series of informal introductions to "our elder brothers in sanctity," my message being that since saints were originally as humanly weak as ourselves, we could become as heavenly strong as they. I called it *Handclasps with the Holy*. The Catholic Literary Guild readily offered publication and gave me a flattering send-off, but though the book received critical approval and brought me many pleasant letters, it was no financial plum; and when the Society of the Divine Savior, assuming the commitments of the Guild, offered me a small sum for the rights, I gladly accepted. This money went out on more repairs for the roof of Joan of Arc rectory, because by this time my assistant and I were using umbrellas as we moved from room to room when it rained.

Irish and obstinate, and now in semi-desperation, I got together yellow copies of articles of mine on the Negro, which had appeared sporadically in *America, Commonweal,* and *The Sign* during my years in Newburgh, and amplified them into a humanized essay or quasi-novel. For a title I chose *The Tenth Man*, since every tenth person in America, according to the statistics of the time, had Negro blood; a fact, if it was a fact, that meant practically nothing, because Negro blood has since been shown by chemical analysis to be just blood—like anybody else's. But I did not know in those days about the four types of vital fluid, A, B, AB, and O, found in all races; and I thought my selection quite arch and clever. The Dolphin Press in Philadelphia, publishers of the *Ecclesiastical Review*, to whom I sent the manuscript, liked and accepted it; but this being their first book on the race theme, they had their doubts about its salability. Mr. Galbally, the editor, wrote me, "The public, comfortable in the star-spangled-banner conviction that our U.S.A. is unequivocally the land of the free and the home of the brave, seems hardly disposed to welcome anything that does not fit into this Francis Scott Key pattern. Which is all the more reason why some of us should attempt to arouse them by asserting, as you do, that it is difficult for colored citizens to sing 'My country, 'tis of thee, sweet land of liberty' with a thick lump in their throats. We can only hope for the best and sustain ourselves with a realization that, anyhow, *The Tenth Man* is a good intention."

The book never earned me a nickel. It was praised highly by Father John La Farge, the renowned Jesuit; but another clergyman wrote a review in a diocesan weekly to air his astonishment that I should be as concerned about the state of the Negro as if it were unique, and to remind me that there were other suppressed groups in America. As if that made the Negro's condition perfectly normal and acceptable! And still another, this one a layman, took me to task for daring to lift the cross that the Lord himself, in His inscrutable wisdom, had permissively placed on a people's shoulder. Getting marriage and martyrdom mixed, he even quoted at me, "What God has joined, let no man put asunder," and was evidently unaware of his identification of divine wisdom with human incompetence and cruelty. So I exhaled unhappily, charged *The Tenth Man* up to experience, and concluded that the best way to help my mission was to forget literature and depend solely on the day-by-day routine and technique with which my fellow missionaries were so well serving the Gospel. Let the roof leak! When umbrellas should give out, Father Conahan and I could use raincoats. Or could we? Well, no. Come to think of it, he had given his—and mine—away.

But now this faithful assistant, whose heady schemes always floated bright until they burst, received word that he was being transferred from New Orleans to Birmingham. Though I'd miss him much, perhaps I'd rather like missing him. Life would be duller but smoother. The day of his going I promised that I'd always remember him, and, quite moved, he "borrowed" my last ten dollars.

It was as easy as breathing not to forget this extremely per-

sonable, picaresque young apostle. How eloquently he had induced me, when we were planning the silver jubilee of Joan of
Arc, to bring out hundreds of copies of a souvenir booklet em-
bellished with his photograph and mine, which he swore would
sell like mad and enable us to start building a new school! But we
actually got rid of only a measly dozen, and I found myself ob-
ligated to the printer for ninety dollars. . . . How he had tried to
help me meet that debt by getting up a series of boxing matches
for the young men of the parish and charging a five-cent admission! But after he paid off the pugilists and presented me with
a bill for the paraphernalia, I was fifty dollars deeper in arrears.
. . . How devotedly, as chaplain, he had accompanied the Xavier
football team on their out-of-town games, thereby causing me
to shift for myself on Saturdays and Sundays when his presence
was needed most! But he so sang the praises of my "understanding" that I had to keep silent. . . . And what cheerful news, such
as, "Well, we certainly out-pointed our opponents," he'd bring
back from every field of defeat! . . . How hospitably, when I
happened to be away on this or that errand, he'd fill the rectory
with guests and set the domestic help hopping almost to the point
of quitting! But when I'd return he would invariably treat me to
such a buttering up about being missed that I could only beam.
. . . And what good white friends he secured for our mission! —
especially the stanch Toye family who lived nearby and could
never do enough for us. But he liked so many people that it
seemed impossible for him safely to concentrate on the tried and
true; and, social ornithologist that he was, he certainly collected
some "birds." . . . And the way he'd hang onto the words from
the humblest Negro's lips, as if Sir Oracle himself were speaking!
Many a time I'd mildly rebuked him for this and declared that if
I were colored I'd be downright embarrassed by it. "Why not
treat our people normally?" I proposed one day. "If one of them
says something wise—all right, show your appreciation. But if the
utterance is quite ordinary, why go into such a spasm of interest? Last week you were dozing at Archbishop Shaw's con-

ference, yet you're always wide awake if Alice Murray says, 'Irish potatoes ain't so good,' or if Philip Odin says, 'It looks like we're goin' t'have a shower.'" But he only grinned and reminded me, "Everybody listens to the archbishop, and nobody to the colored. I have to try to make up for it."

Ah, I was never to be associated with his like again!—so warmhearted but unreckoning, so unselfish but impulsive, so able to make philosophy laughable and laughter philosophical and pain a pleasure, so blessedly but tryingly himself, and—often—so correct.

Soon the loss of him was offset by the arrival of tall, intelligent Father Paul Lannigan, my new curate, and by a piece of luck. Xavier offered me a summer vacation abroad. And though I was now too taken with my work to welcome any respite from it, the appeal of far-off places was still strong. With official permission I made ready again to see what the Old World was doing. For me the New World seemingly had not done much, nor had I done much for it. Was life all preface? When—how—might one's real contribution begin?

XI

One of my suggestions to Xavier was that an honorary M.A. be given to a rising young Negro named Richmond Barthé. I had never met him personally but felt that I knew him well from what Father Kane, the rector of Epiphany, had often told me.

When a youth, Barthé had been a member of Blessed Sacrament Church in New Orleans, where Father was pastor at the time; and one day he brought him, as a donation for a fair, a beautiful picture of the Savior's face. "Where did you get this?" Father asked in surprise; and the surprise became astonishment when the youngster replied, "I painted it." Then Father could not rest until he had scraped together a little money to send such talent to an art school in Chicago. There Barthé studied for some years, supporting himself with odd jobs, however hard and menial, holding to his purpose of becoming no mere artist but an excellent one, and developing steadily. From painting, he turned to sculpture, and even more at ease in this field, he was already being watched by serious critics as the future Donatello of his group. Xavier, I felt, would be honoring itself in honoring him; and, Mother Agatha agreeing, the M.A. was granted.

But Barthé lacked funds to entrain from New York, where he was then living and working, to receive the degree; and on my way North for a sight of Salem before embarking for Europe I brought it to him in his plain little Manhattan studio. His face was a study as his fingers stroked the parchment, and his gratitude exceeded speech. To make conversation, I mentioned that I'd soon be en route to France, and he looked at me as if I were the prime favorite of fortune. "I'd give half my life—even this scroll—to see the Louvre," he said. And why—I thought—

shouldn't he, a real contributor to the realm of art, visit the very center of it? He had far more right to do so than I. If it had not been for the risk of Xavier's thinking I disprized a generous gift, I'd have offered my trip to him then and there. But suddenly an inspiration came. There *was* a way of getting both him and myself to Europe—and such a simple one! My first-class round-trip passage could be changed into two third-class tickets! When I told him this, he tried to demur, but his eyes lit up.

Two weeks later, after I'd been to Salem and satisfied myself that all was well at home, Barthé and I boarded the S.S. *Champlain* in New York. Not even a hint of race prejudice was to mar that voyage, for the French line, as cosmopolitan as Paris itself, seemed to attract a kindred clientele, and Barthé's combination of quiet dignity and affability charmed everybody. Lolling in deck chairs when the evenings were balmy and the risen moon was scattering silver on the sea, we exchanged ideas and ideals; and our uppermost thought was that, since life is a voyage from time to eternity and all men are passengers in the same strange ship of existence, skimming the same perils below, viewing the same stars above, bearing the same misgivings within, a certain mutuality should prevail. Here on the *Champlain* peace reigned, with old ties temporarily severed and another world lying beyond the horizon. The farther we launched out into the deep, the smaller the past became, the more intimate the present, the larger the future. We were as one family with a single destination. Why could it not be continually so? And Barthé and I wove patterns of interracial harmony in the moonlight, envisaging a sphere ruled by the smile of God instead of the frown of man, and quoting Countee Cullen's verse, "When the body's death gives birth to soil for spring to crown, men will not ask if that rare earth was white flesh once or brown."

I spoke to him one evening about Father Uncles, the colored priest, recently deceased, who had taught me Latin at Epiphany. "Everything about him was admirable," I said, "except his habit of going around the college opening windows even on wintry days. That has always puzzled and annoyed me. Do you think there could have been anything—racial in it?" And he answered, "It would not be strange for a colored member of a white community to have a shut-in feeling." I then emphasized that Father Uncles had always kept his own windows shut tight. "Perhaps it was to show how shut in a feeling can be," he offered. "Not that as a missionary among present and future missionaries he could have needed or wanted to make a direct demonstration, but since you folk were the only whites with whom he came in daily contact, I suppose he had to express himself somehow to you or to nobody. And probably your very lack of prejudice made him think of the many who have such a lot of it."

It chanced that just as he finished saying this an elderly woman reeking with perfume passed by us on deck, and we veered to the topic of odors. A satiric line from a Latin comedy that I'd once translated under Father Uncles's direction came to my lips: "He who smells good lives bad." Barthé smiled. "Have you ever experienced such a thing as a—a Negro odor?" he suddenly asked. "Under soapless and waterless conditions—yes," I replied, and appended weakly, "At least I think so." He insisted that I describe it, and I reluctantly mumbled something about roasted, rancid old chestnuts. Laughing, he told me in turn how the unwashed white affects a Negro's nostrils. "Like an old goat," he said.

During that crossing I found out many things about him. The sorrows of his people were heavy on his heart, but he had no hate or resentment and sought only to give forth his best, no matter how it might be received and interpreted. He mentioned his ambition to create a new kind of *Pietà*, a statue of a Negro mother receiving into her arms at the foot of the tree of dolor the body of her lynched son. Today that piece of sculpture is a *fait accompli*, and some say that it affects them like the sighing of autumn or the moaning of winter, but that there is in it also a strange stirring of spring. And this stirring is not strange at all to me, knowing, as I do, that the faith which inspired

Barthé's very first work—a picture of Christ—has preserved hope and charity in him ever since.

That summer I tried to see Europe through the bright eyes of my companion, but there were clouds and a rumble as of thunder not far away. One night in Paris, when we were eating our meal at a windowed nook of a small restaurant, a sound rolled down the Boulevard Montparnasse and grew loud, and I pushed aside my plate of too reddish tomato soup with a sudden nauseous sense of mobs, tumbrels, and guillotines. Then a troop of young Frenchmen, not unlike Hitler's own robots that I'd viewed in American newsreels, strode by. Were the dragon's teeth, sown by the war-to-end-all-war, so soon sprouting with an evidence of fresh misery for mankind?

The next morning I witnessed a student riot in the vicinity of Boulevard Saint-Michel and thought of F. Scott Fitzgerald's words in the twenties: "A new generation—grown up to find all wars fought." What would he write of these thirties if he were still around? What had become of him?

But Paris, the perennial, was as fair as ever and seemed as calm in the rising unrest as Socrates drinking the hemlock. And I prayed with Barthé in Notre Dame, the Madeleine, and Sacré-Cœur that if evil days must again fall on this capital of civilization they be shortened. Somehow his limpid delight in the town, and particularly in the treasures of the Louvre, made me certain that no matter what happened the love of finer things would live on in choice souls as a guarantee against any sweepingly triumphant return of barbarism. He represented a people who had known every misfortune and indignity; and yet, not at all fixated in futility, he was self-dedicated to the best. There must be many others like him; and, if so, culture could not be quite lost.

For a week I left Barthé in Paris visiting an excellent colored family whose son he had met and associated with in New York, and I went on a tour to Our Lady's great shrine in Lourdes. And there I had not only the pleasure of finding Fulton J. Sheen but also the profit of learning one of the secrets of his ever increas-

ing influence. It was his annual custom to come for spiritual renewal to this holy spot where a little peasant had found a healing
beauty and shared it with an afflicted world. Also, I met at
Lourdes George M. Cohan's gifted daughter Georgette who, an
ardent admirer of Sheen's character and career, was drawn to the
shrine by his example; like Eve Lavallière, she found here a gleam
which exceeded all the glamour of the theater that she knew so
well. We talked much about Eve, who had been a personal friend
of Ethel Levey, Georgette's mother.

Refreshed and stimulated by his sojourn on Parnassus, Barthé
returned to New York that fall to do even better work in his
studio than before, and his outpouring of thanks to me for my
having "opened the ever new Old World" to him caused me to
blush. He seemed unaware that he had doubled the satisfaction
of my journey by affording me an opportunity to share it. Too,
he had brought home to me a needed lesson that would-be
helpers of the Negro might well remember how much the Negro
is capable of helping himself—and others—when not hindered.
Without ever having attended a university, Barthé had acquired
enough merit to be honored by one, a fact which, every time I
think of it, causes me to feel as proud of him as critical of myself.

Back in New York again, I visited Eddie Dowling and Ray at
Bayside. Ray looked much the same as on the morning of the
wedding in the Newburgh chapel; but there was less sparkle now
in Eddie's eyes, and more seriousness. His song-and-dance days
over, he had been doing much reading, reflecting, and self-
improving, and had become interested in politics. His friend Al
Smith having taken a walk from the Democratic party, he was
now a Roosevelt man. Franklin D.'s photograph, affectionately
inscribed, held a prominent place in the drawing room, and in-
vitations to White House affairs were so frequent that he and
Ray flatteringly utilized my visit by having me dash off for them
a note to decline the latest. "We need to be very, very diplo-

matic, Father, and you know just how." Ray smiled. My, oh my. Me, if only as a proxy, refusing the President of the United States!

Because of Eddie's civic connections, there was at the time even a possibility of his becoming a senator of Rhode Island. "By act of Providence?" I quipped, quoting Father Leonard when he told me this. But he still belonged mainly to the theater and wanted to do things in it that would leave a lasting rather than a fleeting effect. He showed me a playscript, his expression dreamy as he placed it in my hands. "A fellow overseas called Paul Vincent Carroll wrote it," he said. "I've bought the rights from the Abbey Theatre in Dublin, where it was produced with great success; but I'm afraid that it's—well, too-too for Broadway. Take it along with you to New Orleans and read it carefully. Tell me just what you think."

Ray suggested coffee on the cozy back veranda. And until the light turned lavender with sunset we talked on, reliving the excitement of the days of *Sally, Irene, and Mary, Honeymoon Lane,* and *Sidewalks of New York.* I learned that Marguerite Zender was again wedded, this time to one worthy of her, and finding the happiness she well deserved; that Walter Plimmer, a handsome young actor who had worked for Eddie and who, during my stay in Newburgh, had consulted me about a plan to leave the stage and seek the priesthood, was nearing ordination; that Kate Smith had made history at the Palace Theatre and was making radio radiant; that Ruby Keeler, one of the brightest stars in "Sidewalks," had become Mrs. Al Jolson; that Bob Hope, Eddie's understudy in "Lane," seemed bound for big things.

But there were sad happenings to be recounted too, for some well-loved characters had passed out of the picture: Jack Donohue, of the laughing feet; Gordon Dooley, Ray's own great comedian brother; Jimmy Hanley, who had composed the tuneful scores of Eddie's shows; and Eddie's own perfect mother. All were gone. "I bet Ma's bossing the cherubs right at this moment for flying all over the damp skies without their woolies on, or bringing hot chicken soup to some poor old sick saint lying on a bed of clouds," said Eddie, a smile on his lips but moisture in his eyes. "It could never be heaven for her up there unless the Lord let her lend a helping hand." And falling in with his mood, I declared that I could imagine her and my own mom sitting in a quiet supernal corner, talking about us down here and breathing a prayer that we might always find, as they had found, "the substance of things hoped for, the evidence of things unseen" in the shadows of life. "Why, that's a paraphrase of the title of the play I've given you to read," he said. *"Shadow and Substance."*

Just before I left, he asked me whether I had ever used his letter to Huey P. Long. And I told him no. Not that I hadn't wanted to use it, but what with parochial and university interests, I'd never gotten around to it. Once or twice I had seen the big man in the lobby of the Roosevelt Hotel, but he was too surrounded by admirers or his bodyguard for an approach. "You'd better hurry up," said Eddie. "I've a hunch that he won't last. From what I hear, he's made some real enemies down there." He stroked his chin and murmured moralizingly but, it seemed to me, not too pertinently, " 'Shadow—substance.' " And I could see that the play rather than Huey P. Long was on his mind.

Riding back to Manhattan from Bayside, I began perusing the script and become so absorbed that the Long Island train pulled in at Pennsylvania Station before I knew it. And that night, as I lay in an upper berth of the Crescent Limited bound for the South, I read on, held by Paul Vincent Carroll's three characters: Canon Skerritt who loved the past—old friends, old paintings, old wines, old truths; O'Flingsley, the schoolmaster, who loved the future with its fresh allure and challenge; and the little servantgirl, who loved both men much but her patroness St. Brigid more, and symbolized the faith of Ireland torn by the demands of past and future alike. The style reminded me of Thackeray's description of Erin's scenery, "wild, sweet, and a little sad even in sunlight." The delineations were vivid. Significance pulsed through the plot like clean blood in an athlete's

winning body, and played over it as moon sheen on a river's measured flow. And I finished the last page with a feeling that here in
my hands lay a piece of literature almost worthy to be placed
beside Hawthorne's *Scarlet Letter*.

The next morning, right after breakfast, I sat in the lounge
car and wrote Eddie a long letter, urging him to take a chance
with this play, arguing that the mysticism in it might have an
appeal to a worldly many as well as a pious few. Wasn't the collapse of postwar prosperity making everybody think? Wasn't
there faith even on Broadway? We had both seen so much of it
at St. Malachy's! Wasn't man naturally religious? And I quoted
the skeptic alleged to have said, "I am an atheist, thank God."

It was good to be again in New Orleans. The Mississippi, so
different from the Seine, seemed an image of a deep calm inner
flow of American life; and steamboat whistles, anything but
melodious, somehow were violin and cello to me. Cypress trees,
darkly green, so emphasized the clearness of sky that at last
I understood Lafcadio Hearn's tropes: the Infinite Breath, the
Pneuma, the Divine Ghost, the Great Blue Soul of the Unknown.
I had heard it said that to tarry on the delta for two years was to
be held captive for life. But what a pleasant thralldom! With
contentment I resumed my pastorate at Joan of Arc, watching
my curate, Father Lannigan, filling his days with good deeds, and
Xavier entering a fall term with the largest enrollment to date.

That November sadness came to the city with the decease of
Archbishop Shaw; but his passing was gentle, and our spirits
were sustained by the tidings that, come spring, Omaha's great
Bishop Rummel would receive the pallium and fill the New
Orleanian vacancy. One of Archbishop Shaw's last acts had been
the granting of a request of mine that Xavier be permitted to im-
provise a chapel in her administration building and keep the
Blessed Sacrament there; and I knew that with the Presence in
our midst his successor would find Xavierites at their best.

Higher education for Negroes in New Orleans was now progressing rapidly. Our Protestant brethren had just merged two small colored colleges into a single and potent one, which they named Dillard, after a Southern gentleman who was to them what Mother Katherine Drexel was to us. Never shall I forget a certain note in the dedication of that new institution. As I sat admiring the dignity of the celebration, the master of ceremonies came forth to introduce Dr. James Hardy Dillard and pay high tribute to him. He cited many proofs of the honoree's humanitarianism and dwelt on the fact that, several years before, he had stepped down from eminence at Tulane University to devote himself entirely to the interests of the Negro. The kind-faced, white-haired doctor, rising, acknowledged the praises gratefully but emphatically made one correction. "You have just heard," he said to the large colored audience, "that, sometime ago, I stepped down to help you. That is inaccurate. I did not step down. I stepped *up*." And how they loved him for it! I myself could hardly resist an impulse to cheer aloud this apt and simple utterance, for it afforded me a new glimpse into the goodness of the South and made me think of many other southerners who, as I now realized, were doing their utmost for interracial betterment and giving the lie to inertia.

Some months passed. The atmosphere of New Orleans was getting ominous, because Huey P. Long, all-powerful politically and angry at opposition, was adopting methods which rendered his friends doubtful and his opponents determined; and suddenly, out of the mounting unrest, radios and headlines blared news from Baton Rouge that the climax had come. Long's bullet-pierced body was borne to Our Lady of the Lake Hospital, and there, as a nun leaned over him, he gasped, "Sister, pray for me." Softly she said, "Not for you but with you"; and she recited the Act of Contrition, his lips faintly moved to the words, his eyes closed, and his career ended.

For days and weeks the deeds and untimely ending of Louisiana's foremost son were the chief topics. And as I reread Eddie Dowling's letter of introduction which I had never used but which I had kept among my few papers so long that it was now only a yellow leaf, I thought of *Shadow and Substance* with its fable of human tensions solved only by fate and faith. I could see in Long's once so loud and now so silent figure the story of every man, the struggle called life and the leveler—death—at the end of the shadowy road. And I supposed that the most substantial act of all in Long's career had been his echoing of a little nun's prayer.

I wrote to Eddie, again urging him to bring his significant play to the public. But he was so busy with the Broadway aspects of the New Deal at the time that his personal plans were in abeyance. A year—two—slipped by; and then he wrote me that he was ready. Soon after, he let me know that rehearsals had begun and that his cast was headed by Sir Cedric Hardwicke, "as fine an actor as ever crossed the pond"; and Julie Hayden, "frail and lovely as a Botticelli figure or Keats's blessed damosel"; and Sara Allgood, "so good an actress that she does not act a role at all but lives it." His P.S. ran: "We are bound to succeed if you pray hard. Do. Do."

Success was coy and elusive at first. The show opened in Pittsburgh, and its worth shone too dimly there. "Pray harder," Eddie telegraphed. A week of tryout in Washington proved much more encouraging, and by the time the company reached New York every facet of the production was working perfectly. What a première at the Golden Theatre! The first-string critics praised it, the public were won, Paul Vincent Carroll was discovered as the best of the younger Irish dramatists, Sir Cedric and Julie Hayden found themselves acclaimed, and Eddie, who a year before had distinguished himself as co-producer with Maurice Evans of *King Richard II*, now stood shiningly alone.

Though miles and miles away, *Shadow and Substance* seemed very near to me, because Eddie kept me informed. "It's bringing a breath of moral spring to old Broadway," he almost sang by phone. "Why, people who never patronized shows before are eager for this one!" And to crown the New York run came a

Drama Critics' Circle citation for the play as the finest importation of the year.

Meanwhile, Eddie had sent me a copy of "Shadow" in book form, autographed by every member of the cast. All the inscriptions more than pleased me, but one did better than that. This was Sara Allgood's, and what she had written was a unique Irish blessing: "Father dear, may you be in heaven half an hour before the Divvil knows you're dead!"

Happy Sara. From Broadway she was to go to Hollywood and win fame in *How Green Was My Valley*, and I was to receive from there many a little note expressive of her blithe and beautiful spirit. Often have I used that blessing of hers, and every time I do so nowadays there is a tug at my heart and a tickle in it too, for I suspect that, when she recently passed away, she nimbly exemplified her own words by slipping into glory well before Old Nick could sit up and see.

When *Shadow and Substance* finished its Broadway and road showings, Eddie lengthened his list of generosities by giving me first amateur rights to it. "If you have a drama department in Xavier," he wrote, "this play will be just the thing for you to put on." With much interest, I considered the idea; and while I was doing so, something happened. A personage—premier novelist, Nobel and Pulitzer prize winner, acute individualist, Sinclair Lewis himself!—arrived in town.

The newspaper announcements of the visit instantly drew my attention, for I had done a chapter in *New Psychology and Old Religion* on modern authors, in which some acrid opinions were aired: that Ibsen was the running sore of Scandinavia; that Tolstoy, Rolland, and d'Annunzio were poisoners of the rills of laughter and sounders of the wells of despair; that Anatole France was a mind smeared with sex and inclined to see only Nature's lust in the pollen on the petals of a rose; Thomas Hardy, an exponent of chaos stirred around by a monster with a stick; Theodore Dreiser, a mere pitier of humanity; James Branch

Cabell, a snobbish refugee from it; Sherwood Anderson, a wincer at it; and Sinclair Lewis, an arch contemner of it with a gift for sardonic amusement. And of all the littérateurs, Lewis stood out the most vividly for me, because I was more familiar with his works than with those of the others. I wanted to see for myself whether he had any humanhood at all; but nothing was less likely than a meeting, since I knew no one who might introduce me and could not conceive of his caring to know a clergyman anyway. Yet chance had a plan of its own.

One morning Mr. Bernard Szold, the director of Le Petit Théâtre du Vieux Carré, phoned me to say, "I noticed in the papers that Eddie Dowling has granted you first amateur rights to *Shadow and Substance*. And this leads to a request. Sinclair Lewis, who's been making some stage appearances in other cities of late, was out sight-seeing here yesterday and stopped in at Le Petit. He approved everything, and when I told him we'd appreciate having him perform for us, he liked that too. But he said there's only one drama, one role, that he'd care to do— *Shadow and Substance* and the role of Canon Skerritt, which his friend Sir Cedric Hardwicke played on Broadway. Well, there we are, Father. Would you consider letting us be the first group to do the show—with America's leading novelist as the star?"

Superfluous question. Xavier was busy on an opera. Le Petit, with a long record of successful offerings which had placed it in the front rank of little theaters, would be just right. And to think that my small hold on the play was enough to open a door like this! I readily gave Mr. Szold what permission I could, and gratefully he asked me to assist in the selection of the cast, to act as clerical adviser at rehearsals, and to let him bring Mr. Lewis and me together.

The chancery permitted me to have an active interest in the project because of the religious genre of the play, and then I was free for my first contact with the personal source of *Main Street*, *Babbitt*, *Elmer Gantry*, *Arrowsmith*, and *Dodsworth*. We met at Le Petit Théâtre, near St. Louis Cathedral; and the old steeple bell that had tolled in and out so many historic changes was sounding the timeless Angelus. I had read that, in the mad spirit of the twenties, Lewis once ascended some strange pulpit and gave God exactly ten minutes to prove Himself. *If you exist, strike me dead.* And it had made me think of a louse looking up at a human being, too big for its infinitesimal eyes to see, and blustering, "If you're there, man, prove it by quashing me!" Just as nothing would have happened to the louse, so nothing had happened to Lewis. Now here he was before me, a tall, thin, gangly figure with corrugated brow, sparse hair combed flat, pale-blue agate eyes, a not too prominent nose, and mottled cheeks sloping to a vague, slightly bulbous mouth. And the instant I saw him, I liked him, for I surprised a wistfulness which somehow suggested that of a little boy kept indoors for misbehavior and peeking out a window. Too, the face seemed a parchment on which many things had been written, erased, and rewritten; and I began to wonder whether any past God-challenging on the part of this celebrity had been only a perverse form of truth-seeking.

In our handclasp the feel of those frail, almost skeletal fingers that had dissected social hypocrisies and pretenses galore with a scalpel pen was strangely pleasant to me; yet I did not forget that traces of those hypocrisies and pretenses might still be sticking to the anatomist from so close a dealing with them. I recalled someone's remark that America was made up in equal parts of movie double features, chewing gum, swing, straight eights, and Sinclair Lewis—and that Lewis made lusty literature of all the rest. But as a priest I knew something of the dreams and sighs of humanity and now asked myself, as I looked at this lofty man of letters, whether he would ever do for orthodoxy what he had done against sham. That wistfulness in his eyes made me wistful too. What kind of convert might he make if blinded with light on the road to Damascus and healed by faith in the street called straight?

But there was little time for speculation as the rehearsals of

Shadow and Substance proceeded. Soon it became evident to me that at least a part of Lewis's worldly success was an ability to plunge wholly, like the saintly Mother Katherine Drexel herself, into a task. He was the first to report at Le Petit each evening and the last to leave; and he drained Bernard Szold, the director.

I can still see Szold, whom everybody loved, pacing up and down the middle aisle, running his fingers through his tangled mop of hair, and quivering. In pity I'd light up a cigarette and put it between his lips for him; and, puffing away, he'd relax a little. One night when I was out of smokes and things were going worse than usual, he jumped up on the stage, grabbed a hunk of scenery with both fists, and sank his teeth into fresh paint and old canvas; then, proving how much farther gone he was than I'd thought, he turned to the actors and begged, "Let us be calm."

Another night during a tense moment when Lewis was in the midst of a long speech, Jill Jackson, a bright little blonde holding the prompter's sheets, laughed involuntarily at the distracting horseplay of somebody in the wings, and Lewis, thinking that the laughter was at his acting, went Vesuvian and ordered her out of the place. So Le Petit lost one of its most attractive and talented young members; but another sphere of entertainment won her, and before long she was brilliantly busy at Station WWL, where she has remained a prize asset ever since, thankful for having been scared by a celebrity into becoming one herself.

Yet another night when Ethel Crumm Brett, expert designer of sets and effects, was training the spotlight on Lewis, his tired, watering eyes blinked in the glare. Any real actor would never have complained; but Lewis, just a novelist afield from his regular art and avid for the atmosphere of little theaters which were to be the theme of his next book, burst into a rage and, shouting that his vision meant more to him than this confounded play, stomped off the stage. I followed him. "Here everybody's bending backwards to please you," I rebuked in the privacy of his upstairs dressing room, "and you won't be pleased." His head slightly down, he gave me a sly, slant look which, to my astonishment, twinkled, and then he laughed. "Good act, wasn't it! Now I guess they'll admit I *can* perform when I let myself go." Two minutes later he was down on the stage again, and Szold was regarding me with the kind of awe that is usually reserved for wizards.

Only once did Lewis and I have a contention, and it amounted to nothing but a sprinkling of pepper and salt to season our harmony. As an Irish canon in the show, he had to wear a special cassock. I maintained that the pipings on it should be white, but he demanded red. "Don't you want to be ecclesiastically correct?" I asked. "I want to be theatrically effective," he returned, with a smile like a persimmon trying to be a peach. "Red is better for that. Anyhow I prefer it. Call me 'Red,' Father. All my friends do." And that closed the matter as far as we were concerned; but a report got out that he and I were at each other's throat, and echoes of the imaginary ruckus reached not only the local but even the metropolitan press. Little had I dreamed when I first read *Main Street*, away back in 1920, that I should ever share journalistic space with the author himself!

As for *Main Street*, he mentioned to me one night during a lull in the rehearsals that he remembered less the praises accorded him for that book than a certain wordless commentary. Shortly after publication he set sail for Europe and noticed, the second day out, that a large number of deck loungers had copies. One woman especially attracted his attention, for she kept beetling her brows and chewing her lips as she pored over the pages. Suddenly, mumbling to herself, she sprang up from her chair, leapt to the ship railing, and hurled *Main Street* with all her might into the sea. Recounting this to me, he chuckled as if it were just about the best criticism he had ever received.

In our few free moments I talked with him about religion, since he seemed so taken with the spiritual vistas of Carroll's play. Up in New York, Father (now Monsignor) Fulton Sheen had recently converted Heywood Broun; and this prompted me one night to say to Lewis with affected casualness, "Why don't you do a 'Heywood Broun'?" He scrutinized me for a second and then, out of a quirk in the corner of his lips, suggested, "Why don't *you* do an 'Elmer Gantry'?" And no farther than that did we get, at that time, on the road to Damascus. But once, when rehearsal was over and we were having coffee in a nearby restaurant, we fell into a discussion of the role of the Church in an era menaced by Communism. " 'Onward Christian Soldiers' may yet be drowned out by the 'Internationale,' " he said. And I thought, "Now I have him," because he sounded rather sad. My hope died, however; for he began to tease me by singing—low— the "Internationale" itself. His voice was so unsuited to any song, and his rendition of this one so full of flaws, that I simply had to indulge in a little raillery: "Say, Caruso, the Catholic Church could probably save the world from Communism just by hiring you to chant the praises of Moscow on street corners. Every hearer would run to the arms of Rome for protection." And leering good-naturedly, he replied, "Just for that, Aquinas, I will henceforth be as silent and inscrutable as Eleanor Roosevelt."

After a month of rehearsals *Shadow and Substance* was ready, and yet we were not quite satisfied, so to try it out we put on a special performance for the clergy of the city. They liked it in the main, but some of them gave me a ribbing. Said one, "What a clerical adviser you are! Why, under your learned tutelage Mr. Lewis, as a priest, can't even bless himself." And I groaned within, because over and over again I had had Lewis practice the Sign of the Cross; but this simple little act of faith was either too much for his genius or a resistance lurked in him to a symbol that he was not yet prepared to accept. But he played Canon Skerritt with conviction; and when we gave yet another trial performance, this time exclusively for Sisters, there was not the least criticism. They caught and laughed at every bubble of humor; and the laughter of nuns, an innocent as a child's, makes a music of its own. They wept at the pathos, as if every throb of it were personally theirs. "An audience of angels!" declared Lewis to me during intermission. He was really moved, and I felt him now nearer to orthodoxy than ever before, for at last I saw him, when the second act was in progress, making a perfect Sign of the Cross.

The night of the formal opening the thermometer was at a January low, and New Orleans society came perhaps reluctant, certainly ashiver, to the little theater on St. Peter's Street. But once inside they found the season changed. Just as to old Broadway, so now to the Vieux Carré, *Shadow and Substance* wafted a breath of spring. Its plot unfolded with warmth and color, and its lyrical phrases were heather fresh. The bells of St. Louis Cathedral, sounding the hour, blended with the beauty of the production like a planned offstage effect; and it seemed to me, sitting in the orchestra rear, that a ghostly audience was smiling down on the spectacle of yesterday's God-challenger and today's still tough cynic portraying a minister of grace.

As a matter of record, Lewis's portrayal that night had sincerity but not much else. Still, it was far better than his singing of the "Internationale" had been, and I'd always resent—a little —a certain Manhattan critic's later witticism, "The real Red menace in the American theater is the acting of Sinclair Lewis."

A few days later, after putting several questions to me about Negroes, he expressed a desire to visit Xavier; and I brought him there. Sister Frances, our new dean, attracted him instantly, and in the graciously warm atmosphere that nuns create, his wintry surface melted away. He asked that we let him confer with some of our colored teachers, which we gladly did. Wondering a trifle about his intent, but not questioning it, I absented myself from the conference after seeing it started, because somehow I felt that he preferred to have the group to himself. And not until some years later was I to understand the significance of that round table, for then there would appear a book, *Kingsblood Royal*, in which, with all his power, he'd champion the group I served. And then I'd know that at Xavier he had begun to learn about his subject from the very best of sources, Negro intelligence itself.

The day after his visit to our university, I brought him to meet

Archbishop Rummel, and they had a long conversation. It was his first contact with a Catholic prelate, and the effect on him was great. "A true man of God," he said after we left. Several times during the remainder of his stay in New Orleans he quoted His Excellency to me, and always with the same fondness and respect that I detected in his tone whenever he referred to the writings of Dorothy Thompson and the sayings of his close friend Dr. Cornelius Traeger. But it was rather embarrassing when, after praising me in a press interview, he went on to tell the reporters that the archbishop was "a swell guy too." I'd not have minded, had not the remark appeared in print exactly as he made it.

It was with real regret that I saw him off on the train for the North when the week of *Shadow and Substance* ended. But he promised to keep in touch with me, and so he did. From time to time he phoned or wrote, and I was glad to learn that, still fond of the play in which he had enacted a priest, he was touring the New England straw-hat circuit in the same role with a company emanating from New York. Later, the tour over, a large package containing his neat cassock, cape, and biretta reached me. I was surprised that he had not kept them for souvenirs, but soon realized that *Shadow and Substance* was so fixed in his best memories that he did not need clerical garments as reminders. Perhaps, too, they had become so precious to him that he wanted them genuinely used in the service they were meant for, and certainly he knew what a saving they would be to a missionary whose income was microscopic.

Twice he returned to New Orleans; when he had a special personal worry which he felt I could ease, and when he and Lewis Browne were on a lecture jaunt. And once when I was on my way to earn a few dollars for my mission by delivering an address at Ford Hall Forum in Boston and stopped off in New York for a few days to visit Father Will, now filling the office of novice master at Epiphany College, I saw him yet again.

This time he was presenting a play, *The Good Neighbor*, a comedy drama of "just plain folks," which he earnestly invited me to attend. As the curtain rose on the Broadway première, I leaned forward in my chair, eager for every word, glad to be present at the commencement of a new phase of Lewis's career, confident that he who had admired Paul Vincent Carroll's play so much would not permit a single reprehensible line or scene in this one. And I was right about the irreprehensibility; but the show itself —that was another matter. The first act, though well performed, seemed to zigzag on to nothing in particular, yet the audience applauded the close. I did not know whether this meant an approval of the play or a welcome to the intermission. George Jean Nathan, the most stringent of critics, whom I recognized from pictures in newspapers and magazines, left and did not return. This was ominous enough, but not conclusive, because Nathan was well known to have retched at many a production that the paying public found quite palatable. But the second act, as far as I could judge, showed no improvement on the first; though the final curtain, to my puzzlement, evoked even more applause. Did this indicate that the house was filled with Lewis's friends, or merely that pain—when it stops—amounts to pleasure? Anyhow, the exodus from the theater was cheerful, and not a few individuals, myself included, tarried in the lobby to offer Lewis congratulations.

He insisted that I join him at his hotel to await the verdict of the press in the early morning editions; and there in his suite I met Sylvia Sydney, Luther Adler, Dr. Cornelius Traeger, Dudley Digges, Samson Raphaelson, and several other notables who had been merely names to me. A scintillant group they were, until a bellhop brought in the papers. Then a pall fell. But Lewis read the ghastly reviews stoically and winced only once. That was when, trying to penetrate the gloom with an optimistic ray, I said, "Well, the critics are not the last word. Remember 'Abie's Irish Rose.'" For the first and only time in all our association, he gave me a dirty look.

I was with him the following night and wished that I wasn't. We walked on Broadway, and as we approached the theater of

The Good Neighbor, so alive only twenty-four hours before, we saw comparative death. The foyer did not have a single light on, and not a customer was standing at the box office. We turned into the stage alley, which smelled of decay, and the members of the cast were hovering there like ghosts. Thanking them for having tried to make something out of nothing, he paid them off, his hand trembling a little. He had had far more success than most men of his time, but wasn't this now only making failure the harder to bear? I looked up at the stars over Broadway, all the bigger and brighter to me for the dreary well of an alley which served as a kind of telescope, and hoped that he would look up too. But he did not.

I was to hear from him only briefly, though still intimately, after that; but I'd meet him in books coming rather rapidly from his pen—a weapon against time and loneliness. *Bethel Merriday, Gideon Planish, Cass Timberlane, Kingsblood Royal,* and then one quite different from any of the others. The public would not like this one so much, missing in it the Lewis of bygone days who used to dissect characters with such saturnine cleverness and hurl the pieces to the four winds. They would say that his art had deteriorated, but I'd feel that it had deepened. The very title of this novel was to express what I had long suspected him of being, *The God-Seeker.*

Far from the scenes of his triumphs, he was to spend his last days meditatively in Rome, and his last hours in a hospital there, repeating gratefully to his nurse, a nun, "God bless you," and calling his physician "Father."

XII

WHILE in New York at the time of the Lewis play, which could have inspired Heywood Broun's memorable critique, "It opened at 8:40 sharp and closed at 10:40 dull," I found that Eddie Dowling was master of ceremonies for the big radio program, "We the People"; so I availed myself of the opportunity to attend one of the broadcasts, eager to see him and knowing, from his efficient handling of Flo Ziegfeld and many another "name" on the Chrysler Hour some years before, that a treat was in store. But it was more than a treat that I got. One of the ushers in the radio theater led me 'way up front; and when Eddie came out on the stage to win the audience before the show went on the air, he spied me and gave me such an introduction as only an Irishman, unashamed of sentiment, would dare. Certain on his say-so that I was somebody, the crowd clapped and clapped, and I had to take a bow.

The guest speaker that night was Dr. A. J. Cronin, author of the current best-seller, *Keys of the Kingdom*. A man of great dignity, he spoke briefly, in a soft cultured tone, about his work; and it astonished me at the end of his neat discourse that he received little more response for having written the novel of the year than I for not having done so. But, then, he had not been so boosted as I by one who, at the sight of me, must have remembered a wedding day in Newburgh when the skies were forget-me-not blue and the Hudson a river of gold, and a ring was slipped onto the finger of "the best little girl in the world."

The hit of the broadcast was a modest colored boy who had composed the exceedingly popular song, "I Don't Want to Set the World on Fire." He sang the verse, and Dinah Shore the chorus; and the house went wild. My own enthusiasm was heightened by anticipation of a day when, with all America cognizant of Negro talent, prejudice would be superseded by appreciation.

The following morning, after celebrating Mass in the chapel of the Leo House downtown, I attended a requiem at St. Malachy's Church. Father Leonard, the good shepherd of Broadway, was no more. But living memories of him filled me as I knelt in a pew and felt his spirit-presence like the fragrance of incense that still clings to an altar when Benediction service is over. I saw actors and actresses shedding real tears; and, like everybody else, I was more than affected when the celebrant of the Mass mentioned in his eulogy that Father Leonard, after the purchase of a burial ground for members of the profession, so many of whom would die indigent, had requested that he himself be laid to rest there. How in keeping! "He loved his own and loved them to the end." His heart, in death as in life, would be literally with his children of the stage. And I thought, too, of the missionary priests and Sisters who were sleeping in nameless graves in the Southland, one with the forgotten whom they alone had remembered and served.

From New York I proceeded to Boston for my scheduled talk on "The Church and Democracy"; and as the train pulled into South Station up there, my mind turned to Sinclair Lewis. When I'd told him about that intended talk, he warned me, "You'll have to face the possibility of a lot of heckling, because your subject is an invitation to roughstuff in an open forum. Communists and fellow travelers will surely be there and they'll toss you on the horns of a dilemma by asking your opinion of Father Coughlin. If you say you approve of him, they'll rip you apart; and if you say you disapprove, they'll involve you in arguments against your own Faith." And to my question as to how he'd side-step such a trap if he were in my shoes, he tongued his lips for a moment, his eyes shrewdly aglint, and replied, "I'd say, 'I

believe in justice and truth. Therefore you can infer for yourselves what I think of him.' And I'd let it go at that. Shouldn't add
another word but pass right on—quick—to the next topic."

That night Ford Hall was filled. Dr. George Coleman, the
founder of the forum, who had met me during one of his winter
visits to New Orleans and Xavier and been interested enough to
arrange this lecture, must have provided a good build-up in the
Boston press. Besides, the unusualness of a priest appearing on a
secular platform with special permission from Cardinal O'Connell
must have stimulated some expectancy. In the lounge I saw a few
individuals who might well be "Reds," the way they lynx-eyed
me; and I was sure of this when one of them said, "The Church
had better be up on her toes tonight, Preacher. The day of
reckoning is near." As Dr. Coleman led me onto the stage, he
whispered, "Don't be nervous now," and made me very nervous
indeed. But once I opened my mouth, I forgot myself and
poured out the political doctrine of St. Thomas Aquinas, with
which I had so long been familiar. The experience was almost
zephyr smooth until, the address finished, the question period
began.

"If the Church is the champion of human rights, as you say,"
cried a bearded man from the floor, "why does she hold to her
bosom a man who——"

There it was. Anti-Coughlinism, just as Sinclair Lewis had
predicted. It rolled on with all the stock charges and reached a
climax: "What do *you*, as a churchman, think of your fellow
priest?" My reply was ready. "I believe in justice and truth.
Hence you can infer what I think."

The effect was perfect. Both sides of the house were appeased,
for each evidently thought it had cornered the market on justice
and truth. Applause thundered, and I silently thanked the Lord
for having let His challenger's astuteness guide me.

But then a diehard jumped up. "If the Church stands only for
what's right, why doesn't she strike out any minister of hers who
doesn't?" he shouted.

"The Church deals in the things of eternity and can afford to take her time," I responded blandly, not even noticing that at last I was stepping into the trap. "She lets the cockle grow with the wheat until the time of harvest."

Fortunately Dr. Coleman, an old hand at directing discussions, now threw in a wholly divergent question. He knew his Catholic Boston, well represented at Ford Hall that night, and its admiration for Father Coughlin.

The whole affair, after all, seemed to culminate in good feeling, and with my sister Annie and her husband who had come to hear me I departed serenely for my home in Salem. I slept well. But the next day I felt that I'd never sleep again, for a daily headlined its account of the lecture, "Priest Says Church Bides Time with Coughlin."

Back to New Orleans I hurried, but that was no salvation, because New England Catholics pursued me with letters, the tenor of which was "How dare you compare Father Coughlin to cockle?"

I explained in my answer to every one of those letters that I had not even mentioned Father Coughlin at Ford Hall but merely stated a Gospel principle. And feeling that so well informed a man as Coughlin must have caught at least a faint echo of the affair, I wrote him, too, at his Shrine of the Little Flower in Michigan. His prompt reply gave me my first breath of relief and also a fresh estimate of his stature. Of all the mail I received, his note alone was calm. "Thanks. Do not give it another thought, Father. I understand."

The trip to Massachusetts, apart from controversy, was profitable to my spirit. I had seen my sister Agnes in the house where Mom died, living a life of simplicity and piety; my brother Frank and his wife raising a family well; Annie rejoicing in the ordination of her elder son John, who had followed his uncles into the life of missionary service; and the parents of other boys whom, years before, I'd led off to study for the Order of St. Joseph, taking pride that those sons, now men, were affording Salem the prestige of having supplied more vocations to Negro evangelization than any other town in New England.

Having finished two terms at Joan of Arc, I was now sent to Blessed Sacrament Church, which Father John Clarke, our devoutest Josephite, had started a quarter of a century before. Making the rounds of my new parish, I found the memory of this first pastor as green as the winter grass that renders a southern lawn more beautiful in December even than in May. Most homes had a picture or some other keepsake of him, and several were burning vigil lights in his honor. There had been a succession of good pastors during the twenty-five years, but only one Father Clarke. Clearly the best way to begin my shepherding here was to study this model, and it delighted me to discover in his old desk a ledger on the first page of which was written in an almost schoolboyish hand, *My personal thoughts and reflections*, J.C. How fitting that Jesus Christ and John Clarke should have the same initials! Eagerly, I turned to the next page, certain of a mental and moral treasure-trove. But there was only one sentence there: *Time is wingèd, and as we grasp at it, it is gone.* Riffling the other pages, I stared. They were all utterly blank.

Disappointment was not to remain, however; for soon it became clear that Father Clarke's record lay in a second ledger—the minds and hearts of his people. Too busy to write it, he had simply lived it, and their reverent gratitude and retentiveness had done the rest.

I preached to those good people, but it was they who, taught by him, taught me. Three generations were represented in the parish. He had personally molded the grandparents, and they in turn had reared their sons and daughters strictly according to the virtues instilled by him; and now those sons and daughters themselves were fathers and mothers, breathing into their own little offspring the spirit of one who had long since passed out of this world.

The Blessed Sacrament Mission seemed to go along largely on

its own momentum, and consequently I could now devote more attention to Xavier and the general field of Negro interest and need. I read as many pertinent books as I could find, and attended as many helpful conventions as possible. More and more, requests were coming to Xavier for data on the Negro, since the subject of racism was to the fore, what with Hitler so loudly emphatic about Nordic superiority. Asked by an American statesman, "When do you intend to cease persecuting Jews?" he had replied in effect, striking home at us powerfully, "When you liberty lovers over there cease persecuting Negroes." And this appeared to be somewhat stirring the American conscience. Moreover, Cardinal Pacelli, destined to become Pius XII, had written a rebuke, which, aimed at Germany, hit prejudice everywhere: "The Church can never make peace with those enemies possessed by superstition of race and blood."

It really looked at last as if the Negro would no longer be "mere." Already his status had changed from that of a caste to that of a minority group, and his vote—though limited—was beginning to count. Moved by the improvement, I donated my mite to it by stimulating the establishment of a Negro historical society at Xavier and also a press for the encouragement and dissemination of the researches of our students, in whom I tried to arouse a reasonable pride of group not only with Gospel truths but also with talks on such subjects as the three great African Middle Age kingdoms (Ghana, Mellestine and Songhai) and the brilliant Negro university in Timbuktu which, eight centuries ago, used to exchange professors with the leading schools of Europe. Also, I kept in close touch with Father John Gillard, whom I had taught Latin at Epiphany and who was now giving a vigorous account of himself as editor of *The Colored Harvest*, the magazine of the Josephite Order. We fed facts to each other, and one of the results was that he wrote and published two highly informative books on the Catholic Church and the Negro. For my part, I was content to do some articles; and among them was the following survey, which the newly formed Catholic Committee of the South invited me to read at a convention in Richmond.

THE NEGRO IN AMERICA

If America is to be saved for democracy and to serve as its mental and material arsenal, certainly the Church has no small part to play in the great enterprise. There is no other organization on the face of the earth better fitted to proclaim human dignity, rights, and worth, and to uphold the torch of truth in our darkening times.

By the light of that torch we can see many things to which the would-be worldly are always blind. And perhaps we should especially discern, for the immediate future, the need of knowing not less about the Maker—of whom we can never know enough—but more about our fellow man, so as to be truly democracy-conscious.

We cannot love God and hate man—His masterpiece on earth and the bearer of His image. To be anti-Semite or anti-Negro is to be both anti-Christian and antidemocratic. But in order to be pro-humanity we have to know humanity; and unfortunately a large number of our citizens here in America have been shunted into the shadows, away from our knowledge and interest. Lost, these must be found, for they seem to have become the very test of the sincerity of our democracy and Christianity in the eyes of the world.

The Negro is not a problem but a person—a fellow being—a brother. As such, he should be accepted and given his place, not beneath but beside us. Justice, charity, our Constitution, our Bill of Rights, and simple social grace require this. And the over-all need is understanding. If we do not meet and settle a minor challenge at home, how shall we deal with the major ones abroad? Where, then, is our leadership?

Many Americans hold that the Negro has offered too little to warrant his incorporation into the body politic. They argue, "Can any good come out of Africa?" just as, two thousand years ago, the thoughtless questioned, "Can any good come out of Nazareth?" Yet the truth is that long before the shining of Bethlehem's star the light of civilization shone below the Isthmus of Suez, and the land of Egypt was settled by Negroes, and some of the greatest Pharaohs were as dark-skinned as any cotton picker in Alabama today.

The predecessor of our present Holy Father sent scholarly researchers to the so-called Dark Continent, and they excavated objects which would indicate ancient cultures there to have been of as high a degree as—perhaps higher than—those of corresponding periods in Europe. Early explorers have left records of kingdoms and cities that flourished in defiance of the Sahara. Far from having slept through the centuries, Mother Africa taught her children to domesticate the sheep and the ox and endowed them with art, a homely philosophy, and a rich folklore. Best of all, she told them of God; and not a single tribe without faith has ever been found among them. Hence it is necessary for us to concede that when the Negro came to these shores he had something to give.

He figured importantly in our national history, but our school children are never told that, in a sense, he was a co-discoverer of America. Alonzo Pietro, the pilot of one of Columbus's three ships—the *Niña*—was black. "Il Negro," the record of the voyage describes him. The Negro stood with Balboa when the Pacific rolled for the first time before the white man's eyes. He was among the first explorers of Arizona and New Mexico. He accompanied De Soto into the Mississippi Valley. With Menéndez he shared in the founding of the oldest city in the United States, St. Augustine, decades before the Pilgrims landed at Plymouth. And he played his part in the war that made America by making America free, for his was the first blood to be shed in the Boston Massacre. He fought at the Battle of Bunker Hill in the person of Peter Salem, and dispatched an important enemy, Major Pitcairn. He defended the Colonial Army in the Battle of Long Island and was heartily praised by Lafayette.

He was in the War of 1812 with Commodore Perry and gave a good account of himself with Andrew Jackson in the Battle of New Orleans. After the victory there Jackson spoke: "Men of color! Soldiers! I have expected much from you, and you have surpassed my expectations. Your country will honor your valor."

In the Civil War the Negro acted in a manner beyond praise. His was the great task of keeping the plantations going and protecting women and children while the masters and their sons were off in uniform; and he remained loyal to it, a classic example of returning good for evil.

In the Spanish-American War he distinguished himself at the Battle of San Juan Hill and won the commendation of Theodore Roosevelt.

In the World War over 200,000 Negroes crossed the Atlantic. They are said to have been the first of the American Expeditionary Forces to go into action, and some of them were among the first to win the *Croix de Guerre*. Four whole regiments were decorated for bravery.

Since the Emancipation Proclamation the Negro has made more progress than any other group, similarly handicapped, in the same space of time; showing himself a genuine asset to America, because such an advance could not have been effected without intelligence and stamina.

By the early thirties, he had fifty-one banks, doing seventy-five million dollars' worth of business a year. Industrially, his contribution to the commonweal is very high. His fingers keep bringing up the white gold of cotton from southern soil, and his inventive ability has been noteworthy. Politically, he has given evidence that he can stand on his own feet. There are over fifty villages and towns and ten settlements in the United States populated and administered by the colored, notably Mound Bayou in Mississippi and Boloy in Oklahoma. In the former place, quite significantly, the jail has been dispensed with as useless.

The story of the Negro is particularly commendable in its educational chapter. At the time of the Civil War ninety per cent

of the group could neither read nor write, but in the statistics of
a decade ago, hardly sixteen per cent were shown to be illiterate,
and now the record is nearer to five. Today the group has 109
colleges in America with 45,000 students, and each year the
graduates number from two to five thousand. There are many
doctors of philosophy, and more than one hundred Negroes
have already been honored with biographical sketches in the
American Who's Who.

Aframerica has reared 42,000 churches, and attendance exceeds
5,000,000. The Baptists claim 3,000,000 or more; 1,350,000 are
Methodists; and the Catholic total is less than 400,000. Why the
smallness of this last percentage? The explanation has to be sought
far back. Only one of the thirteen original colonies was settled
by Catholics, and even there, in ten years' time, the Catholic
influence declined, while the Protestant increased. As for Catholic Louisiana, it did not have enough priests even for the white
apostolate. Then again, Catholics settled mostly in cities, while
the colored were attracted by and large to the soil. But now the
picture is changing, with the colored flocking into urban life.

What does the Negro want today as he "stands at the gate and
knocks," like One who was despised twenty centuries ago? He
dreams of a larger share in education, without which he cannot
duly be fitted for his full share in the benefits of democracy.
Every American should be educated, since this was evidently the
intent of the Founding Fathers; yet from two to twenty times as
much money has been spent on white children as on colored, and
the disparity is a glaring one.

The Negro wants more justice in the courts, which often rule
fantastically where he is concerned.

He wants the right to work and jobs to be offered on the basis
of ability—not withheld because of the color of skin.

He wants adequate police protection in his districts.

He wants a share in civic improvements and a chance to live
humanly. In a recent study of two thousand cases of colored
planters in the Deep South, it was discovered that the average

annual income was only $125, or $1.78 per individual per month.

He wants to be acknowledged as having the same needs as other men, and to walk in dignity with his God.

What has the Catholic Church been doing for him? In the field of education, much. From the very beginning, she set about her task. In 1829 the Oblate Sisters of Providence founded their congregation in Baltimore, to be followed in 1842 by the Sisters of the Holy Family in New Orleans. In 1871 the Josephite Fathers started their apostolate, and then the order of English Franciscan nuns appeared. A half century ago a great blessing was bestowed on the Church and the country in the person of Mother Katherine Drexel. Just as the stars in the sky shine down on this earth, so the works of this holy woman through the South and the West gleam heavenward.

Today hundreds of priests, representing twenty-two religious orders and the diocesan clergy, are devoted to the teaching of the Negro in the South; and also two thousand Sisters are giving their all.

But socially our program has lagged, and it is essential that Catholics—and all Americans—learn more about the historical background and the human possibilities of the Negro if their attitude toward him is to become more sensible and constructive. They should note organizations like the National Association for the Advancement of Colored People and the Urban League. The work of the Interracial Commission in Atlanta and the Catholic Interracial Council in New York should be studied, appreciated, abetted, and subsidized. Protests against any gross example of racism should be organized, for if the voice of Christian democracy is not raised to protect our colored brothers, it is neither democratic nor Christian.

In fine, the Mystical Body of Christ, in which souls are cells, is not a theological speculation but a vital revelation. And now is eminently the time for a readjustment to it, as America, looking out on a vast scene of human wretchedness beyond her borders, is girding for a crusade. To be worthy, she must set her own house in order and have clean hands with which to dispense her blessings.

It would be pleasant to record that this paper, so earnestly read and expatiated on by me at a morning session of the Richmond convention of the Catholic Committee of the South, immediately produced a good effect. But it didn't; or at least not quite. One of the gentlemen who heard it became very ungentlemanly when he saw a colored priest at our luncheon in the Jefferson Hotel that noon. The fact of a Negro—priest or no priest—sitting with whites at table was more than he could endure. He left the dining room and fumed in the lobby about "this flaunting of the color line, this social outrage, this heinous thing." He even prophesied for the Jefferson a doom by fire. And sure enough! Not long after, as I was to learn, fire did break out in the gracious old hostelry. A really damaging blaze. And perplexedly, until the return of a little wisdom, I'd wail within myself, "O Lord, why do you not give more co-operation to those of us who wish only to do your will? Why must bigotry rather than brotherhood appear to be vindicated?"

From Richmond, the day of the address, I rode over to Washington to see the papal legate himself. Like the Holy Father in the Eternal City, the Most Reverend Amleto Giovanni Chicognani was quite accessible, and courteously I was admitted to him. We conversed for more than an hour about the missions. There was nothing I could tell him that he did not already know, but he listened attentively, drawing me out and relieving the tensions that every laborer in a thwarted field is bound to feel. And he especially helped me by hinting that soon an expression of Rome's mind on evangelical matters would be reaching these shores, so that I was personally prepared for the message of the new Pope's second encyclical, *Sertum laetitiae sanctae*, which would do much for the advancement, prestige, and encouragement of the Clavers in the South with its tenor, "We confess that we feel a special paternal affection, which is certainly inspired by heaven, for the Negro people dwelling among you; because, in the field of religion and education, we know that they need special care and comfort and are very deserving of it. We therefore invoke an abundance of heavenly blessing, and we pray fruitful success, for those whose generous zeal is devoted to their welfare."

Strange—the sublimity of a missionary career, blessed by the Pope, and the absurdity of so many of its incidents! Perhaps *le Bon Dieu* permits the absurdity so that His ministers' humility—and sense of humor—may be preserved. But whatever the reason, the fact of the matter was that, pastoring my flock back in New Orleans, I repeatedly met the ridiculous in my pursuit of the ideal. Examples were various. . . .

There was the sober delegation of women who, planning a chicken-salad supper for the benefit of the church and wishing to hold down expenses so as to jack up profits, called on me for permission to mix a little—well, a lot—of cheaper veal and canned tuna with the chicken, since the consumers wouldn't notice the difference. And when I told them that God would notice the difference, one almost floored me by retorting, "Well, Father, didn't He hisself stretch a few loaves'n fishes as far as we wants to stretch our chicken?"

And there was Lucille Page!—a fervent old soul who sang out so raucously at services and grated on so many nerves that I had to beg her to temper her love for the Lord with a little consideration for man, and even threaten smilingly that if she didn't, a "Page" would be missing from the annals of our parish. So, in her own individualistic way, she tried to please me. One stormy night, thoroughly unfit for human being or beast, I noticed from the sacristy that the church was empty or, rather, that it would have been if Lucille had not been leading in a stranger. Both were drenched, but the stranger was the more pitiable sight, elderly, shabby, and evidently blind. Lucille assisting, he groped his way into a back pew and fell on his knees. Then she sloshed up by herself to her usual place near the Blessed Mother's altar, and I came out into the sanctuary to conduct our regular novena. When I had finished the prescribed prayers, I turned full-face to my scant congregation. Lucille, with no singing to keep her awake, was sound asleep. But her poor man in the back pew, his head bowed down, his hand trembling before him surely in an effort to thrust aside the veils that separated his soul from light, looked so appealing that, overcome, I went right into my sermon as if the church were filled, and even rose to such heights of elo-quence as I'd seldom or never reached before. But when, at the finish, I went to shake hands with this great listener, I found that he had not been listening at all. He could not have been. Worse than sound asleep like Lucille, he was drunk. *Blind* drunk.

(When I told this experience to a fellow priest the next day, he laughed and said, "Well, it wasn't exactly unique. There's the one about a similar souse who strayed into Benediction service and snored so loud that an usher had to shake him awake. The fellow rubbed his bleary eyes and, seeing lights all around and Sisters coming down the middle aisle, muttered to the usher, 'Some night club you got here, bub. But what a dumb floor show!' ")

A very good old man of my congregation was arrested for driving his Noah's ark of a car, with which he earned a bare living, through a red light on Canal Street. "Why did you do it, Sam?" I asked when I went to get him out. "Mah brakes is all gone an' Ah couldn't 'ford t' git'm fixed, an' they jus' slipped," he said morosely, "but that ole machine couldn't hurt nobody, seein' how it moves lak a snail." Knowing that it would go hard with him when his case should come up in traffic court, because one of those periodic campaigns for safe-and-sane driving was on at the time, I pondered the Gospel counsel that we should be as wise as serpents and harmless as doves; and perhaps, too, I did not forget what Sinclair Lewis had taught me in preparation for that Ford Hall appearance of mine. So after getting Sam's car reconditioned, I primed him; and when he went before the judge shortly after, he said nothing about his "brakes slippin'." Instead, true to my instruction, he told him, "Y'r honor, Ah saw all the white folks goin' through the green light, an' Ah jus' went through the red." The judge smiled and the case was dismissed.

Then there was the time when Clailee, my housekeeper, wishing to surprise me, so neatly rearranged the books in the parish library—according to size and color—that for weeks I could hardly find a thing. And the day a woman, brandishing a license, pushed a highly intoxicated man into the rectory and demanded action! "But he is in no state for marriage," I said. "It's the only state I can get him to come in," she snapped.

One morning, when about to leave the house, I called to the maid who was working upstairs, "Can't find my hat. Must've left it in my bedroom." And instead of her bringing it to me as I had expected, she shouted down a comment which amounted to a cheery invitation to come and get it myself: "Well, them that ain't got brains has t'have laigs."

Another time one of my most faithful but least literate female workers approached Monsignor Wynhoven for a donation toward the refurbishing of Blessed Sacrament rectory. The word "rectory" being too big for her to pronounce or even remember, she amused him by explaining, "Po' Father Murphy wants t'have his whatcha-ma-call-it painted green. Me—I likes gray." He gave her a five-dollar bill; but his beneficence did not end there. The following week, at a special dinner in the archiepiscopal residence, to which I was invited as Xavier's representative, he teased me amiably and purposely by retailing the woman's remark to the guests. They all smiled at me. "How much, Father, will the job on the 'whatcha-ma-call-it' cost?" asked His Excellency solicitously. When I told him, he pledged seventy-five dollars; and that set the ball of generosity rolling. "Put me down for fifty, Father," said one of the bishops present. "I'll give the same," volunteered another. And so on. Before I left I felt like Croesus; and soon the rectory was duly painted—but not green. In deference to my humble parishioner who had helped me so much by not being able to pronounce a word of three syllables and therefore substituting one of five, I had chosen a wise gray.

But the seriousness of mission life kept pulsing under all the trivialities. Out of many examples of that seriousness, I remember most the murky night when a rooster crowed on the back steps of the rectory and my housekeeper said to me, "That's a sure sign someone's gonna die." Thunder was rumbling, rain falling, and the telephone jangling.

Having read a good deal about mobs and lynchings, I'd often wondered just how well I'd measure up against any such diabolism. Would I have the spirit that our Father Warren showed when he bearded Ku Klux Klan kidnapers in Norfolk, or would I simply go to pieces? And now the time of test had come, for the voice on the phone was telling me that one of my best Holy Name men had just killed a little white girl. Almost cut her in two! His automobile, impelled by another behind it, had crashed over a sidewalk and caught the child, who was passing by, in the wreckage.

Though the case was purely accidental, the very idea of black slaying white in the hot-blooded South conjured up awful possibilities. Would my man be torn limb from limb, before I could get to him? Schooled only in peace, was I at all capable of dealing with a rabble? Might there be a finis for pastor and sheep alike? What could I do?

A cold sweat on me, I said an Act of Contrition, committed myself to the Lord, and dashed off to the scene of violence. What I found was largely anticlimax. True, a crowd had gathered, but the police were in perfect control. A path opened up to me, and I entered the patrol wagon where the "killer" sat cowering. His chin was on his chest. One of his hands grasped mine, the other clutched his rosary. He could say nothing.

We were driven to the nearest station, and there I testified to his character. He was paroled, the word of a clergyman meaning much in New Orleans; and I went to the parents of the child, to plead for him further. Good Christians, they tried to understand and, despite their overwhelming grief, promised not to press charges.

The moon was releasing itself from thick blankets of clouds when I returned to the rectory at a late hour that night. Soon the sun would be rising, and the dawn of a new day in interracial attitude seemed to me to be nearer than ever before.

The successive priests who shared my second mission in New Orleans were Father Tom Brophy, a smiling shepherd around whom lambs flocked as around the Savior himself; Father John McShane, a tireless worker and a born leader of youth; and Father Dom Marchese, as gentle and devoted an apostle as I have ever known.

Because time was beginning to show—white in my hair, and a thinning out on top—they spared me many an effort that I still wanted to make; and this irked me a little, for Archbishop Rummel had renovated the old archdiocese with his energy and interest, and it was the ardent wish of all his clergy to please him with a fullness of service. I refused to believe that middle age mattered, and succeeded fairly well in my illusion until truth glared at me. That was on a day when, realizing that my dingy felt hat ought to be discarded, I entered a Canal Street haberdashery and bought a brand-new one. On the way out I glanced at my reflection in the plate-glass window of the store and nodded, feeling younger and sprightlier already. What a boost to a man's morale, as to a woman's, a mere change of headgear could be! But on arriving home, I removed my fresh possession only to discover with astonishment and chagrin that it was not fresh at all. In fact, it was the same hat that had been serving me so long, my purchase having been left where I had made it.

But I hardly dared admit, even then, the end of life's heyday. There was too much yet to be done, and so little had been accomplished. I thought of St. Philip Neri's customary rallying of his community, "Well, Brothers, when shall we begin to do good?"

It almost appeared to me that so far I had not even warmed up for the work required of me. Father John Albert, one of our senior Josephites, could boast of at least two thousand converts; and what was my handful alongside a record like that! The voice of Holy Scripture rang in my conscience, "The night cometh, when no man can work." How near the end to the beginning!

As if to make my reflections more somber, about this time a colored man asked me point-blank, "What has the Church done —what is she doing—for my people?" I had already answered such a question aggressively in the paper delivered at the convention in Richmond, but now that I was on the defensive, I had to use something more than speech. Bringing him to my mission classrooms, I said, "See how the seeds of decent living are being sown." And from the school I led him on my round of sick calls, so that he could witness how the Church remembered the poor. Maybe he was impressed, but he murmured, "The 'Reds' also teach and remember." And I warned him that, as far as I knew, the "Reds" taught men to remember their woes rather than their blessings and inflamed society rather than relieved it. Was the leftist "comrade" any improvement on the Christian "brother"? What admirer of Moscow wasted time at a lowly sickbed when there were showy rostra like the Scottsboro case from which to shout? Whether I really convinced my man I never knew, for he was a transient visitor to town; but at least he came to the novena in honor of Our Lady of Perpetual Help that night.

Ah yes, each missionary in the South had worked as grace works, beginning at the beginning and proceeding not with sound but soundness, not with panaceas but principles. My own Josephite Order, as the first to espouse the Negro cause exclusively, had kept the sanctuary lamp of an ideal well trimmed and agleam through the years, showing the way. Other orders were now being attracted, and the prospect of a wide evangelization, though still dim, was growing brighter. As a matter of fact, the small colored harvest was already, proportionately, somewhat larger than the white harvest.

Father Gillard, young, energetic, brilliant, impatient for spectacular results in the field he loved, remarked to me in one of his many letters, "Any society, to have life in it, needs a few good funerals"; and that, as much as the episode of a new hat left in a haberdashery and an old one worn out, made me the more sensitive to my season of decline. But shortly after writing of funerals he himself passed away, and our older men were still carrying on, bearing the heat and burden of the day without complaint, seeking no praise, setting a quiet standard for young apostles. Could not—must not—one's last phase, enriched by experience, be the most fruitful time of life?

While this question was preoccupying me, another playscript, as uncontrived as a blossom, and as tangy as the huckleberries of my boyhood days, came to me from Eddie Dowling. It presented a gallery of characters not only exteriorly but interiorly, and its theme seemed to be that no life is valueless, that each makes a contribution to the treasury of existence by fostering some ideal, however humble. "Give me your opinion pronto," wrote Eddie in an enclosed letter. "The author is a young fellow whose ideas are dreams or whose dreams are ideas, I don't know which. Anyhow, I'm depending a lot, just as before, on your reaction."

He did not have to wait long. After two good readings, the second more pleasant than the first, I was all for this strange comedy drama, which defied every rule of construction I'd ever read, but displayed in its very lack of recognizable technique what a poet might have called "the graceful gracelessness of boughs" or "the careless carpentry of snow." The only character in it that seemed unconvincing to me was Kitty Duval—a childlike, almost ethereal victim of the night. But thinking of the Magdalen and the Lord's words, "Many sins are forgiven her because she has loved much," I felt that I better understood what the author was trying to express. And then, satisfied that here was a play as good, in its way, as *Shadow and Substance*, I telegraphed Eddie: "Fresh as April and a new moon. Just right for a jaded Broadway. Do produce it."

He did produce it, with himself in the chief role; and it won both the Pulitzer Prize and the Drama Critics' Circle Award. *The Time of Your Life* went down in theatrical history, and a new playwright, William Saroyan, became the theater's white-haired boy.

Seeing the Saroyan career all abloom under the right touch, I now thought that the talent of one of my own boys might be similarly given release from the fate of blushing unseen and wasting its sweetness on the desert air. Ralph Cager, a Xavierite, had what seemed to me to be one of the finest of baritone voices; and right after graduation he expressed his desire to offer it to the public and asked, "Would it be foolish of me, Father, to attempt New York?" No, I didn't think so. Paul Robeson had more than made good with his voice. Too, there was the Negro boy whose song, "I Don't Want to Set the World on Fire" had brought him fame; and I remembered the three entertainers whom Eddie Dowling discovered in Harlem and featured with happy effect in *Honeymoon Lane.*

Cash was still scarce, but I got just enough together for Ralph's train fare. His eyes were wet as he thanked me.

Two weeks went by and I received a depressing air-mail letter. Yes, Ralph had arrived and had been auditioned. "But your charity rather than your wisdom must have recommended him, Father," wrote Eddie, to whom I had sent him. "He is very likable, but his singing, I am so sorry to say, did not sound even ordinarily good to me. Well, we all make our mistakes. . . . I forced some money on him, and I gave him a note of introduction to the manager of the company doing *Porgy and Bess,* on the chance that he might get into the chorus. Haven't heard from him since."

I read this letter over and over, trying to understand. Was Ralph's failure to make a good impression due to his having been worn out from the long trip North in a day coach? He had not looked any too well when he left New Orleans, maybe he had eaten little or nothing on the way. An awe of Broadway, and a too tense effort to please, would have increased his disadvantage.

Days passed, and at length there came a full account of what happened. Ralph had found employment not in *Porgy and Bess* as a chorister, but in the Hotel New Yorker as a busboy; and one night an official who had taken a fancy to him and learned of his ambition gave him a chance to sing in one of the floor shows. This time, better prepared, he did so well that his audience clapped and cheered. Encore followed encore, until, exhausted, he had to extend his hand in a mute plea that they let him go. And his triumph, doubly precious because of its delay, did not go to his head but his heart. In the hotel that night, he took ill. Before dawn he died.

Soon many a city knew of Ralph Cager, because Louis Sobol devoted one of his widely syndicated columns to his memory, captioning the article, "That's Why Darkies Were Born," and expressing in it the poignancy of a success which, so unexpected and complete, had been more than meekness could bear and which had therefore not only begun but ended a career.

My little army of the Lord, recruited in my home town during the earlier years of my ministry, was now a developed reality. Out of the thirty-five youngsters who had come to the Josephite Order from Salem and vicinity, a dozen or more had persevered to the priesthood; among them, John Lundergan, a cousin of mine, and John O'Connell, my sister Annie's son. They both were now sent to churches in New Orleans, and their arrival made me so want to be young again that I almost felt I was.

They shared their enthusiasms, and we created a little Pierian spring of our own. Father Lundergan liked to preach and did it so beautifully that, proud of having been one of his teachers at Epiphany, I had him invited everywhere. His pastor, wiser than I, requested me to limit these displays, observing that plaudits might not be the best thing for a young priest. As for Father O'Connell, he did not concentrate on pulpit excellence but showed an interest in all forms of parochial service. During the Lenten season of his first year in New Orleans, he wanted his sodality to put on a Passion play and asked me to suggest one. Recalling my own little drama, *Mary of Magdala*, I unearthed the script for him. "Great," he said loyally, scanning the old pages. "Will you help me direct it?" Help him? I determined to do more than that. Like Eddie Dowling and a young Salemite constructing a diving board for a pool in Lime Rock long ago, he and I—nephew and uncle—should work as a team.

There were handicaps from the start. Except for pretty little Teresa Ferguson, a Xavierite, who was to be the Magdalen, the only actors we could secure were wholly inexperienced; but we felt sure that strenuous rehearsals would take care of that. Our scenery was no good, but dim lights, like charity covering a multitude of sins, could conceal most of the blemishes and effect something like a simple Biblical setting. Costumes and props could be borrowed from Xavier. The only thing that seemed to elude our resourcefulness was caused by my having added to the script a Last Supper sequence suggestive of the institution of the Blessed Sacrament. How could this be best handled? After some headaches, we decided that a group of apostles rendering a hymn offstage would be just right; and the relief from this solution was vast until we realized that two more difficulties were entailed. First, there was no room backstage for choristers; secondly, nobody in the cast but Teresa Ferguson, whose role required her to be out front practically all the time, and whose sex certainly disqualified her for an apostle, could sing well. It occurred to us, though, that Werlein's, the music store on Canal Street which had given the country in antebellum days the great song "Dixie" and which had been fostering music along the Crescent Bend ever since, might lend us a phonograph and a suitable male-chorus record. "Ask and ye shall receive." So we did ask and we did receive; and at long last we considered ourselves quite ready for the unveiling of our masterpiece. "It can't miss," said Father O'Connell. "It has everything."

Our first performance, on Palm Sunday afternoon, was a special one—for the kind of audience that Sinclair Lewis had called celestial. From their convents the good Sisters, ever ready to encourage a parochial project and lend themselves not only as angels but also as trial balloons, came and filled the hall. A hush enfolded them as the curtain rose on our cheesecloth conception of "a room in Jerusalem." The first act began on a note of casual calm and assurance, achieved by many a hard rehearsal, and interest smoothly ascended. Behind the scenes, in a narrow windowless little space lit by a single electric bulb, coatless Father O'Connell and I were working the props and occasionally peering through a hole in a drape at the fine account the actors were giving of themselves. *Success, success.* And now, without a hitch in the buildup, the time was come for the wafting of the audience to the very peak of experience. Piously Father O'Connell plugged in the phonograph. Reverently I handed him our precious male-chorus record of *"Panis Angelicus,"* and he placed it with infinite care on the already revolving disk.

Just as he was about to touch needle to wax and release the harmony that would impart to the audience a sense of the holy unseen, the back door of the stage swung open and revealed the boyish but stodgy presence of Father Ed Hennessey, second assistant of Corpus Christi and last person we wanted to behold.

"Hey, can I be of any help?" He spoke in a whisper which sounded to us like a blast.

Nervously we gestured him to go away, knowing that though his heart was big, his awkwardness equaled it. An elephant would have been more welcome at the moment than this—this benignant flubdub. Our mute dismissal became almost frantic, but he lumbered right in, slamming the door behind him. Next, true to type, he tripped over an exposed electric cord on the floor, instantly causing a fuse to blow out and thereby plunging everything into inky darkness. The machine gave a *gr-r* and went dead.

Father O'Connell gasped at me, "We'll have to be the Twelve

Apostles and do the singing. Confound that Hennessey! I—I'll be tempted to strangle him if he dares join in."

Neither he nor I had memorized "*Panis Angelicus.*" The only other hymn we could think of, and somehow we thought of it simultaneously, was "Nearer My God to Thee," although God had never seemed farther away from us before. Atremolo, we burst into would-be song but got no farther than "E'n though it be a cross that raises me" when, choked with embarrassment at our miserable rendition, we broke down. *Failure, failure.*

To make matters even worse, if possible, Hennessey *did* dare to take up the strain and carry on for us, until he himself, convulsed with suppressed laughter at our predicament, likewise had to quit.

After that we just stood in agony and gloom as the actors out front continued to deliver their lines and the play somehow continued to its close. Then, taking a deep breath, I went alone and miserable to mingle with the audience and offer an apologetic explanation, my partner being too ashamed to do anything but shake his fist in Hennessey's face.

But what was my surprise to find the Sisters sitting as if under a spell!—their hands like lilies in their laps, their gaze mystical. Before I could speak, one of them came to and said, "Oh, Father dear, it was all so lovely! So moving!" And another chimed in, "Almost unbearably beautiful." And a third sent me reeling as she sighed with utter sincerity, "Particularly that offstage part where the singing voices, so perfectly timed and trained, quavered with emotion and cadenced into such a wonderful, soul-stirring silence."

Three other performances of *Mary of Magdala* were given, and even without the aid of Father Hennessey's fuse-blowing feet and "Nearer My God to Thee," they were successful. Hence, when Lent rolled around again and Station WWL honored me with an invitation to furnish something suitable to the holy season, I once more thought of my sturdy little play.

All that I had to do was adapt the old script to the new medium. This I cheerfully did, and WWL was pleased.

Immediately after Mass the Sunday morning the play was to go on the air, I went to my room in Blessed Sacrament rectory and seated myself in front of a decrepit Crosley set which, originally a donation from some well-meaning person with no further use for it, had been palmed off among the prizes at three of my parish fairs, for it had always been re-donated to the church by the ungrateful and slightly indignant winners. Not even Lucille Page, who lacked all sense of suffering, wanted it. But how glad I now was that I had not thrown it away!

There was difficulty in finding my station, or any other, on the old thing. I kept dialing and dialing, but evoked mostly static; and when I finally did tune in on WWL, my unhappiness only increased, because what I caught was no more than a line of my script. A line spoken by a Pharisee astonished at the spectacle of the Magdalen throwing herself at the Savior's feet and washing them with her tears. "Mary—Mary of Magdala! This is the most infamous woman of the town!" But it came forth from the decrepitude of the Crosley as a scratchy squeak. "Marie—Marie of Mag-dah-la! This ees the most in-fame-ous——"

My heart and ear all ache, I turned it off. Like Sinclair Lewis's *The Good Neighbor*, this radio offering of mine was as bad as bad could be. Never should my reach exceed my grasp again! Yet within an hour the telephone summoned me several times to receive congratulations from listeners who had either enjoyed the broadcast on instruments with exceedingly better reception than mine, or who were downright liars. And before the day was out telegrams of praise arrived from such definite sources of truth as Bishop Desmond of Alexandria and Archbishop Rummel himself; making me feel that, after all, the disappointments of life may be nothing more than the reverse side of its blessings.

After that the saga of a woman of many loves, fallen from grace, groping in darkness, and at last finding the Light—white with death and ruby sacrifice—at the feet of the Lover supreme, became my favorite meditation. Timeless, it seemed to me to typify the modern world. What prostitutions had involved humanity since the Age of Faith!—naturalism, rationalism, positivism, pragmatism, materialism. And now the weirdest *affaires du cœur* of all: nazism, fascism, and communism. But surely the tried soul of man, like the Magdalen's, was still seeking the Way, the Truth, and the Life. Surely it could and would find peace and renewal where she had found them. How much longer might grace be resisted? Why were shadows so repeatedly embraced?

Asking myself this, I yearned to see a surge of penitence sweeping modernity to the Source of salvation. So late the hour! Already Mars was again claiming Europe; and the Orient, under the might of Japan, was trembling; and now I read in a newspaper that F. Scott Fitzgerald—symbol of an era marked for decease from the start—was no more. Then, overnight, Pearl Harbor. . . .

Most of those who had lived through the former world war had neglected its lessons, and the new generation were having their eyes opened to the enormity of problems unsolved. Perhaps all would now come to realize that the ways of the world never end the woes of the world; and perhaps, too, it would be manifest that a vision cleansed with tears finds the path of wisdom best.

Hoping and praying, as all ministers of the spirit were hoping and praying, I watched the effect of the times especially on the people to whom I was vocationally committed. Seeing their sons going off to fight for everything the nation held dear, I was sure that, as a result, their rights would no longer be denied. The fostering of this confidence required some forgetting of the apparent thanklessness that had followed Negro service and sacrifice in the last war, but it was not hard to wax hopeful when the press announced that Robert Brooks, colored, was the first soldier of our armed forces to lay down his life in the present strife. How deeply and enduringly America, awakened as never before, would be affected by that!

Soon, however, other stories appeared, dismaying my fellow missionaries and me. It seemed that there was relentless—even bitter—racial division in Army and Navy alike. And on the home front conditions did not improve much. As the wounded were brought back, instances of the old animus appeared most painfully, seemingly in proof that its vigor had not declined, but increased. There was the report of a maimed Negro veteran who, ordered to give his place on a southern trolley to a white and hardy civilian, could only tear off the coat of his uniform, crying, "I fought for decency across the Pacific—I guess I'll have to fight for it here too." And there was the alleged case of our national enemies—German prisoners of war—being fed in a Dixie railroad-station restaurant while the colored American soldiers in charge of them were served through a back door where they might not offend white sensitivity by being seen. But most irrational of all was the bigotry that demanded the separation even of the blood plasma donated by Negroes to the common cause, an absurdity high-lighted by the reply of a doctor to some of the screamers, "Segregate it yourselves, if you can. *I* can't. Plasma is plasma."

But such evidences of intolerance were no more a proof that harmony was impossible than the bluster of winter is an argument against the eventual return of spring. Bewilderment, knotted nerves, and the terror of the times gave explanation, if not excuse, for them. One could now almost see America sinking to her knees and searching her soul; and what was this but the mood of the wounded thing named Magdalen who, twenty centuries before, writhed to the feet of the Divine Physician?

Indications of a spiritual and moral stirring in the nation multiplied; and even Hollywood, alert to the change or trend, was catering to it. Religious pictures were being produced with care and received with acclaim.

About this time a priest whose travels had taken him to the Coast in the interest of his just published book, *Men of Maryknoll,* stopped off at New Orleans on his return trip to New

York. A local literary group who had arranged a reception at the Roosevelt Hotel invited me to introduce him; and this I felt more than pleased and honored to do, because I had read his little volume and been deeply affected by its tales of missionary spirit. One of his heroes, Father Robert Cairns, had been a classmate of mine in seminary days at old St. Mary's in Baltimore. Red-haired, smiling Bobby, always with a luster in his Scotch-blue eyes and a heartiness in his handclasp! He had written to me from his field afar, and I'd sent him what few dollars I could spare to help relieve a poverty greater than my own; and somehow space had drawn us closer together, his gratitude reaching out to me and my admiration for his enterprise growing. But for some time now I had not been hearing from him or about him; and at last I knew, from *Men of Maryknoll*, that his life was over. Stationed on the very isle where St. Francis Xavier, greatest missionary since Paul of Tarsus, dreamed of adding Cathay to his conquests for Christ and died, Bobby refused to abandon his post when word reached him that the Japs were on their way to take over; and his remaining meant the attainment of the martyr's crown for which Xavier himself had yearned.

Noticing how the ladies present at the reception in the Roosevelt were inspired by the mere sight of the priest-author, so tall, slender, softly mesmeric-eyed and spiritual, I presented him, in an effort to be bright, as "the ecclesiastical Sinatra." For that I should have been drawn and quartered, because this recorder of apostolic deeds was Father James Keller, soon to be founder of one of the most idealistic, yet most practical, projects ever to bless America—the Christopher movement.

His talk that day left an indelible memory, and I again longed to do more than I had been doing for the Lord. I thought of the many little ways in which good civilians were straining to preserve a normal community. I thought of the uncertainty of the future, the prayers beneath the determined but sore-tired hope of the nation; the purged, the penitential, the Magdalen mood. Then I thought of the Magdalen herself and began to write, or rather rewrite, that play of mine which had come through the hazards of stage and radio production. Why could it not be made into a helpful readable thing? Perhaps a novel . . .

That night my pen flew. And when dawn was creeping into my room, ten full pages lay before me. Too, some poinsettias showed themselves above the nearest windowsill. Like great lilies reddened with sunrise, they spread their gorgeous but humble coronas; and I remembered having seen in my Bible dictionary that the lilies of the Holy Land were scarlet, and that their heads bowed toward earth but their petals curled heavenward. Back to me came one of Thomas Carlyle's assertions to the effect that he would give all the paintings of Raphael for one glimpse of the countenance of the earnest young rabbi delivering long ago the parable of the lilies of the field. I imagined the rabbi's countenance in the risen sun, and considering those poinsettias at the window, I found a title for my ten pages.

Through December and January all my free moments were spent at my desk, and by mid-February *The Scarlet Lily* was finished. Putting it aside, I turned my attention to a play that Eddie Dowling had just sent me. This one pleased me, in several respects, even more than the others. It lacked the spiritual quality of *Shadow and Substance* and the colorful vignetting of *The Time of Your Life*, but it had assets of its own and seemed to mirror the pathos and bittersweetness of human existence in its crystal stream. I felt as grateful to the author for having written it as to Eddie for having sent it, and my letter of commentary brimmed with enthusiasm. A few days after I mailed that letter, a telegram came from Eddie. *Thanks. Agree with you that Glass Menagerie and Tennessee Williams have something. Am going ahead with production.*

Meanwhile Father Conroy, my latest and highly efficient assistant, had picked up *The Scarlet Lily* and perused it with interest. And now he made a suggestion. "*Extension Magazine* in

Chicago and Bruce Company in Milwaukee are running a literary contest," he said. "The winning novel will be serialized in *Extension* and brought out in book form by Bruce. Good cash prize too. Why not compete? I'll wrap up the manuscript and mail it for you if you'll let me."

With nothing to lose, I let him.

A month later a special-delivery air-mail letter arrived from Father Joseph Lux, editor of *Extension*, telling me that my story had possibilities but, for one thing, was too long. Would I be willing to cut it down to about eighty thousand words in accordance with a ruling of the contest which I must have overlooked? For another thing, the second half should be recast, because it let the Magdalen of the first chapters melt like a mist in the shining presence of the Savior. This, though factually good, was fictionally bad. Readers liked to have their heroine kept vital to the very last page. In short, would I come to Chicago for an editorial conference?

The next day I boarded the Panama Limited. One sunrise more and I was sitting in the office of *Extension*, vis-à-vis Father Lux himself ("Call me Joe") and Miss Eileen O'Hayer, his executive secretary. Never had I met two keener or kindlier personalities. Within a half hour they had told me more about authorship than I could have gotten out of textbooks; and they knew what they were talking about, for their periodical led its field. They analyzed my work thoroughly, generous in their acknowledgment of whatever merits it had, frank in their exposition of flaws. We say eye to eye on everything. I remained in Chicago three days, practically rewriting one half of the story and amending certain points in the other. This was cricket, because the only other manuscript that had won the judges' serious attention was also being revised by its author.

"Hope the 'Lily' wins," said Father Lux the morning I was leaving, "but whether it does or not, we'll publish it in *Extension*." And he handed me a substantial advance check. Eileen merely bestowed that floral Irish smile of hers, worth a mint.

From Chicago, I carried away a heart-warming memory of my two new friends and of a meeting with Samuel A. Baldus, the much earlier editor of *Extension* who had bought my first short story in seminary days and chided me mildly for having had a character in it walk up two flights of stairs and then lean out a window to receive a letter from the postman in the street: "How far can one's fancy—and psychological suspenders—stretch?" Well, my imagination had stretched far enough to evolve a whole novel from the very few texts in the Bible about Mary Magdalen; and my elasticity was now such that almost as soon as I got home I snapped right back to Chicago. The reason was that the judges of the literary contest, having immediately gone over my revised *Scarlet Lily*, had come to a unanimous decision that it be awarded the prize; and Bruce Company and *Extension* had decided that the prize be given with ceremony in the Gold Room of the Drake Hotel on the Gold Coast.

When I stepped once more into the *Extension* office, representatives of the press were there. Never having been interviewed since Emmanuel Margolies's funeral, I felt as ill at ease now as then. "What caused you to write your book?" asked a sad-faced, gray-suited young fellow, pad and pencil ready. "Mosquitoes," I blurted, trying to get back to the start and remembering how the little pests had helped by keeping me wide awake throughout an unseasonably warm midwinter night. "That's a good angle, Father," he said, suddenly grinning. "You mean you were too poor to buy screens for your windows 'way down yonder in New Orleans, and couldn't sleep, and just had to do something; so you got up and wrote a winner. Bitten, as it were, into success, eh?" Confusedly I replied, "Something like that." He whistled softly, jotting a note. Then came a swarm of personal questions worse than mosquitoes, and I almost wished I were back in Blessed Sacrament parish visiting the sick or talking to Lucille Page. But soon Eileen O'Hayer—bless her!—appeared and freed me by announcing that I was wanted in Father Lux's private office.

There within the sanctum I found him reading to a visitant bishop from the manuscript of *The Scarlet Lily*. He paused only to greet and introduce me, and I had to join the bishop in listening to the episode of Salome's dance, which was an integral part of the story. Such language! "With her hands—a pair of lotus blossoms—held high above her unruly tumble of curls, and her little bosom thrusting itself through a thin silk half jacket, her lissome body as erect as a young sapling, her bare feet fluttering, she was visible music." Was *that* my description of the daughter of Herod? I gazed worriedly at the bishop's face, trying to catch his thoughts, sure that he could not possibly approve; but it was a face that told nothing at all. And Father Lux read on: "Now a quiver ran from the hollow of her slim throat to the soles of her dainty feet; then from the twinkling toes up to the twilight countenance in which her eyes glistened like live beryls." Where, in the name of holy water, had that lush wordage come from? Though it was certainly mine, I did not know. Fidgety now, I again scanned the episcopal visage, hoping that Lux would cease, but he did not. His excellent voice was rendering each phrase the more vivid. "Her hips swayed—her skirt threw out its folds in the shape of a bell. She tore a flower from her hair, parted its beauty with her teeth, white and sharp, and tossed the petals to Herod. He strained forward——" The bishop also strained forward and his lips opened as he adjusted his pince-nez and turned his eyes to me. I braced myself for the worst. "Father Murphy," he said, suddenly asmile, "the weather must be very warm in New Orleans."

That day I met and dined with the Bruces, co-sponsors of the contest and as sterling a family of publishers as any author could wish. From the grandfather of the firm, with the gray beard and cultured benignity of a Longfellow, to the clean-cut grandson and personable granddaughter, the evidence of worth was so solid that I felt extremely proud to be admitted to the circle of their interest. And that night I was guest of honor at the Cathedral Book Club, which under the auspices of Father Emmet

Reagen had become a most flourishing concern. There I met people who had been only bright names to me: Maureen Daly, the young and very pretty author of *Seventeenth Summer;* Eddie Dogherty, the worldly-wise *Sun* scribe whose gifts had grown mellow with spirituality and altruism; Baroness de Hueck, whose heart had gone out to Harlem and the underprivileged everywhere; Fanny Butcher, the handsome and accomplished book appraiser of the Chicago *Tribune*. And what a special treat it was to see Father Joe Morrison, a dandy old classmate of mine at St. Mary's whom I'd not even glimpsed for years and who was now rector of the cathedral and a monsignor!

The following night the Gold Room of the Drake Hotel seemed a preview of paradise. Hospitality flowed in a warm, candle-lit stream; scores of literati, genial and congenial, were there; and the ensemble was perfected by the arrival of Archbishop (later Cardinal) Stritch, who personally presented the prize check. The big moment, I suppose, was my acceptance, for applause punctuated it. But it admitted the ridiculous too. Never having handled anything so valuable as that check before, I transferred it for safekeeping, and as fast as if it were a hot coal, to John F. Reilly—a loyal friend who had accompanied me from New Orleans but who had been so busy with business affairs in Chicago all day long that he had not had time to don his tuxedo. In a striped suit and soft collar, he looked more like a sports fan than a patron of literature, and I overheard somebody whispering to him as he pocketed the guerdon for me, "Are you Father Murphy's manager, sir?" Which made me feel more like a prize fighter than a prize winner and less like a pugilist than a race horse or an ass.

Nobody present, except Father Lux, Eileen O'Hayer, and the Bruce literary editor, had yet read my story; but everybody talked about it, assuming that it must be something, else why the celebrating? So a swirl of publicity began; and, some weeks later, when galleys were available and I was deep again in the life of old New Orleans, proof of the far-reaching effect of that swirl reached me. A telephone call from the land of Aladdin and his wonderful lamp! I could not believe the honeyed voice announcing itself as that of a Hollywood agent and telling me that a major studio was interested in purchasing my story. Would I accept some thousands of dollars? I thought the whole thing a ribbing on the part of a fellow clergyman; but when I realized that it was nothing of the sort, I had just enough breath left in me to gasp yes. Bells were ringing in my brain.

Next morning Elsa Neuberger, of the Vanguard Films staff in New York, phoned to tell me that her big boss in Hollywood, the purchaser of my *Scarlet Lily*, was delighted with the deal, and read for my approval the account that would appear forthwith in the New York *Times* and other papers. Her accents seemed melody itself as she went on to say, "And Ingrid Bergman is to be the star. Mr. David O. Selznick plans to make this picture his biggest production since *Gone with the Wind*."

When the book issued from the press, life became a carrousel for me. Jack Lester, an energetic young reporter, wrote me up in the New Orleans *Item* so glowingly that I had a feeling of being slightly mistaken for God. There were radio interviews, photographs, letters, telegrams—the heartiest and most congratulatory from Sinclair Lewis, requests from the Coast for a look-see at any other stories I might have up my sleeve, an attempt of a Manhattan bureau to sign me for a lecture tour, paragraphs in Hedda Hopper's and Louella Parsons's columns, an inclusion of *The Scarlet Lily* in Dorothy Kilgallen's "tops-in-town" and national best-seller lists.

Testimonial dinners. In the Rex Room of Antoine's Restaurant kindly and generous Frances Parkinson Keyes gave me the first—and the best—of a series. At another celebration, this one at the Roosevelt Hotel, a bewildered toastmaster presented me as the author of "the already well-known and widely read *Scarlet Lady*." But catching himself, he tried to correct his lurid mistake by smiling toothily and chuckling miserably, "Do forgive me,

Father Murray, for my pardonable slip of the tongue. What I meant to—er—say, of course, was *The Scarlet Letter*." . . . At a third affair I failed to be present because the time and place escaped my mind, but a certain personage, brought in unexpectedly by a gentleman of the press, took over completely. This was a female star, headlining that week at the St. Charles Theatre and rejoicing in the success of a book that she herself had recently written and published. The next day I met John Reilly and apologized to him, as the provider of the feast, for my absence. "Oh, weren't you there?" he twitted. "Well, anyhow, your name came up, and comparing notes with Gypsy, we found that your *Scarlet Lily* is just now probably selling better than *The G-String Murders*. How does it feel to be outstripping the most famous Lee since Robert E.?"

Extravaganza. The really modest sum that Hollywood paid me (later on Barbara Stanwyck would call me "a babe in the woods" for having accepted it) was blown up in a press release; and a Chicago paper, accidentally adding a cipher, made it look so much bigger that a snowstorm of letters from down-and-outers and dead-beats blew my way. Then an announcement appeared that Mr. Selznick was planning to produce *The Scarlet Lily* in Palestine, even with the war going on, to the tune of five million dollars. But that was topped by the news that he, who had created so much interest for his *Gone with the Wind* by scouring the United States for an actress with enough southern allure to play Scarlet O'Hara, was now seeking an actor with perfect legs for the role of Tullus, my Roman soldier hero. It seemed that neither Gary Cooper's underpinnings, nor even Robert Taylor's, were good enough, at least for Selznick, who had neither of these gentlemen under contract; but client Joseph Cotten's—ah, they were right out of a sculptor's dream! How extreme, I asked myself, could extremities get? A cool breeze, however, fanned my brow when Ingrid Bergman herself communicated with me. Hers was the simplest and sincerest missive to come out of the whole hullabaloo. She merely expressed her joy at the prospect of playing the Magdalen and promised to give the part her best.

Reactions. Though *The Scarlet Lily* soon reached and swept past the hundred-thousand-sales mark, achieving—I was told—a record as the first Catholic novel from an American Catholic publishing house ever to have done so, and causing the happy but harried Bruces to dub it *The Scarlet Fever,* there was bile along with balm for me. One journalist berated me and a certain fellow priest author for writing best-sellers, as if worst-sellers represented literary perfection. Another, who liked Hemingway, stigmatized me as a lover of Shakespeare. A third, possibly missing the tang of *Forever Amber,* complained that I did not make him "feel" the Magdalen. A fourth opined that Biblical characters should be left in the Bible, and seemed quite unaware that if this were so Christ ought to be kept out of sermons. A fifth, Father Gregory de Witt, a Louisiana Benedictine artist whose modernistic technique still amounts to a genius so stark and original as to hit one between the eyes, told me frankly, "I do not like your book"; and just as frankly I told him, "I do not like your paintings." With our mutual frowns he looked so funny to me, and I to him, that we burst out laughing, thus becoming good friends.

Dismissing the unreasonable criticisms with a smile, I appreciated the reasonable ones the more and might have comported myself calmly enough, only that a clergyman up North now went berserk at my "prostituting religion by selling it to Babylon." "Examine your conscience," he wrote, "and remember both the Old Testament crime of those who delivered their brother Joseph to slavery and the New Testament betrayal of the Lord for thirty pieces of filthy silver. Repent, repent." To this I made no reply, but wondered how anybody could have forgotten how reverently and effectively Hollywood had handled *King of Kings, Keys of the Kingdom, Going My Way, Bells of St. Mary's* and *Song of Bernadette.* My uneasiness at the attitude of a man of God—even though the accent in this case was probably less on the divine than the human—continued until, shortly after, I learned that Cardinal Spellman was permitting Hollywood to transfer his memorable poem, "The Risen Soldier," to the screen. Also at this time I read in an article in the *Saturday Evening Post* that Cardinal O'Connell, far from despising Hollywood's better phases and achievements, had once contemplated writing a movie scenario, and that when some unconscious Pharisee indicated the oddity of a prelate's name being associated with, say, Greta Garbo's, he had spiritedly replied, "What's wrong with *her?*" Then I happened to learn that the list of names enrolled in the Devotion of Our Lady of the Miraculous Medal ranged from Pope Pius XII to Mae West. So, free from all fear of "prostituting religion" by my very slight link with cinemaland, I smiled again and ceased worrying.

But, as the "Lily" went into its several editions and foreign translations, I kept wondering how so modest a literary effort as mine could have succeeded so well; until, while in New York to talk over some matters with the metropolitan office of the Bruce Company, I visited Eddie Dowling. He was playing in *Glass Menagerie*, and during our confab I asked him, "How is it that this fine show of yours has not yet been bought by Hollywood, though my *Scarlet Lily* was grabbed up even before publication?" He looked at me, his eyes narrowing and glistening with Broadway acumen. Then he let me have a reason which seemed to make the whole puzzle of the "Lily's" quick success as clear as *lacrimae Christi.* "Just think of the heroine you have," he said. "*Mary Magdalen.* Two thousand years of publicity and advertising!"

XIII

HOLLYWOOD's interest in *The Scarlet Lily* went on and up, and
when it was at its height I heard that the famous painter of the
Four Freedoms was being commissioned by Selznick to do a portrait of Ingrid Bergman as the Magdalen. At the same time,
through my good friend Irv Kupcinet of the Chicago *Times*, I
met Varga, the creator of the light-clad girl who was pleasing
so many a lonely G.I. joe; and he confided to me that he wanted
to resume the serious work with which he had begun his career
and would be happy to illustrate my forthcoming Spanish edition.
(A cynical New York columnist, getting wind of this, promptly
wrote, "South American postmasters, beware!") Then I read an
interview, granted by Miss Bergman to the press, in which she
declared that her abiding ambitions were to play Mary of Magdala in the screen version of my story and, on the stage, Joan of
Arc. Next came the news that, her contract with Selznick having run out, she was deciding against a renewal. He had helped
her to fame and she had helped him to fortune, and the relationship could well be a closed book. Now free to essay Broadway,
apparently she would be unavailable for pictures. Besides, at this
juncture the war came to an end; and so, it seemed, did the religious cycle in Hollywood.

Curious about the future of the "Lily," I asked permission
from my superior to spend a week or two on the Coast. Mr.
Selznick had indicated that when—and if—the picture was successfully made, a financial bonus would be offered the Society of
St. Joseph; and this naturally facilitated the granting of my request. Without a connection with the main object of my life,
the Negro missions, all this business of having written a book from

which a photoplay might even yet be adapted would have been pretty empty stuff; but now, under the circumstances, it seemed important enough to warrant a Westward-ho for the purpose of possibly blowing a dying ember to flame. And off I entrained for Hollywood, not so old as I'd thought myself; in fact, rather young again, with the vision of America's most colorful industry ahead of me.

Before the sale of the "Lily," I'd conceived of Hollywood, when adverting to it at all, less as a place than a jumble of old questions. What had happened to David Wark Griffith after *The Birth of a Nation?* Had Fatty Arbuckle really been a moral monster, and was Charlie Chaplin of the baggy pants, trick mustache, and floppy shoes a great artist? Theda Bara! Was it true that royal Egyptian blood explained her brooding beauty? I'd seen somewhere that, urged by a reporter to tell about her "native" Africa, she gave the question serious thought and then replied, "It is very, very hot." And Clara Bow . . .

If it wasn't for the improved viewpoint that the purchase of my story had brought me, I believe I'd have expected to see a tinsel town, full of blue lagoons, Chinese pagodas, synthetic beauties who changed husbands and hairdos every other day, and males with the morals of jack rabbits. But now I felt, especially from the recent output of religious pictures, that there must be much good in Hollywood; and what I actually found was, for the most part, a normal community where people worked as hard in studios as New Englanders in mills and factories. My discovery was facilitated by Monsignor Devlin, pastor of St. Victor's Church and adviser to filmland in Catholic concerns, whom I visited first. Busy as two or three clergymen, he took time out to listen to my questions and share his intelligence and experience.

Providentially, Father Walter Plimmer, who had once, as an excellent Broadway actor, worked for George Cohan and Eddie Dowling, and who at the height of his success had come to me in Newburgh to discuss his plan of studying for the priesthood, was visiting his sister Helen and his niece Rosemary in Hollywood.

We ran into each other near the Brown Derby on Vine Street and thwacked palms. Many years had passed since my last sight of him, but he looked as young and dapper as the Dowling of *Sally, Irene, and Mary* and seemed to be at the threshold rather than in the midst of his second career. "I've had only bit parts so far in the priesthood," he said characteristically when I quizzed him. "My big role, if any, is yet to come."

On the way to his sister's home, where he was staying, I asked whether he still kept in touch with the theatrical world. "Certainly," he said. "Ordination does not require me to ignore good friends who follow the same profession that supported my dear father and mother." And reflecting how well football and grand opera were being put to an ideal purpose at Xavier, I suggested that he use his unique background ideally too. He smiled and asked how. "Well, there's St. Genesius," I reminded, and went on to indicate that, as a former actor and now a priest, he might be just the man to make Hollywood and Broadway conscious of possessing a heavenly patron. And as we walked along we talked over the story of Genesius, who in the early era of Christianity had been the most popular of pagan performers in Rome. While playing the part of a bishop on the imperial stage and derisively pouring baptismal waters on the head of a Christian priest arrested and thrust into the spectacle to heighten the satire of it, he was so overcome by the man's purity and dignity that, instead of proceeding with the false ritual, he submitted to the true by falling on his knees and begging to be received, even at the cost of martyrdom, into the Church that produced such souls. "Maybe I could start a Genesian movement somewhat on the order of Father Keller's Christophers," said Father Plimmer. And so, out of our casual conversation in the heart of Hollywood, came the beginning of an organization which, taken up since by the Catholic Actors' Guild, has grown large and is at present working toward the achievement of a national foundation in honor of the thespian who, long, long ago, found Reality, gave it his all, and slipped into the eternal role of saint.

It so happened that Jill Jackson, at whom Sinclair Lewis had once been so annoyed in New Orleans because he thought she laughed at him, was visiting Hollywood at the same time as myself, to obtain firsthand material for her popular broadcasts over WWL; and her personality was opening every door. Hearing of my presence, she got in touch with me, and through her I met Frances Marion, who had ventured from San Francisco to Hollywood when moving pictures were an ambition rather than an achievement, and had advanced with the industry steadily. Hers were the scenarios that supplied Mary Pickford's ascendancy; hers was the hand that led Marie Dressler to astounding popularity; hers such stories as *The Champ*, which established Jackie Cooper, and *The Big House*, in which Wallace Beery reached the top; hers the inspiring skill that moved Fred Thompson to give young America the wholesome "Silver King" series. Sculptor, concert singer, pianist, novelist, linguist, humanitarian, she was now committed to a simple program of study and hospitality in her perfectly appointed Selma Avenue home.

I gave her an autographed copy of my *Scarlet Lily*, and the next morning she phoned me at my hotel to say that, sitting up most of the night, she had read it through. Her estimate was heartening and she requested that I let her have some friends meet me. "Is there any star you'd particularly like to see?" she said. I was on the verge of replying, "Clara Bow," but bit my tongue.

The only time I had ever glimpsed Miss Bow on the screen was when, teaching at our college in Newburgh and seeking to relieve the occasional periods of snowbound tedium there, some of us Fathers induced the rector to buy a movie machine for the boys. We rented a few films, sight unseen, from a New York supply house, and the very first one shown turned out to be a Bow feature. It began with such fire that the rector scrupulously ordered it to be run as fast as possible, and the result was a furious flicker in which everything became a safe blur. Next day a sharp letter went off to the supply house, demanding, "Do you not have *any* photoplays suitable for boys studying for the priesthood?" Quickly came a blunt reply: "Hollywood does not invest its capital in making pictures for boys studying for the priesthood. Would *you*, if you were Hollywood?" It was travelogues and shorts that reached us after that, and a vague curiosity as to what the famous "It" girl really looked like, devoid of blur, persisted in me and possibly the whole community.

But now, instead of "Clara Bow," I found myself murmuring over the phone to Frances, "Mary Pickford." And to my delight and awe, she replied, "I am sure this can be arranged. Will eight tomorrow night be convenient?"

The following morning the telephone rang and I hurried to answer it, for this would surely be Frances with more news about tonight's affair. Eagerness causing awkwardness, I slipped on the polished floor and nearly broke my nose. Bleeding profusely, I somehow got to the instrument and found that the caller was Father Plimmer. "How are you?" he asked, sounding so replete with well-being that I detested him. "Horrible," I moaned, catching my bloody reflection in the bureau mirror. How could Hollywood's gentry be faced with a busted nose? What would they think of the clergy!

But by dint of prayer and a neat application of court plaster, I felt sufficiently presentable after sundown to sally forth; except that, on my way out, I noticed a tiny spot or two on my only good suit and had to go back to use some cleaning fluid. In my haste I spilled the stuff over me. The odor was powerful, and now I not only felt again that I looked bad but knew that I smelled worse. Ah, if the night were only ending instead of beginning!

On arriving at Frances's home, I learned that the reception was to be held not indoors but on a velvety, jasmine-scented, candlelit lawn. Just perfect for imperfectly conditioned me. Now it was possible to feel less like an imposition and to look around with a little confidence. As if stepping from another world, people appeared: Walter Pidgeon, Doris Kenyon, Igor Gorin,

Mario Lanza, and at least a dozen others. Who was that white-armed Juno—or rather that bright, personified plume—approaching? "I am Hedda Hopper, Father," she said, "and I am going to sit beside you at table. Want to hear all about New Orleans. Is the French Quarter really so wicked?" And I answered by telling her of such noble Vieux Carré assets as the Cathedral, the Holy Family Convent, St. Mary's Italian Club House, the Holy Redeemer Negro Mission, and the Cabrini Day Home. Her ear was as good as her tongue, and her interest better than both. In no time we were old friends.

Then came a couple like the candied figures on a wedding cake—Mary Pickford and Buddy Rogers, she as golden and girlish as I had hoped, and he hardly less handsome than in his days of stardom. All the guests were formally attired, but their manner was relaxed. Frances, perfect hostess, moved quietly everywhere, making each and every one feel the very center of interest and attention; and Katherine Porter, her attractive companion, helpfully whispered to me so much pertinent information that it was possible to talk to the personalities as if I had been following their careers for some time. They liked that, and in turn inquired about my work among the colored in New Orleans, which Frances must have mentioned to them. By now I had forgotten all about the court plaster and cleaning fluid. I was in my glory.

From Hollywood little information about the future of *The Scarlet Lily* could be gathered, but I did acquire friends who have been loyal ever since. And those friendships were not only for me but also for the apostolate I represented, because I had spoken earnestly, not only to artists but also to executives, of the Negro's struggle as known to missionary Fathers and Sisters, and hinted at the rich picture material that lay in it. This was at best a very small seed that I planted out there; but many other and abler agents must have been sowing too, for a vivid cycle of interracial plays, among them *Pinky* and *No Way Out*, was soon to resume what Fannie Hurst had begun in the thirties with her tender and touching depiction of Negro psychology in *Imitation of Life*.

Bruce Company was eager for a story to follow *The Scarlet Lily*, and I belabored my brain until another, *The Road from Olivet*, came forth. This one, too, was about the Magdalen. I had shown her in Jerusalem, and in as much as, according to tradition, she brought the Faith to France, I now visualized her tarrying in Rome while en route to her destination, and having many a spiritual adventure in her quest for souls. "Why not write a whole series on the same theme?" suggested somebody jovially. "Mary on the Riviera, Mary in Paris, Mary at Oxford . . ."

Vanguard Films in New York, to which the story was submitted, sent a very favorable report to Mr. Selznick on the Coast and recommended a purchase with a view to combining the two tales in his final scenario. A rescrutiny of the "Lily" contract, however, showed that he might take all the time he wanted for making up his mind, there being a clause which gave him first option on any sequel.

The Road from Olivet, paved with good intentions, went well and headed the New Orleans best-seller list for a spell, but it did not equal the success of its antecedent, perhaps because I had given my plot so large a scope that my characters seemed rather dwarfed in it and more like puppets than people. But at least I saw that I had a lot to learn, and a publicity tour from Milwaukee to New York, which the Bruce Company now arranged for me, served as good experience. It was not without incident.

In Chicago I went on a radio program in which literary guests listened to microphone artists reading excerpts from various novels and then tried to name the books and authors. One of the excerpts, the night of my appearance, had a scriptural smack to it; and the master of ceremonies called on me first, since I was the only clergyman present. But I failed. So did everybody else, and the master himself had to give the identification. "Why,

Father," he declared, "it is your own *Scarlet Lily!*" And I could only say with Shakespeare, " 'It is a wise father that knows his own child.' "

In Manhattan I was elected a member of the theater club, the Lambs', which agile Douglas Fairbanks had often entered by swinging monkey-style up to a window on the second floor, and where Jack Barrymore had given some of his best impromptus and George M. Cohan had pegged out on a piano the immortal song of World War I, "Over There." This election pleased me much, because Father Plimmer, already a member, so wanted me to help him get his Genesian movement started where impetus would count most, and my interest in the spiritual welfare of the stage had lived on since the days of Father Leonard.

At the Lambs' there were many personalities. Just listening in this warm, relaxed, friendly atmosphere made me eager to grab a pen. Everybody from dear old David Warfield at a card table down to the omniscient barber in the basement, was a two-legged story. But wasn't this true of any human being anywhere? The older I'd grown, the more I'd come to recognize that nobody is without uniqueness; and a would-be author, I now knew, could find his characters at every turn. The question was how to deal with them when found. Should they be adapted to a preconceived plot, or should the plot be permitted simply to evolve from them? The former method seemed to please the general public more, but the discriminating public less. If I should try to produce a third novel, I'd have to make a choice or a blend of techniques.

The notion of a third was already astir in me, for Tess Crager in New Orleans had just telegraphed that, as scout for Doubleday & Company in New York, she had been asked to have me get in touch with them about a contract. This required some pondering, my purpose in life being evangelization and not authorship. But could not authorship be put to evangelical use? Away back in my time of teaching at Epiphany, I had had the boys memorize a verse which I now recalled: "There are strange ways of serving God. You sweep a room or lift the sod; and suddenly, to your surprise, you hear the whir of Seraphim and find you're under God's own eyes and building palaces for Him." Indeed, it seemed strange for a missionary, living so much fact, to write fiction; but no stranger than the divine call to a career of "all things to all men." And hadn't the Lord himself adopted the story form called "parable"? If my pen could continue to interest some readers and serve an apostolate, ought I not go ahead, utilizing my leisure and working when sleep eluded me in the long stretches of the night?

I visited Doubleday and when I took my leave, a signed document and a sizable check lay neatly folded in my inside pocket. But then an unease possessed me. Here I was, committed to deliver a manuscript within a matter of months, yet at the moment I had not a single idea as to what it would be about.

One of the many Josephite rules prohibited travel by air; but the superior, having recently taken advantage of this means of transit when it was essential for him to get to a certain mission sooner than soon, had become so pleased with wings as to lift the ban. He must have known, though, that coach trains and busses would remain the custom for us missionaries who could not afford any better. Nevertheless, with emolument temporarily mine, I did not feel poor; and I flew back to New Orleans in style for once. The sensation of zooming through space would have rendered me exuberant, only that the question, "What shall I write, what shall I write?" kept distracting and disturbing me. Until it was answered, any extra convenience or comfort would have to seem purloined. When, still inspirationless, I deplaned at Moisant Airport on the Crescent Bend, it seemed to me that a good meal might help a little; so, still extravagantly, I decided to betake myself to the nonpareil restaurant known as Antoine's.

While busy there with a plate of crawfish bisque, I overheard two women at a nearby table. Tourists, they were speaking rather loudly and volubly of what they had seen that day, and "Père Antoine Alley" kept bobbing up. I well knew this pathway alongside St. Louis Cathedral, and now remembered that Tess

Crager and her husband Bob had spoken to me more than once about the historic character after whom it was named, a priest so strong as to have frightened governors, yet gentle enough to have won the hearts of the people. Leaving my food unfinished, I taxied to Blessed Sacrament rectory, took down from a shelf my copy of Roger Baudier's *History of the Catholic Church in Louisiana*, thumbed the index, and made notes and outlines deep into the night. The next day I visited the public library and discussed Père Antoine with Librarian Margaret Ruckert, a regular mine of information and a wonderfully willing dispenser of it.

The complexity of the character of this Antoine, who according to historian John Gilmary Shea had been "the scourge of religion in Louisiana" but whom the preacher at the "scourge's" funeral lauded as a saint, fascinated me. I wondered what a pious laity would think of him, but felt that a story based on his human faults and moral triumphs might have the good effect of making readers more cognizant that an ecclesiastic must engage in the same spiritual combat he preaches, and that in this he needs as much prayerful help from souls as he gives to them. And my next novel took shape and form.

Doubleday, pleased with the book, afforded me, right after publication, an autograph tour of the South; and this enabled me to see at close range the excellent work that Josephites were doing. I recalled what one of them had told me in my early priesthood when I threw up my hands at the sight of his shedlike church in a rice field: "Come back ten years from now and you'll be surprised." Much more than a decade had passed, and the Father had gone to his reward, but the shack was now a beautiful structure flanked by a school and a convent, and a goodly life for a whole colored community flowed from and around it. This was typical, for not one shoddy or shabby mission did I see in my entire circuit.

My novel, *Père Antoine*, "hit" the New York *Times* and *Herald Tribune* best-seller lists. Cinemactor Vincent Price became quite interested in my hero; and Mrs. Evelyn Soulé Kennedy, a talented New Orleanian, did a dramatization which was tried out at the Dauphine Theatre. But my chief reward was the new vision of the South that the book occasioned for me.

Now better known in town, I was invited to assist at various affairs, one of which particularly stands out in memory. A great fund raising for the relief of the sufferers in the catastrophe of Texas City, it was bringing a planeful of Hollywood stars to us; and the Arrangements Committee requested me, as a missionary among the colored, to take care of Jack Benny's Rochester who, as a gentleman of tint, could not be accommodated at a leading hotel with his fellow artists. But Joe Geddes, an old friend of mine and also the biggest Negro undertaker in town, so begged me to delegate the honor to him that I did. The stars arrived at the airport after midnight and, waiting rather impatiently in the damp breeze from Lake Pontchartrain for taxis, suddenly stared at a palace-on-wheels rolling near. They had no way of knowing that this ultimate in limousines was straight from the Geddes Funeral Parlors, and thought it to be for themselves. Soundless as perfection it came; snootily it by-passed Frank Sinatra, Phil Harris, Alice Faye, Diana Lynn, Jane Powell, and even Jack Benny; purringly it paused before the only one left; and out of it stepped an ebon-hued chauffeur in a brass-buttoned uniform, bowing from the waist and announcing in a resonant basso, "Mr. Rochester, your car, suh!"

The eyes of the famous comedian bulged. Then, with a dawning consciousness that this swank was not a spoof, he straightened his shoulders, smiled, flipped the rim of his fedora, and swung languidly forward. Away to an Eden on Louisiana Avenue he was whisked in cushiony comfort, there to be dined, wined, cosseted, and bedded like royalty itself by his very own.

After seeing how much Rochester and the other stars enjoyed what New Orleans had to offer, I wanted more than ever before to get Eddie Dowling to come to us, knowing how much the town figured in his memories of the early days of his trouping, the days when his salary was so small that he had to live on hope and ham sandwiches. "Your success may not be considered complete," I now wrote him, "until you've dined well in Deepest Dixie. Besides, Father John Toomey, founder and director of the very popular Loyola Forum, not only wants you to deliver a lecture here but insists that I get you." And the letter brought results. As soon as his Broadway commitments eased off enough to give him a breathing spell, down he came.

He had with him his prize-winning dog, worth five thousand dollars, that he wanted me to see. Accommodation had been secured at the St. Charles Hotel, but the unexpected canine posed a problem, because pets were not admitted there. The solution, however, seemed simple enough, Eddie agreeing to my offer to take the creature home with me. "What does he eat?" I asked. "Oh, a chopped sirloin steak will suit him fine," said Eddie. But when I got back to my rectory, dog under arm, I certainly found no such luxury as sirloin in my larder. Half a bottle of milk and a few crackers were all I could locate, and breaking those crackers into a saucerful of the liquid, I set this strictly plebeian pap before the little aristocrat, expecting him to turn up his nose. On the contrary, he consumed all of it and licked the dish clean, as if to assure me that even prize winners could condescend; and my opinion of him went high. But five thousand dollars! A sum that could have launched a mission. I'd seen more than one braving existence on less; and I wondered whether, after all, I had chosen the better part.

The thermometer registered low that night, and my house felt like a refrigerator. Fearing that this four-legged champion might get pneumonia, I wrapped him in my old woolen bathrobe which usually served as an extra blanket. He thanked me with a big moist look.

When Eddie dined at my rectory the following night, his eyes saucered like Rochester's. Never had he seen a finer meal. Yet it did not cost the parish a cent. I had had only to tell three of my sodalists, who cooked *à la Creole* for some of the best families on St. Charles' Avenue, that a very dear friend was to be my guest for dinner, and they took over from there. First, they informed their exceptionally generous madames that their pastor needed "eats" for "a special swell occasion" and had "nothin' but a big empty icebox." Secondly, laden with hampers, they came to my kitchen. Thirdly, they pinned on their aprons and plunged into their art. Three mansions, minus their *cordons bleus*, must have had only cold cuts that night, but for Dowling there was the height of cuisine. *Bouillabaisse*, perfected with a first-class French dry wine; *calas tout chaud*, those hot rice cakes that the North never knows, spooned up out of deep fat, fried crisply, and sprinkled with powdered sugar; *daube glacé*, so seasoned with thyme, parsley, bay leaf, pepper, garlic, and onion, that it seemed to be magic instead of mere veal; *truite Marguéry*, covered with Hollandaise sauce supreme; lemon meringue pie, deep, high, light as foam; and *café brûlot*, as black, strong, sweet and hot as the fussiest N'Orleanian taste could demand.

"Guess I should have been a missionary, not an actor," said Eddie delightedly, loosening his belt. "Do you dine like this every night?"

"What do you think?" I smiled.

"Can't think," he replied. "My envy's too great."

I made no mention of the milk and crackers of yesterday and possibly the morrow, but let him have his own idea of life on a mission. Somehow, though, I did feel richer than he and satisfied that my "part" was better.

Eddie was not the only Broadwayite that Father Toomey and I lured to New Orleans. In between a Saturday and a Monday night performance of *Harvey*, Frank Fay flew to us from Manhattan and filled the Forum with merriment over his unique theatrical experiences. More than pleased, Father Toomey was stimulated to aim even higher. He wanted Monsignor Fulton Sheen who, having achieved the poetic justice of influencing

Colonel Horace A. Mann—the person most responsible perhaps for the blocking of Al Smith's White House hopes—to enter the Church, now had to his credit such converts as Clare Booth Luce, Fritz Kreisler, Grace Moore, Henry Ford II, Jo Mielziner, and Louis Budenz. Here would be the biggest of drawing cards. And, coming to me at Xavier, he said, "You were a classmate of Sheen's. Busy as he is, he'd surely favor us if you'd personally ask him."

I doubted my influence, all too mindful of a certain mistake that I'd made when preparations for a great Eucharistic Congress were afoot in New Orleans some years before. As chairman of the Nominating Committee, I had proposed my classmate for leader of the list, and the other members were so elated that, thinking the matter settled, I wrote him to expect the official invitation that would soon be on the way. But it happened that higher authority then decided on utilizing southern orators for the most part, since the Congress was to be an expression of the faith of the Southland; hence our list had to be changed, and it was necessary for me to write Sheen again, this time in apology for my precipitateness.

But Father Toomey was now so bent on my trying to get him that I had to put in a long-distance call to Washington. "Yes, I'll gladly come," said the monsignor, "and my only stipulation is that my good friend Bishop Toolen's mission work will receive whatever honorarium the forum offers." When I turned to Father Toomey with the news, his face shone. And how he prepared for the coming!—hiring the huge Municipal Auditorium, infusing his own remarkable energy into co-workers, placarding the city with announcements, and praying that nothing would happen to the plane in which our Chrysostom was to fly. As the excitement reached its height, I received a calm phone call from Mobile: "Here I am, Eddie, with Bishop Toolen. He and I will slip over into New Orleans by automobile. Beyond the lecture for the forum, my time is yours." And I knew that years and astounding success had not changed Fulton J. in the least from the simple, loyal, and sincere young priest whose first audiences were little orphans.

He took New Orleans by storm, yet with meekness and dignity; and brilliant as he was in the packed Municipal Auditorium, he seemed even more so to me when he addressed the modest student body at Xavier. As I listened to his discourse, his fine, flexible voice, as much as his words, set me thinking. I could see him as he looked the first day I met him. So much water had flowed under life's bridge since then, and still he evoked for me the impression of Amos emerging from Tekoa. But more than that now. Great service for the Gospel had put a spiritual stamp on almost every phrase and expression of his, and that was why I found myself looking dreamily ahead. If *The Scarlet Lily* were ever to be produced on the sound screen, the role of the Savior in it would have to be suggested by a rare voice, uttering the immortal words of Holy Scripture; and what vocal cords were more attuned to the Master's personality and message than those of my own classmate?

The theme of the Master and Magdalen, so useful to me in *The Scarlet Lily* and *Road from Olivet,* had been away from my mind since the writing of *Père Antoine.* But that day of Sheen's address at Xavier, what with my imagining his voice pouring all its beauty of tone into the text, "Many sins are forgiven her because she has loved much," it came back to me. And when I got home, I searched among my books for one entitled *Eve Lavallière: A Modern Magdalen.* Though I had read and meditated on this little volume more than once before, it exercised a wholly fresh appeal for me in the hours that followed, and I did not put it down until dawn. By then I knew that I was going to write a fourth novel, this time about the woman of Montmartre who, like her sister of long ago in Magdala, saw a gleam of grace in the moral dark and followed it to the very Source.

I really believed that this fourth attempt would be my final. But when it was finished and published a year later, it brought me so much response that the will to go on increased rather than declined. A prelate wrote, "It may surprise you to know that in my episcopal ring one of Eve Lavallière's diamonds is sparkling. Just as she came to the Church in a roundabout way, so did this jewel come to me. As you know, her problem child Jeanne valued nothing. One of the girl's companions was a young American reveling in Paris. She tossed him the diamond and afterward, when he returned contrite and repentant from abroad, he gave it to me. So, like Eve's own soul saved from the world and given to religion, this little symbol speaks to me of divine grace every time I look at it."

Imbued by this story with a fresh awareness of the beauty and mystery of Providence, I got to thinking of a scriptural character who, in pagan Moab, much worse even than Montmartre, had found and never lost perfection, the faithful Ruth of the Old Testament. And the result was yet a fifth book which, since it depicted the romance that began the royal line which begot David and culminated in Christ, I called *Song of the Cave.*

Fulton Oursler, after reading the galleys of "Song," raised my spirit high by declaring, "You have taken the beautiful Bible story of Ruth and rendered it even more beautiful. What greater could be said of any writer?" Smiling to myself, I wondered what he would have thought about the version of that same story which, back in my seminary days, I had given in Scripture class and in the presence of a teetotalist professor. That gauche introduction! *Ruth, the Moabitess, was gleaning in the fields of Bethlehem and found Booz.*

XIV

THE Chicago *Tribune* was now sending me books of a New Orleanian genre to review; and to qualify for the pleasant chore, I made myself better acquainted with the local literary world queened by Frances Parkinson Keyes, kinged by Harnett Kane, princed by Robert Tallant, and high-ministered by Hermann Deutsch, who knew his city inside out, David Stern, whose *Francis* had set the whole country chuckling, and W. F. Fitzpatrick, whose pen was to spear a Pulitzer Prize. Lyle Saxon and Roark Bradford had recently laid down their scepter pens and departed, but their standards still fluttered in the breeze; and from the neighboring state of Mississippi the dark star of William Faulkner and the white one of Eudora Weldy were gleaming. Alice Graham's prose, chaste and warm, was winning a large public; Dagmar LeBreton's scholarliness, lending dignity; Gwen Bristow's colorfulness and sweep, opening panoramas; Thad Saint-Martin's Delta delineations, still being read and appreciated; James Feibleman's philosophical treatises, stimulating thought; the Jesuit Father Quirk's voice, rising gently in exquisite sonnets; John Chase's one book, *Frenchmen Desire Good Children*, creating a demand for more. And knowing my interest, several Orleanians with an inclination to authorship began to seek me for advice and assistance.

I told them what Sinclair Lewis had once told me: that when the students attending an English course of his in a mid-West university expressed to him their ardent desire to be writers, he dismissed them with a single sentence, "Then go home and write, write." But this was not what my approachers wanted to hear. Secrets and short cuts were their object, and I knew none. Indeed, the whole business of books still puzzled and humbled me. Even with a wealth of effort and talent, some authors failed and none absolutely succeeded. From Shakespeare to Lewis himself, there were con's as well as pro's. Hadn't Samuel Pepys branded *Midsummer Night's Dream* as the most insipid and silliest play ever seen? And hadn't Voltaire referred to the Bard as savage, low, unbridled, and absurd? As for Lewis himself, I could not but think of the woman who hurled his *Main Street* into the sea. So for the most part I tried to steer clear of literary aspirants, realizing full well that my opinion amounted to little or nothing and that only a publisher's was vital to the launching of a pen career.

But one day my doorbell rang with what seemed an especial insistence, and peeking down from the shutters upstairs, I saw a neat-looking woman with a portfolio under her arm. "Another one," I said to myself, returning to my desk. Then came a second ring—and a third. Annoyed, I was now more than determined not to answer. After some moments of welcome silence, the telephone whirred. Taking up the receiver, I heard a soft voice: "Father, I knew you were there. One of your neighbors told me. Do forgive this importunity, but I must see you about a personal matter. It will take only a few minutes. Let me come." Hardly subduing a note of impatience, I said yes; and I shudder now to think that a no would have robbed me of one of the most precious experiences of my whole life.

When I opened the door, a man was standing beside the woman. I invited them in and asked them to be seated. And the woman began a tale which took much more than a few minutes to tell but riveted my interest from the first word to the last and made my feelings go out in a rush.

For almost twenty years, under assumed names, they had been living a life of social death as victims of the disease that men dread most. Stealthily and inexplicably it had entered the days of their youth, extinguished the light, and driven them from their homes to the relative tomb of a leprosarium. They might have gone mad with wretchedness and despair only for some blessed circumstances. Sisters of Charity moved and served in the gloom of the colony, and there was a little chapel to which the patients could repair for the touch of One who never shrank away; as well as a clinic where noble men of science and research toiled continually that at least a faint hope might linger on in the bosoms of the afflicted. There in Carville these two present visitors of mine had met and, in the meeting, found the mutual and compensational love to which Providence had been all the while leading them through a maze of woe. As time went on, new techniques and remedies appeared for the treatment of Hansen's disease, and now, their youth gone, this wedded couple were discharged as cured. Strangers to normal existence, they felt bewildered. So long lost to life, how could they earn a living? Harry Martin—this the assumed name the husband must even now keep—had gotten a little manual labor, but his healed hands were still too weak; and Betty, his wife, had been trying to help him in the only way she knew. At the hospital she had made a few timid contributions to the *Star*, a paper which the inmates themselves issued; and, with this sparse experience, she had gone so far as to record Harry's story and hers, in the forlorn hope that somehow it would sell. But so far there was no success. "Would you glance at what I've done, Father, and—and make some suggestions?" she begged.

As she took the manuscript from the portfolio and passed it to me, I did not know what to say. How could I tell her that business is business and that one's sad needs might hardly be expected to influence a publisher to accept a work? But as my eyes swept over the pages, I could see that here was direct and honest writing, with the kind of appeal that I had found in the plays sent me by Dowling. And within a half hour I had Tess Crager on the telephone. Yes, she would be glad to interview Mr. and Mrs. Martin. Yes, she would present their material to Doubleday if she should find in it as much promise as I indicated.

Three or four weeks passed, in which I breathed many a prayer. Tess had mailed the biography, and now came the report from New York. Doubleday was sending Evelyn Wells, an expert, to consult and collaborate with Betty Martin, and a contract would be drawn up, and publication could be expected in the spring.

What a spring that turned out to be for Betty and Harry! The book appeared under the title *Miracle at Carville*, and *Reader's Digest* promptly paid a good sum for the rights to a condensed version. It won a Christopher award and received praises from every direction. Never in all my days did I more thoroughly enjoy another's enjoyment.

The "Miracle's" message of the gleam of God in every trial was especially helpful to me at this time. A priest—very dear as a cousin and my first recruit for the missions—was bending under a burden of ill health but still trying to carry on; and I made his worries my own.

One very hot morning in summer, there came a terse report which chilled me to the bone. Father John was dead.

Never had a sense of loss pierced me more keenly. But consolation was mine when a complete account of the demise reached me and was followed by a clipping from the Salem *Evening News:*

HONOR FATHER LUNDERGAN
FOR HIS DEED OF BRAVERY

In commemoration of his unselfish courage and heroism, a posthumous citation will be bestowed upon the late Rev. John Lundergan of this city, by the B'nai B'rith of New Jersey, for sacrificing his own life to save the life of another on the bathing beach at Long Branch, N. J.

The citation, in the form of a plaque, will be made in Salem the latter part of this month to the family of the late priest, by the Salem B'nai B'rith chapter on behalf of their brother lodge from Asbury Park, New Jersey.

The citation is one made annually by B'nai B'rith for an outstanding act of heroism beyond the normal line of duty.

Notification that Father Lundergan's act had been selected for

the Distinguished Service Award for 1949 came to the Salem
B'nai B'rith chapter last week in a letter from Wayne D. Mc-
Murray, chairman of the Service Award Committee:

"On July 7, on the bathing beach of North Long Branch, a
twelve-year-old lad was drawn into the sea beyond his depth.
The Rev. John Lundergan, taking a rest cure at the Methodist
Jefferson Fresh Air Home at 142 Ocean Avenue, Long Branch,
witnessed the boy's difficulty and plunged into the ocean to
rescue him. After bringing him to the beach, he collapsed from
a fatal heart attack. So his action was beyond the call of duty
and performed at the cost of his own life. . . . In commemoration of this example of unselfishness, the Distinguished Service
Award Committee of the Shore Lodge, B'nai B'rith, of which I
have the honor to be chairman, bestows this posthumous citation
upon the Rev. John Lundergan in order that public attention
may be directed to his deed, and that others, through the knowledge of his sacrifice, may re-dedicate themselves to the service
of their fellow men."

My first recruit was not a failure. And, in his victory, I felt as
if achieving one of my own.

There was scarcely time for me to adjust myself to the loss
of Father John when I received word that Father Will, my
brother, lay in a Baltimore hospital. Though he had been unwell
for months, he had never complained. I flew to his side and found
him very weak, but he smiled as he opened his eyes and extended
his hand. "You'll soon have to do for both of us, Eddie," he said.
"It's been a long day, and yet so brief. . . ."

The flesh of him was almost gone, but fiber was still there; and
in the next few days he recovered sufficiently for a removal to
St. Peter Claver Church on Pennsylvania Avenue, where he had
served his first curacy and last pastorate. There he lingered on
in a small plain room, caring to leave it only for visits to the
Blessed Sacrament and the Masses that he managed to read even
though his vision was very dim.

I remained with him as long as possible; and, when the days
were sunny, we would sit in the little convent garden adjoining

the churchyard, just as we used to sit when we were young on the Salem shore, gazing at the sea. His gaunt figure, in a cassock hanging loose on his bones, was scriptural-looking; and the garden became Bethany as the Sisters—Marys and Marthas—gathered around to listen and administer to him. I could see something of Lazarus in his pale drawn face, but even more a suggestion of Christ in his liquid patient eyes.

When I was back again on the Delta, and it was winter, there came a letter from him, written in a remarkably firm hand for one whose sight had failed. "The past is now so clear, and the future too," a paragraph read. "The present is a narrow stream that I can step across the instant I hear 'Come.' This morning at Mass I saw Dad and Mom just as plain! They were kneeling and waiting, and they seemed the same as on the day I gave them my first blessing, only that Dad's shirt was shining like the Thabor garment of the Lord, and Mom had a mantle on her head and shoulders. It was a soft white mantle, and it made me think of those lace curtains—remember?—that she gave poor Marie Manski long ago. I felt Tom, Joe, and Jim there too; but I couldn't take my eyes from Mom and Dad."

Early in the New Year I hurried again to him, this time too late. He had heard the "Come" and had already passed over the narrow stream.

Friends gathered for me the tributes which the press surprisingly paid one who had lived so unobtrusive a life; and I more than prized some paragraphs from the Salem *News:*

> As a boy of fifteen, Rev. William Aloysius Murphy, S.S.J., sought admission to the poorest religious order he could find, reasoning that such an order might well be the richest in merit. The then pastor of the Immaculate Conception Church, where William was baptized and confirmed, directed him to St. Joseph's Society, which, with headquarters in Baltimore, prepared young missionaries for labor among the colored all over the South.
>
> Forty-five years ago William Murphy became Father Murphy and began his ministry of meekness, zeal, and self-effacement.

During most of that time of arduous travel through the South he never even dreamed of occupying a berth in a sleeping car or partaking of a meal in a diner. "So much the more for the poor," he told himself as he economized the few nickels and dimes that came his way. And whether the congregations that heard him were encouragingly large or pitifully small, he always gave his eloquent best.

In the early days of his service, Negro churches were mostly shacks, and to work among a forgotten people was to be forgotten along with them. But he lived to see comparative desert spots bloom and, better still, to behold many young apostles, whom he had trained and directed in St. Joseph's Seminary and Novitiate, going forth to reap the spiritual harvest.

No son of Salem, perhaps, ever prayed himself into meeker efficiency; and it is literally true that everyone who happened to come under his influence learned to cherish him. "One of the kindest men I ever knew" was a commentary frequently heard at his obsequies in Baltimore. White and colored passed wet-eyed around his casket.

Several priests followed Father Murphy's remains to honor them at their last resting place here in Salem. And unnumbered souls in the South, mindful of his unselfish ministry and rare personality, reverence this town as the birthplace of a true man of God and a true friend of man, faithful to the end.

Some of my fellow Josephites kept repeating to me that the loss of so good a brother as Father Will was heaven's gain, but I needed no such reminding. How could heaven's gain be anybody's loss? Now the Negro apostolate had Will as one more advocate in the group of Clavers around the Throne. Now our sisters in Salem, used to his being away through the years in southern fields, seemed to feel that all separation had ended and that he had come home to stay, for heaven and home were practically synonyms with them. And now, with memory focused more vividly than ever before, I could see him as clearly as he had seen Mom and Dad. I recalled that when he first went away to study for the priesthood the emptiness in our hearts had been compensated by a strange soothing, as if, in following a dream, he had opened a door and let in a breeze from a better world. It was the same now. And again and again I was to feel that breeze, for other hands were opening other doors. . . .

There was the case of Father John Neifert, my predecessor almost twenty years before in the pastorate of St. Joan of Arc. A developer of several missions since then, he had just returned to New Orleans, this time to be pastor of Holy Redeemer Church on Royal Street. Knowing the deep regard for him that had endured in the hearts of the colored of New Orleans, and feeling a kinship with him because of my having been privileged to assume his former endeavors, I eagerly anticipated a reunion. It seemed inconceivable that, to see him, I should have to go to a hospital, and that I'd never hear his voice again.

On my way to greet him soon after his arrival, I bought a newspaper and, scanning the front page, almost stopped dead in my tracks. Such an incredible tale of brutality smote my eyes! That very morning, while he was making his thanksgiving after Mass, a Negro had crept up behind him at the altar railing, and with a blunt metal weapon had delivered himself to an orgy of assault. No longer young, the priest was incapable of self-defense and perhaps too worn out from service even to attempt it.

It was not at Holy Redeemer Church but the Hotel Dieu that I found him. Battered, insensate, scarcely breathing, reduced to this condition by one of the very people to whom his entire career had been devoted! The grim irony of it all unnerved me, and I cried within myself perplexedly to the Lord as at the news, some years back, of the "punishing" fire in Richmond that followed an instance of Christian interracialism. But when Father Neifert's eyes closed forever, I began to understand. Though the slayer, as everybody now knew, was demented and irresponsible, the colored bowed their heads as if their group were to blame for the deed, and Holy Redeemer Church was filled with the sobbing of non-Catholics and Catholics alike. With a suggestion, too, that more souls might be won by his death than he had won with his life; and it was only for souls that he had lived. The suggestion grew to a certainty for me when, while preaching at the funeral, I gazed down from the pulpit on the open coffin. A sunbeam was shining on the white lips which had uttered no word of condemnation from the first blow to the last breath; and the countenance was not that of a victim but a victor.

Then came another strong indication of light in darkness and life in death, together with a proof of the significance of a certain poem that I had loved since my student days at Epiphany. And, as in the case of *Miracle at Carville*, I almost side-stepped the experience. . . .

One morning a nun phoned to say that she could give me a true story to write, if I were interested. I was not. But to please her, for her voice was sweet and earnest, I listened and promised to visit the scene and meet the subject of the tale. That day, after calling up Father Miller, the chaplain, I entered the New Orleans Parish Prison and was taken to a cell to see a young man who had only five days to live.

At the age of fourteen he had run away from his Utah home and plunged into a jungle of temptations. His few good principles were torn to shreds, and his career slithered on through a decade of shadows to a climax of murder. Tracked down in a Louisiana swamp by the law, he brought to his imprisonment a character as glisteningly hard as a cobra's stare. And yet, when a little Sister of Mercy came to him, the stare melted and blurred, for she told and re-told how God so loved the world that he sent His only begotten Son to save it, and how the Son so understood and pitied men as to have assumed their wretchedness and died for them on the Cross. He listened incredulously at first, then yearningly. Who could resist such lips as Sister Basil's! And the need of faith induced the dawn of it. There in jail, after following the chaplain's and the nun's series of thorough instructions, he was baptized, made his First Communion, and received Confirmation from Archbishop Rummel himself. Then, enrolled in the Third Order of Saint Dominic under the name of Dismas, the penitent thief that Christ forgave and canonized on Calvary with the words, "This day thou shalt be with me in paradise," he set about erasing every vestige of the past and preparing, as he awaited death, for eternal life. And now, the sands of earthly existence almost run out for him, I was making his acquaintance.

My very first moments with him astonished me. Here I had come with the idea of dispensing a little consolation, but was finding more than I could give. And the astonishment increased when he told me simply, "You have already been with me in this cell." His eyes bright with gratitude, he went on to explain that a friend had loaned him a copy of my story, *The Scarlet Lily*, and to express the effect that my message of spiritual regeneration had had on him. If writing meant nothing more, it would still have been eminently worth while, for never had I seen anybody more sustained with holy hope.

I tried to remember that he had killed an innocent man; but the "still, small voice" in the whirlwind of life drowned out the memory and left only a sense of the boundless sea of grace with the echoing words, "If your sins be as scarlet, they shall be made as white as wool." And surely the acquired merits of a reformed slayer, applied to the soul of the slain, had gained rest for it. Surely the intense and heroic effort involved in redeeming the time, when opportunity was so brief, must have redounded to the salvation of two souls instead of one. "With what moanings and groanings through the night," I thought, "the peace in this convict's face has been won! And it could never have been won without some inner assurance from above that the winning is for another too."

I returned to him on each of the few remaining days and always came away with a feeling of profit. Here was no pauper in spirituality but a millionaire. Not a single expression of gloom or fear came from his lips, but many and many an evidence that he had advanced as far on the road to sanctity as he had gone in that of sin. He smiled often. A shining smile.

In the course of our last afternoon together some noises penetrated the quiet of his cell, and I asked him what they were. "My chair is being set up on the—electric—train, Father," he said. "I won't have to walk far. They call it 'the last mile,' but I think of it as the first minute."

A few clock ticks after the stroke of twelve the following day, he walked to the "train" with happy dignity, leaving behind him the transformation of a whole line of death cells into what was now named by the inmates "Resurrection Row." All of those men had been bettered by his conversion and example; all were now members of the League of the Sacred Heart and devotees of the rosary; and none broke under the strain of the last good-bys, so tranquil and confident was their brother's passing.

The little nun to whom he owed so much claimed his body. An unknown lady donated a casket, and a Dominican Father his habit. As he lay in the habiliments of holiness, the face of Dismas was as bright as that of a child to whom parental arms are out-flung; and the hand that had been raised against society but was now entwined with Sister Basil's beads, glimmered like alabaster in the candle glow of evening upon it.

The next morning, at his Solemn High Mass of Requiem in a church flooded with sunshine, I preached a sermon on the Love that leaves the ninety-nine that are saved to seek the one that is lost; and all the while I was thinking of Francis Thompson's "Hound of Heaven" and of what Mom had said to me in my boy-hood about a soul: "Son, it is a pearl of great price."

Epilogue

SEATED at my desk, the dimming light of an autumn sunset on it, I scan the elongated moment of my past. How meager the wisdom that has been added to my store since childhood days in old Salem when only a knowledge of the catechism was mine! But time has confirmed that early knowledge, and this in itself is a great gain.

Having repeatedly perceived what the Book of Job calls "the obstetric hand of God" moving through the gloom and folly of human affairs, I remind myself that, since this hand is ever with us and at work, evil can never universally prevail. Base triumphs are but partial and transient. Crucifixions become resurrections, as winters become springs; and life, for all its aberrant and fearsome undercurrents, flows on in the right direction—doesn't it?

But I need a "lift," because a sense of my own shortcomings and mankind's is heavy on me in this twilight hour, and moralizing is not enough. A glance at my watch tells me that it is time to leave my room and drive to Xavier, there to end the day and begin the night with Benediction.

On my way I keep wishing that Moscow were on another planet and that world peace were something more than a sigh.

Soon I am holding the golden monstrance before a congregation of nuns and students, incense drifting around me like the perfume of a mystical May. And I notice one of my kneeling acolytes as he swings the thurible from which the fragrance comes. The sheen of the altar is on his dusky upturned face, his eyes are round and clear, and presently his voice sounds above other voices in the general echoing of the divine praises that I am now reciting at the foot of the altar. Just as it should. A few

swift years, and he himself, having already learned to see substance through shadow, will be giving Benediction and leading
men to God, for tomorrow he is to go from us to a seminary
where he will be trained for the priesthood. And I recall a distant
Sunday afternoon when, as he lay in his godmother's arms, I
poured the baptismal waters on his head.

Now the choir is singing the Magnificat.

"He hath put down the mighty from their seat . . ." Hitler and
Mussolini, the mightiest of yesterday, reduced to dust! A finger
already writing on the wall of history a third dictator's doom?

". . . and hath exalted the humble." I glance again at my
acolyte, son of the lowly, who is destined for an honor sublime;
and I behold him as a living sign that, all through years of human
neglect, his people were heaven-remembered. Else how could a
New Englander like me, to whom this Deep South was originally
no more than a mist, have received the call to serve as one of their
missionaries here? How could St. Joseph's Society and other
sacred agencies have been inspired to prepare young lives to re-
linquish all things for a Claverite cause? And who but the Lord
of Harvests could have fostered the gradual, blessed changes that
enhance Aframerica's prospects today?

The service over, I depart from Xavier. The night is deep
with stars and I feel the Providence that never sleeps. A sentence from some forgotten source rises within me. "Our blessings
are many, our happiness great, but our prayers much too few—
still it is never too late."

On my slow ride home I drive out of my way and stop almost
automatically before a tall dark wall and an iron-picket gate. Out
of the car I step. In the massed shadows behind the gate and wall
stands the Parish Prison, and a light is shining high up in a window, causing me to visualize one who, by finding solace and salvation even there, demonstrated that they are everywhere. And
this, at the moment, is to me no mere moralizing but a fact as solid
as the bars enclosing the window above.

With no one around to think me odd, except the Lord, who

knows everybody is, I touch my finger to forehead, chest, and shoulders. The gesture that Sinclair Lewis once found so difficult, the Sign of the Cross. And I murmur, "Good night, Dismas. Thanks for the lift. Maybe I'm readier now for 'the last mile— the first minute.' "